~ Golf's 100 Toughest Holes ~

OLD COURSE AT ST. ANDREWS, 17TH HOLE

Chris Millard

Foreword by Rees Jones

~ Golf's 100 Toughest Holes ~

Harry N. Abrams, Inc., Publishers

Contents

PEBBLE BEACH GOLF LINKS, 9TH HOLE

for

MOM AND DAD

WESTCHESTER COUNTRY CLUB, 12TH HOLE

"Place the golf course on a level plane; have no traps of any kind; let every fairway be flat; the green unpro-
tected and without rolls; let there be no rough; nothing between tee and green but perfect fairway, and the green
itself absolutely level; and what would be the result?—A thing without interest or beauty on which there is no
thrill of accomplishment worth while; a situation untrue to tradition, and apart from the spirit of golf as it was
given birth among the rolling sand dunes of Scotland."

~ GEORGE THOMAS, FROM *"GOLF CONSTRUCTION IN AMERICA,"* 1927

OAK HILL COUNTRY CLUB (EAST COURSE), 17TH HOLE

AUGUSTA NATIONAL GOLF CLUB, JACK NICKLAUS ON THE 12TH HOLE

Introduction

This book began in December 2002 with a phone call from Margaret Kaplan, my editor at Harry N. Abrams. Her boss had an idea for another golf title. The concept: Uncover and profile the toughest 100 holes in the game.

There are roughly 30,000 golf courses in the world. Accounting for the fact that some of those are nine-hole courses, we can estimate that these 30,000 courses comprise approximately 500,000 golf holes. We can immediately eliminate about half of those holes as having no claim to extreme difficulty. So I was left with about 250,000 holes from which to choose.

I began with the philosophical determination that there is a difference between a "great" hole and a "tough" hole. I found myself in agreement with five-time British Open champion Peter Thomson who once said that tough isn't always a good thing. Consider, he said, steak. Thomson was right: Not all tough holes are great holes and not all great holes are tough. So, while many great holes are profiled in this book, there are also plenty of not-so-great holes that are just plain tough.

After getting semantics out of the way, I turned to the criteria I would use for the book. I relied heavily on PGA Tour, USGA, and PGA of America data. While this worked quite well for courses and holes that have hosted Tour events and major championships, it left the everyday courses out in the cold. The key to an interesting and representative list was including all kinds of holes from all kinds of courses. If I was going to include lesser known but deserving brutes from outposts such as Koolau and The International Golf Club, I would have to expand my parameters.

Information from state golf associations on course ratings and slope ratings helped. I also began speaking to experts. One was Dean Knuth, former director of handicapping for the USGA and the whiz who created the USGA's slope system. Although Knuth left the USGA in 1997, he is still known as "The Pope of Slope." I spoke at length with golf course designers such as Rees Jones, Tom Fazio, Jack Nicklaus, Pete Dye, Jeff Brauer, Bob Cupp, Tom Clark, and Bobby Weed.

Respected golf writers Gary Van Sickle of *Sports Illustrated,* Ed Sherman of the *Chicago Tribune,* and Lorne Rubenstein of Toronto's *Globe and Mail* weighed in with candidates on the local, national, or global level. Ron Whitten, architecture editor for *Golf Digest* and the pre-eminent writer on the topic, generously shared his thoughts. Scotland's John Huggan, the European correspondent for both *Golf World* and *Golf Digest* and the golf columnist for *Scotland on Sunday,* lent his unmatched knowledge of British Isles and international golf. Likewise, New Zealand native Kevin Morris, formerly of *GOLF Magazine*

Properties and of late a researcher at Harvard University, contributed several of the Australia, New Zealand, and Pacific Rim holes you'll be reading about. Editor David Barrett was extremely helpful and insightful in shaping the final list.

That research was supported with insights, anecdotes, and confessions from a galaxy of world-class players including Jack Nicklaus, Tiger Woods, Phil Mickelson, Davis Love III, and Ernie Els. I went through page after page of golf history, reading books by and about Pete Dye, Tom Fazio, Jack Nicklaus, Robert Trent Jones, Alister MacKenzie, Donald Ross, George Thomas, and the forefathers of golf course design. I immersed myself in the mythology that has built up around holes such as the 12th at Augusta National or the 15th hole at Pine Valley in hopes of finding out just what it is that makes a tough hole tough.

The answer? Several factors: length, wind, number and placement of hazards, pin placement, green contour, green speed, the weight of history, even beauty. These are the physical assets of the hole. But the mind of the player has far more to do with difficulty than does any design element. In fact, the great golf course designers act more as mindbenders than backbreakers. Donald Ross wrote that golf is both an eye test and mental examination. "The hazards and bunkers are placed so as to force a man to use judgment and exercise mental control in making the correct shot," he said. You can confirm this anytime you play a classic tough hole: Once you've putted out, look back at the hole you just played. You'll be amazed by how simple it seems from that perspective.

So, is this the definitive listing of the toughest 100 holes in the world? No more than Miss America is the prettiest woman in the country. Aside from the subjective nature of the topic, this list admittedly includes some par fives and medium-to-short par fours and par threes that don't necessarily extract the highest scoring averages from the pros but yard-for-yard present extreme physical and mental challenges. This book represents months of dedicated research into a fascinating subject (and more than a little bruising field work). I am certain that when you've finished this book you'll come up with another five or ten holes that belong between these covers. Conversely, I'm confident that you will find in this book some new, rocky, and relatively uncharted territory and perhaps a new appreciation for some old nemeses. Either way, my hope is that you will derive hours of enjoyment from visiting these dread 100 holes—without losing a single ball.

Chris Millard
Atlanta, Georgia

Foreword

When considering the subject of tough holes and what they mean in a round of golf, I think of the course I grew up on and still play, the Montclair Golf Club in New Jersey. The toughest hole on this 36-hole layout is widely recognized to be the par-four fourth hole on the first nine. During the qualifying rounds for the 1985 U.S. Amateur, this hole played the hardest.

When I was a child playing in the time before fairway irrigation was installed, the hard, tilted fairway provided little room for error. (Even now, with modern maintenance, it is difficult to keep the ball from running into the rough.) The green was treacherously contoured. The penalty if I missed the green to the right was woods, a ditch, and out of bounds. The thought of all that trouble ahead loomed over me as I played holes 1, 2, and 3. To this day, when I play this hole, all I think about is getting through it unscathed.

On Donald Ross's Montclair Golf Club design, each nine has three birdie opportunities, three holes of medium difficulty, and three very demanding holes. Maybe that is why this golf course has intrigued me all my life. It is always interesting to play.

Golf courses should have an ebb and flow. There should be birdie opportunities, swing holes, and holes that supremely challenge par. Today, this balance is a principle of design. Make all golf holes too hard and you never want to play the course again. Make them all too easy and the golfer knows he hasn't been challenged. Give him a mixture, and he will enjoy every round. Golf is the player against the course. I believe golfers derive real satisfaction from *earning* their score on a challenging layout.

When we redesigned Bethpage State Park for the 2002 U.S. Open, we didn't try to make every hole as tough as it could be. Instead, we gave the best players in the game a good chance for birdie on at least a third of the holes. We did, however, create our own "Amen Corner" by re-bunkering and adding length on holes 10, 11, and 12. All the players in the competition knew they had to successfully negotiate the turn in order to have a chance at our national championship.

As an eight-handicap golfer, I shot 77 on Bethpage Black in the tournament celebrating the reopening of the course after the restoration. Even though I bogeyed the last hole, that round—in competition—satisfied me as much as any round I had ever played, because it was achieved on such a demanding layout.

Tough golf holes are not only difficult to play, but they do a number on your psyche, looming in your thoughts as you play toward them. That is why they are especially effective toward the end of a round, as the player is trying to preserve his score, win a match, or win a tournament. I like to design my courses with some tough finishing holes that create a crescendo for the round.

A great example of a difficult finishing hole is Pete Dye's 17th island-green par three at the TPC at Sawgrass in Ponte Vedra, Florida. It is successful because a mistake cannot be made on the 71st hole of a tournament such as the Players Championship. Leaders in the tournament know they haven't completed their task until they get through that hole and the next.

Most golfers enjoy being reasonably challenged. Golf holes that unfold with a variety of shot options requiring intelligent management of the game—choosing the right strategy, selecting the right club, and executing the necessary shot—make for a more interesting and fulfilling round. When making decisions about strategy, a golfer must choose the degree of risk he is willing to take. He can play it safe and studiously avoid hazards, or he may "go for it" and flirt with trouble. I try to offer this kind of risk/reward option in my designs; whether or not the golfer can pull it off successfully is up to him.

Chris Millard identifies the toughest 100 holes in golf and casts a new light on difficulty in this book. He gives the reader insight as to how to conquer these holes, both physically and mentally. He examines the architect's thinking, points out how that thinking is reflected in the design of the hole, and backs up his assertions of difficulty with terrific anecdotes and quotes from victimized players. In short, you'll be reading what designers like me hear firsthand after a player has struggled on one of our designs.

I hope you enjoy this book, and I wish you success on these holes, where so many others have met disaster.

Rees Jones
Montclair, New Jersey

ROYAL TROON GOLF CLUB, GARY WOLSTENHOLME IN THE 2003 BRITISH AMATEUR ON THE 8TH HOLE

The Atlanta Athletic Club dates back to 1898, when it made its home in downtown Atlanta. In 1908, it added a golf course in the East Lake section of town. A true athletic club, the AAC was devoted to a wide variety of pursuits, but ultimately it became known for golf. Players such as Tommy Barnes, Alexa Stirling Fraser, Watts Gunn, Charlie Harrison, Charlie Yates, and the immortal Bobby Jones were all early products.

However, by the 1960s the East Lake area, which was once the envy of Atlanta, had become enveloped in crime and hopelessness. So the Athletic Club members acquired a 550-acre parcel north of the city in Duluth. There, in 1967, the club unveiled 27 holes designed by Robert Trent Jones, with nine more designed by Joe Finger following in 1971. Finger's nine became the front nine of the Highlands Course, which hosted the U.S. Open in 1976.

When George and Tom Fazio redesigned the course in preparation for that Open, they turned Jones's 18th hole, designed as a par five, into a 460-yard par four by building a new tee ahead of the original. With water guarding the front of the green, it was one of the toughest finishing holes the Open had ever seen.

In the 1990s, Trent Jones's son, Rees, did a redesign of his own that resulted in the club being awarded the 2001 PGA Championship. While making extensive changes on much of the course, he left the 18th alone except for moving the tee back to the 490-yard mark, assuring that the hole would play about the same considering the greater distance players were now driving the ball.

Early in the week of the championship, David Toms said, "Number 18 is probably the most difficult par four I've ever played. That green—it's not built for a par four. It's so hard to hold it on your second shot."

There is no quit in either the tee shot or the approach. Off the tee you want to favor the left side to cut off some yardage to the green, but water lurks on that side. Hit too far to the right and, because of the bend in the fairway, your distance to the green may be too great. Even with a dead-center 300-yard drive, the 2001 players still faced a 190-yard approach over water to an undulating green.

"That truly did intimidate them," says Jones of the closing hole. "Now, because they hit it so far off the tee, the water on the left comes into play, so they have to throttle back a little bit. When they put the hole location on the left, that long approach shot is pretty treacherous."

That's where it was when Toms came to the 72nd hole with a one-shot lead over Phil Mickelson. Mickelson had already put his ball 25 feet from the hole for a slippery but makeable birdie. Toms's drive had come to rest slightly above his feet in the first cut of rough. He had a sidehill, downhill lie and over 200 yards to the green. The gallery urged him to go for it. And Toms considered it.

"I pulled out the 5-wood and got to thinking about it," says Toms, who realized that he was unlikely to hold the green with that club from his lie. "The best I could do was hit it over the green and . . . that didn't look very good—you are chipping back toward the water."

He opted for the pitching wedge. "I hated to do it," he says. "The crowd was over there oohing and ahhing and moaning 'You wimp.' I just had to put it out of my mind and go hit two good shots."

With 88 yards remaining to the green after his lay-up, Toms played an L-wedge to about 12 feet. After Mickelson two-putted for par, Toms turned to his caddie and said, "These are the putts you're supposed to make to win a major." He holed the putt for one of the smartest pars ever played in a major championship.

"You know," he said later, "I might still be playing that hole if I had gone for the green."

In the 1976 U.S. Open, Jerry Pate did go for the green and hit one of the best shots in the championship's history, a five-iron from 190 yards to two feet from the hole, turning a one-stroke lead into a two-stroke victory. He had the benefit of catching a good lie in the rough.

But that Open also showed the virtues of discretion on the 18th. Tom Weiskopf and Al Geiberger, playing in front of Pate and trailing by one, both laid up from the right rough, pitched on and holed putts for pars, just as Toms would 25 years later. In their case, all it did was keep their hopes alive for the 10 minutes until Pate hit his shot. John Mahaffey, playing with Pate and trailing by one, found himself more than 200 yards from the green in the right rough—the water to the left probably had something to do with all four contenders missing the fairway to the right—and felt he had to go for it. The shot never had a chance.

Opposite, bottom: Discretion proved the better part of valor for David Toms. His lay-up par on the 72nd hole of the 2002 PGA Championship at Atlanta Athletic Club was one of the savviest pars in major championship history.

Given golf fans' intimacy with Augusta, it would seem that anyone could easily identify the hole that has consistently played toughest since the Masters Tournament started in 1934. Could it be the 11th, where Ben Hogan once said he wouldn't even try to hit the green with his approach in order to stay clear of the water on the left? Might it be the long par-three fourth, which has surrendered only one ace in Masters history? Could it be the 18th, where so many champions have been christened and even more hopes have been dashed?

The fact is that through 2004, the hardest hole at Augusta National has been the 10th. The downhill par four has played to an average score of 4.32, or .32 strokes over par, during the 70-year history of the Masters. In that same period of time, the next toughest hole—the 12th—has averaged 3.30, or .30 strokes over par. Yet while the 12th has always been celebrated for its difficulty, the 10th has never been afforded the spotlight it deserves.

The actual handiwork of Augusta flowed from the combined genius of Bobby Jones and legendary designer Alister MacKenzie. When you take a man who was by far the most celebrated golfer of his time—and one of the most popular human beings—and combine him with a British military camouflage expert who metamorphosed into one of the leading minds in golf-course architecture, it's likely you're going to end up with a course that is elegant, difficult, and deceptive.

No. 10, or Camellia as it is named, is all that. Originally designed and played as the first hole (Jones reversed the nines in 1935), the 10th is a flowing, downhill par four that plays at 495 yards after being lengthened by 10 yards in 2002. Unlike some golf holes where a certain shot—the drive, the lay-up, the approach, or the putt—will determine a player's fate, the 10th makes every shot count. On the tee shot, the fairway turns subtly to the left as it burrows down into a cavernous valley surrounded by loblolly pines. The downhill nature of the fairway helps all players, but those who can play a right-to-left tee shot gain some valuable yardage, while a tee shot pushed to the right leaves a much longer approach. Pine sentinels guard the left side of the fairway and the hole's trademark bunker, the last of the original MacKenzie bunkers on the course, stands handsomely between the landing area and the green. When the course opened, this bunker guarded the front of the green, but the putting surface was moved back some 50 yards in 1937, relegating this bunker to the aesthetic, lightening up this dark corner of the course and giving some definition to the last third of the hole.

The second shot is generally a mid-iron for the pros, sometimes even a short iron for longer hitters thanks to the downhill slope. If the tee shot reaches the bottom of the hill, the second is back uphill, with the green elevated from the low point on the fairway by some 25 feet. The green slopes hard to the left and

back toward the player and is one of the more deceptive putting surfaces on a golf course renowned for deception. Whether played as the 10th hole or as the first hole of a playoff, the green is dappled with shade, making putts very hard to read.

The list of 10th-hole victims is long and distinguished. In the 1982 Masters playoff, Dan Pohl missed a four-foot par putt on the 10th to hand Craig Stadler his only major. In 1987, in the playoff famed for Larry Mize's 11th-hole chip-in against Greg Norman, Seve Ballesteros three-putted the 10th and was eliminated. Who can ever forget Scott Hoch's missed putt from less than two feet on the first playoff hole in 1989 that enabled Nick Faldo to advance with a bogey and win on the next hole? In his 2003 playoff against Mike Weir, Len Mattiace committed the cardinal sin of missing his approach shot to the left and ended up three-putting for a six, allowing Weir to win with a bogey.

In the five Masters playoffs that have been staged since 1979 (prior to that, ties were settled with an 18-hole playoff), the 10th hole has registered six pars, five bogeys, and one double-bogey for an average score of 4.58. That's testimony not only to the pressure of competing for a green jacket, but to the brilliant design of one of golf's most underrated holes.

Opposite. In 1989, the underrated and overlooked 10th hole at Augusta National proved Scott Hoch's undoing.

Augusta National exists for two purposes: to afford club-level amateurs an enjoyable outing and to challenge the best players in the world during the Masters Tournament. In order to serve those divergent interests, two golf courses have evolved since the course's creation: the members' course and the tournament course. In fact, when you compare the Masters setup with the typical members' setup, only one hole plays virtually the same in February for an 18-handicap member as it does in April for Tiger Woods: the beguiling 12th hole.

While Herbert Warren Wind's world-famous appellation "Amen Corner" refers to the corner of the golf course that comprises the second half of the 11th hole, the entire 12th hole, and the first half of No. 13, the heart and soul of Amen Corner is No. 12.

The 12th is the epicenter of Masters lore and drama. In its diminutive size and simple appearance, it is a maddening reminder of the difficulty that lurks at Augusta. For beauty, shortness, and difficulty combined it is unrivaled.

Jack Nicklaus calls the 12th "the most demanding par-three in the world." Obviously, distance is not the issue here—at only 155 yards, the tee shot is at most a seven-iron for a good player. There are four keys to the 12th hole's challenge: Rae's Creek, the green, wind, and history.

Rae's Creek runs at an angle in front of the green, so that while a left pin leaves some room for error, a right pin (Sunday's hole location) courts treachery. In 1992, Fred Couples nearly drowned his bid for a green jacket when his tee shot came up short and flirted with the creek. He was among the lucky ones who stayed out.

Other than a slope toward the tee, the green contours are fairly simple. Next to its speed, the most difficult aspect of the green is the narrowness of the putting surface. The green is only about 18 paces deep and canted toward the creek. A long tee ball can mean a dangerous downhill chip out of the flora or bunkers behind the green. A short shot can mean water or a bunker shot to a close pin. The 12th has all the risk/reward of the famous par-five 13th, but it's compressed into one shot.

"You've got a safe way to play it, directly over the bunker to the center of the green," says Nicklaus. "Or you can be as bold as you want. You can also be penalized accordingly, but you've got to make that decision."

The wind in this hallowed crook of Amen Corner is historically unpredictable. It's not unusual for the flag at the nearby 11th green to blow in one direction while the flag at the 12th blows in another. Because the 12th is situated at one of the lowest areas on the golf course the players are largely guessing as to whether the wind is helping or hurting.

The most subtle force behind the 12th hole's difficulty is its history. The Masters is the only major held at the same golf course every year. This means that from an early age, golfers develop an easily referenced archive of agony. These file folders in the mind call up the misadventures of players such as Dow Finsterwald, who carded an 11 in 1951, or Jeff Maggert, who in 2003 carded a quintuple-bogey eight here and squandered any chance of winning his first green jacket.

When it comes to 12th-hole ignominy, however, nothing can match Tom Weiskopf's encounter with Golden Bell in 1980. In Thursday's first round Weiskopf's seven-iron tee shot found the water. He dropped short of the creek and played four straight sand wedge shots into Rae's Creek. Like a scene from *Tin Cup,* after each splash, he dispassionately extended his hand to his caddie, Leroy Schultz, who supplied him with another load. He eventually carded a 13, the single worst score on the 12th hole in the history of the Masters. For good measure, he knocked two more balls in on Friday for a seven. He played the 12th hole in a two-round total of 20 or 14-over-par. It was the only time in 16 Masters appearances that Weiskopf missed the cut.

Opposite, bottom: Tom Weiskopf in mid-drop during the 1980 Masters. His "deca-bogey" 13 on the 12th hole is a tournament record.

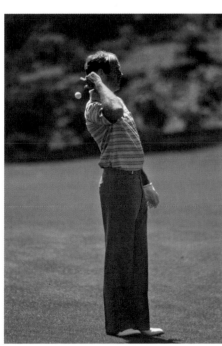

Like Royal Dornoch in the far north of Scotland, it wasn't until the 1970s that the wondrous links at Ballybunion came to the notice of the wider world. Located in a remote corner of County Kerry, it lay largely undiscovered until writers like Herbert Warren Wind in *The New Yorker* and Peter Dobereiner in *Golf Digest* began singing its praises. Tom Watson didn't make his first visit until 1981, by which time he'd won three of his five British Open titles.

Wind went as far as to say that Ballybunion was "nothing less than the finest seaside course I have ever seen." Watson was just as effusive, saying that he had never had as much fun on a golf course as he had had at Ballybunion, and he began regularly preparing for the British Open with a stop in Ireland.

Ballybunion is nothing short of a spectacular place to play golf. Sitting on the shores of the Shannon Estuary amid a breathtaking series of towering sand dunes, it encourages the mind and eyes to wander. Best that you come to your senses in time for the 453-yard 11th. From the championship tee—magnificently sited between the edge of a cliff above the water to the right and the dunes to the left—it is a carry of no less than 200 yards to the narrow strip of fairway that tumbles eccentrically toward the distant green.

The strength and direction of the ever-present breeze determine one's tactics from the tee. If it is blowing hard off the water, the perfect line might be somewhere west of landfall. "The tee pushes you to the right," says European Tour player Raymond Russell, "which is okay unless you go too far down that side. Left is no bargain either. You can't see the green properly from that side."

As Russell hints, the ideal finishing point is hard to determine or, at least, to reach. The fairway has seemingly as many levels as the Pentagon's organizational chart, but one of them is a distinct shelf which many consider the best place to land the tee shot. Down by the green, the fairway narrows between two large sand hills. "The smart play is to the top," continues Russell. "From there you are looking down on the kidney-shaped green."

"If you want to be defensive and play to the front of the green with your approach, there is more leeway," says New Zealander Greg Turner, a veteran of the European Tour. "The ball will feed in. The chip or putt will be straightforward. A miss from a more aggressive play will result in a far more difficult shot. It's just a spectacular piece of real estate."

The green has no bunkers around it (sand would be superfluous here). A pushed approach shot will disappear over the cliff, never to be seen again. A pull will plummet into the long grass on the dunes, perhaps never to be found. A near miss leaves—as at all good links—the choice of a pitch back onto the putting surface or a bump-and-run up and over the inevitable bank between ball and green.

Except for those who follow Watson's lead and spend some time there in preparation for the British Open, the pros don't get much chance to play Ballybunion. An exception was the 2000 Murphy's Irish Open on the European Tour. Even at just 6,651 yards, the course held up well, especially when the wind picked up in the final round and only winner Patrick Sjoland was able to break par among the contenders. With the course set up in a different configuration, the normal 11th played as the sixth. The players were probably glad to get it out of the way earlier in the round.

For five-time British Open champion Tom Watson, Ireland's Ballybunion was the perfect pre-Open preparatory test.

Baltusrol has a long history of treachery and difficulty. Just consider the man for whom the course was named, a thrifty farmer named Baltus Roll, who once owned this patch of land 30 minutes outside of New York City. In February of 1831, Roll was attacked, tortured, and killed by two strangers intent on finding his horde of cash. Two suspects were later arrested; one hanged himself in jail; the other was tried and acquitted but died in prison for another crime. Roll's gravestone in nearby Westfield, New Jersey, bears this unusually succinct epitaph: "Murdered."

About 60 years later, just as golf was setting roots in the United States, Louis Keller, owner and publisher of the New York *Social Register,* acquired the Roll farm, commissioned a nine-hole course, and brought in a few hundred friends as members. A few years later the club scraped out another nine holes and after some more changes to that 18 ended up with a course that hosted two U.S. Opens.

In 1918, the club contracted with A.W. Tillinghast to replace that course with two 18-holers. Tillinghast, troublemaking son of a wealthy Philadelphia couple, was introduced to golf during a visit to St. Andrews, Scotland. After a series of lessons from the game's patron sage Old Tom Morris, "Tillie" had finally found his calling. In 1907, at the age of 32, he designed his first golf course, and suddenly Tillinghast was in demand. He would go on to design nearly 50 golf courses and re-design as many

more. Some of the best-known, most widely respected championship tests in the world, like Winged Foot Golf Club and Bethpage Black, are Tillinghast originals and monuments to his talent for toughness.

Tillinghast's Upper Course at Baltusrol hosted the 1936 U.S. Open. After that, the Lower Course took over with four Opens between 1954 and 1993. One course or another at Baltusrol has hosted seven U.S. Opens, four Women's Opens, two U.S. Amateurs, and two Women's Amateurs for a total of 15 national championships. Only Merion has hosted more USGA events.

In recent times, two names have become synonymous with Baltusrol: Nicklaus (Jack won two of his four U.S. Opens here) and Jones. Robert Trent Jones, who died in 2000, was among the most influential golf course architects of the 20th century. In addition to nearly 500 original designs, Jones was the original "Open Doctor," dating back to the 1951 U.S. Open at Oakland Hills. Jones prepared the Lower Course for the 1954, 1967, and 1980 Opens, and his son Rees got the job when the championship returned in 1993.

In 1993, Lee Janzen shot 272 to tie the all-time scoring record for a U.S. Open established by Nicklaus 13 years earlier, also at Baltusrol. But don't think that those records indicate the Lower Course is a pushover. While there may not be quite as many back-breaking holes as, say, Winged Foot, Baltusrol is plenty tough, especially in its championship guise as a par 70, with both par fives on the front nine converted into demanding par fours.

Since Tillinghast designed the Lower Course with a unique finish of back-to-back par fives, that means there are no par fives until the last two holes. That's a long wait, especially considering that par fives are generally where the pros go hunting for birdies. What's more, the first of those par fives, the 17th, is anything but a birdie hole.

Oh, it will yield birdies to three well-struck shots. But any mistake on either the drive or the second shot leaves even the pros just hoping for a par. In 1993, it was the longest par five in Open history at 630 yards. That's 630 uphill yards. What's more, the fairway was interrupted by a series of bunkers set about 380 yards from the tee. With U.S. Open rough, that sometimes meant a lay-up after a poor drive, leading to the unusual sight of a pro trying to lash a fairway wood or one-iron for his third shot on a par five.

In 1993, big-hitting John Daly came to Baltusrol with a long-range plan: to reach the par-five 17th hole in two.

The exception was John Daly, the man who had given new meaning to the word "distance" just two years earlier when he essentially air-mailed all of Pete Dye's hazards at Crooked Stick and stunned the golf world by winning his first major. In his own inimitable style, Daly came to Baltusrol not so much focused on winning the Open as he did on reaching the "unreachable" uphill 630-yard 17th in two. (Billy Farrell, the son of long-time Baltusrol pro Johnny, had gotten home in two in the 1967 U.S. Open when the hole was listed at 623 yards.)

During the practice rounds Daly, who wasn't carrying any fairway woods in his bag, came within three yards of the green using driver, one-iron. Then on Thursday his drive found the rough. Asked after that round if he would continue his quest through the weekend, Daly responded, "Yeah, why not? It's a par five."

The next day Daly put his drive 325 yards into the left side of the fairway. "I knew that if my drive was in the fairway I was going to hit that one-iron as hard as I could," he said after the round. Facing approximately 300 yards, the last part of it to a seriously elevated and heavily bunkered green, Daly lashed his one-iron into history.

His ball bounded off the edge of a greenside bunker, kicked right, hopped twice through the rough around the green and ultimately rolled some 45 feet past the pin, coming to rest near the back right fringe but on the putting surface.

"They were two of the most solid shots I've ever hit," said Daly, who added, "It was fun. It was just meant to be."

For those with an interest in the Sisyphean: Baltusrol added 17 yards to the hole for the 2005 PGA Championship, making it play at 647.

Arnold Palmer first visited the Orlando area in 1948. The Wake Forest University golf team had come to central Florida for a match against Rollins College. Orlando was still a quiet, rural area, and its sun-warmed countryside, pristine freshwater lakes, and rambling horse farms made an impression on the 19-year-old Pennsylvanian.

"I knew then that some day I would be back here," says Palmer. "I didn't know to what extent."

Palmer is president and primary owner of Bay Hill Club and Lodge, and over the course of the last 30 years has become almost as closely identified with the club and its grounds as Jack Nicklaus is with Muirfield Village. Whereas Nicklaus designed Muirfield Village (with Desmond Muirhead), it was Dick Wilson, not Palmer, who designed the original golf course at Bay Hill. Palmer's impact was not felt until a 1980 redesign. It was then that Palmer transformed what many considered a mediocre par-five 18th hole into a stern par four.

The hole starts out simply enough. A 441-yard dogleg right, the tee shot is played slightly downhill to a wide, largely unobstructed fairway. That's where things start to get complicated. First, there is an eye-catching pond that separates the approach shot from the green. While largely out of play on the tee shot, the pond serves as the centerpiece for the hole's strategy.

The longest hitters sometimes have to worry about a tee shot trundling into the rough just short of that pond, so they might have to hit a three-wood off the tee, particularly if the wind is at their backs. A typical approach shot will measure anywhere from 160 to 200 yards (even Tiger Woods has left himself as much 191 yards). In 1990, PGA Tour rookie Robert Gamez shockingly holed his 176-yard seven-iron for eagle in the final round to beat Greg Norman at the Bay Hill Invitational.

Players who approach the green from the fairway have a huge advantage at 18. The green—diabolically simple in its design—is canted toward the water and stretches out in an inverted J shape around the upper left-hand quadrant of the pond. This design means that the "Devil's Bathtub," as members affectionately refer to the pond, is in play regardless of the hole location, but especially if it is back right. That's where it was when Vijay Singh dunked his approach shot in the water to lose at Bay Hill in 2005.

A drive down the left side doesn't have to carry the water, but the further right you go, the more the water is in play on the approach. While the green is fairly long, it is narrow and the prime landing spots are small. Only shots with precisely the right amount of distance control and spin can threaten the pin, and that's impossible out of the rough. Since Palmer ordered the greens to be firmed up a few years ago, it's pretty tough from the fairway, too.

With water to the right, the bunkers on the left of the green get a lot of action. But that's not a completely safe play: Even a slightly thin sand wedge from any of these hazards will end up in the Tub.

Tiger Woods tied a PGA Tour record by winning at Bay Hill four years in a row, 2000-2003, but even he claims to struggle with the 18th hole. The trifecta of water, a narrow green, and leering bunkers can affect not only the way you play a ball, but even how you talk to it. Once you've hit the ball "there's nothing you can say," explains Woods. "You can't really say 'get down,' or 'get up.' You don't really know."

Coming as it does after the dramatic and difficult par-three 17th hole, Bay Hill's 18th caps off one of the great finishes in golf.

Opposite, bottom: Tiger Woods won the Bay Hill Invitational four years in a row, but even he has issues with the difficult 18th hole.

Every once in a while, the federal government gets it right. Such was the case in the early 1990s when Congress passed the Defense Base Closure and Realignment Act. The idea behind the measure was that in a post–Cold War world, the country should reduce the number of military bases it maintains. While that premise can be debated, the unintended fruits of the act are obvious to avid golfers: the conversion of military-base golf courses—once the preserve of brass and their guests—into public facilities.

For decades the existence, not to mention the quality, of America's military golf courses was shrouded like a national security secret. For instance, since 1963 the Air Force Academy has operated a five-star course—the Eisenhower Golf Club's Blue Course—on its campus in Colorado Springs. It's among the best golf courses in the state, but there was a time when tourist maps of the campus did not even include it.

Since 1990, dozens of military courses have opened to the public, none more difficult than the aptly named Bayonet Course at what used to be California's Fort Ord. The Bayonet, which has a sister course called the Black Horse, was conceived and designed in 1953 by Major General Robert B. McClure, commanding officer of Fort Ord. And because "Bourbon Bob" was a left-hander who tended to slice the ball, the Bayonet is chock-full of doglegs left. Rank does have its privileges.

But the Bayonet is more than a general's plaything. Even though it was the only golf course McClure ever designed (he received assistance from Lawson Little, two-time champion of both the U.S. and British Amateurs and winner of the 1940 U.S. Open), it is an intense test. In fact, golf-shop personnel try to steer high-handicap curiosity seekers towards the Black Horse.

Because of its difficulty, the Bayonet frequently hosts PGA Tour and U.S. Open qualifying rounds, with scores typically the highest of any qualifying venue. In 2000, the Tour held first-stage qualifying at Bayonet, and 12-over par made it to the second stage.

The course's vital statistics tell the story. From the gold tees it measures a wind-riddled 7,117 yards. While par is set at 72, the course rating is a healthy 75.6. There is no out-of-bounds; apparently, that would be superfluous. Instead, the course ambushes visitors in plain sight.

The par-four, 428-yard 15th is the toughest hole on the course. The drive must be directed at the left fairway bunker. Bite too much and you're asking for trouble. If you can hit it 260 or 270, that will put you safely in the fairway about 170 yards from a deceitful green, one that slopes wildly from left to right. Miss it left you're MIA, chipping to a green that runs away.

"Here's the tough part," says Al Luna, head professional at the Bayonet for six years. "It's slightly uphill so you have to take more club, but at the same time you have to hit the front part of the green. No matter where the pin is, smarter players will play for the middle-front and not even mess with the left or high side of the green. We don't even like to put a pin placement left. It's just unfair." How tough could it be? Legend has it that Jack Nicklaus, widely regarded as among the greatest putters ever, once four-putted this green.

Perhaps the most illuminating Bayonet outing in recent memory came in February 2003. Cousins Boyd and Joseph Summerhays were attempting to qualify for that year's AT&T Pebble Beach National Pro-Am. After locking their keys and clubs in the trunk of their rental car, the pair called a locksmith, but by the time he got there Joseph had already missed his tee time. Boyd got his round in but lost a ball on the final hole, costing him a spot in a sudden-death playoff. Locals are still debating who got the better deal.

The two got some revenge later that year when Boyd finished first and Joseph second at PGA Tour first-stage qualifying.

Opposite, bottom: Amateur legend Lawson Little (center), shown here accepting the U.S. Amateur Championship's Havemeyer Trophy from USGA president Prescott Bush in 1935, had a hand in the punishing design of the Bayonet Course.

In 1931, Robert Moses headed the Long Island State Park Commission. Moses, who eventually became famous for reshaping the Empire State, envisioned a public park in Farmingdale and set his sights on a tract of land owned by the heirs to a railroad fortune. There was already a private golf course—Lenox Hills Country Club—on the grounds; after finally acquiring the land for the state, Moses in 1934 hired A. W. Tillinghast not only to redesign Lenox Hills (ultimately renamed the Green Course) but to design three additional courses, the Blue, the Red, and the Black.

The Green, Blue, and Red courses opened for play in 1935; the much more difficult Black opened a year later. For 66 years New York's devoted public-course players quietly embraced the Black. In fact, many local private-club members had no idea that the public was enjoying a golf course that could put many of the region's acclaimed private layouts to shame.

In June, 2002, the world got in on the secret. The United States Golf Association brought the venerable U.S. Open to a truly public golf course for the first time in the championship's 102 years. Once Tiger Woods, Phil Mickelson, and the international media were exposed to a Black Course that had been lovingly restored by Rees Jones, they quickly learned what golf-loving locals had always known: This was a beauty and a brute.

Through the four-day Open test, two holes rose infamously above the others in difficulty, the par-four 12th and the par-four 15th.

There's no mystery about what made the 12th so tough: At 499 yards, it was the longest par four in U.S. Open history. The hole required a drive of roughly 240 yards to carry the large bunker that guards the corner of the dogleg left. Most of the field could manage that carry, but the few that couldn't were forced to play it as a three-shot hole, using a three-wood off the tee to avoid going through the fairway and then hitting another three-wood short of the green (the hole plays even longer than 499 yards taking that route).

The woes of that small minority didn't account for the hole's 4.522 scoring average, however. Those that carried the bunker faced their own set of problems, and they had the competitors in the 2001 New York State Open at Bethpage to blame. Tom Meeks, the USGA official responsible for U.S. Open course set-up, watched that tournament and noticed, to his dismay, that many players were able to cut off a lot of the dogleg and leave themselves just a seven-iron approach. So, not only did he decide to move the tee back 10 yards, he ordered the rough to be grown in on the left side. That way, players had to aim over the right side of the bunker, not the left, and the hole would play to its full yardage. He probably didn't know what a monster he was creating.

"I think what happened in the Open is that when you cleared the bunker you didn't necessarily get to the fairway," says Jones. "There was a cut of rough on the back of the slope. Not only did you have to carry the crest of the bunker, but you also had to carry the rough cut. And if you got hung up in that rough you also had a downhill lie. I think that in the 2009 Open the USGA is going to mow that a little more closely."

While the drive is the key shot on the 12th, the green presents some difficulty, too. It has more contour than most of the greens at Bethpage, and the putting surfaces at the 2002 Open might have been the fastest ever, a combination that one player labeled "Satanic."

Rees Jones's celebrated rehabilitation of daunting Bethpage Black set the stage for one of the most exhilarating U.S. Opens ever contested.

Of the roughly 900 holes played on the PGA Tour in 2002, the 15th hole at the Black played toughest of them all, averaging a heartless .599 over par for the U.S. Open.

Based on length alone, at 459 yards the 15th is a formidable par four. That length does not include the fact that the green is elevated by some 50 feet. The mound on which the green rests is coated with shaggy rough and protected by three of A.W. Tillinghast's trademark bunkers. As if all that were not enough, the two-tiered green itself is the most severely sloped putting surface on the course. For a player who misses the fairway on the tee shot, par is no longer a realistic possibility. In fact, during the 2002 Open, the 15th hole chalked up nine "others," i.e., scores of triple bogey or worse.

"It's a smallish green and it's the most contoured green on the golf course," says Rees Jones. "We tried to make the lower portion of the green usable—we expanded it down closer to the front bunker—but they had to leave the hole locations on the top deck, and there's quite a transition there from the lower tongue to the back terrace. Then if you miss it to the right, it goes pretty far down a precipitous slope. We brought the bunkers all in closer to the green. So it's very well fortified. The reason I think it plays so hard is that if you go for the back terrace and you go over, you have a lot of trouble."

Amazingly, as tough as the 15th is, it could play even tougher in the future. A couple of years after Jones's 1998 restoration of the Black, he built a new tee 15 yards farther back that the USGA elected not to use for the 2002 Open. In future U.S. Opens (including the already scheduled 2009 encore), this tee may well be employed.

The 15th at Bethpage Black proved a thorough examination for the best players in the world, including Tiger Woods, at the 2002 U.S. Open. Things could be even tougher in 2009.

Pete Dye has been given the nickname, "the Marquis de Sod," and anyone who has played the River Course at Blackwolf Run understands why. In terms of severity and difficulty, it doesn't take a back seat to any Dye creation, not even the notorious Stadium Course at PGA West.

In his autobiography, Dye describes his penchant for challenging golfers with demanding shots. "Before my visit to the British Isles, it was a downright mystery to me why a 25-handicap golfer would pay thousands of dollars to fly to Scotland and not break 100. The answer to that question came in 1963 when [wife] Alice and I visited the ancient country. We saw first-hand golfers' tremendous excitement when they achieve a brief moment of glory on one of the legendary Scottish holes. Regardless of their total score, players never forget one challenging shot played on a challenging hole."

Dye writes that he kept that in mind at Blackwolf Run as he tried to design a course with memorable shot opportunities. The up-and-down terrain is nothing like the linksland of the Scottish seaside. Nor do the water hazards that come into play on 14 holes remind anyone of Scotland. But the long, acquisitive fescue grasses off the fairway do. That was the idea of course founder Herbert Kohler, an idea initially met with doubts by Dye.

"My skepticism that public golfers would dread playing a course that featured such conditions was, as Herb continues to remind me, dead wrong," Dye writes. "Playing in and around long grasses on the mounds and dunes provides a unique challenge, and regardless of their score, these dedicated golfers keep coming back for more."

Indeed, only two years after opening the original course at Blackwolf Run, the high demand led to the construction of 18 more holes. Within the next decade came two courses at Whistling Straits, nine miles away, with all 72 holes part of Kohler's American Club complex, which features a first-class hotel.

Score is virtually irrelevant at the River Course. The penalties are so severe for a missed shot that mid- and high-handicappers will almost certainly pencil in a few "Xs." Competitors at the 1998 U.S. Women's Open didn't have that option. It proved to be one of the most difficult tracks ever for that championship. Se Ri Pak and amateur Jenny Chuasiriporn tied for first at six-over par 290. Pak, the eventual winner, shot 75 and 76 in the final two rounds of the championship, then prevailed on a second sudden-death hole after both shot 73 in an 18-hole playoff.

"There's not just trouble out there," said shell-shocked former Open champion Meg Mallon. "There's *massive-number* trouble out there." That was especially true in the third round when the wind blew and the scoring average soared to 77.89.

The 1998 championship was played on the original 18 at Blackwolf Run, incorporating nine holes of the River Course and nine of the Meadow Valleys Course. The four par fives on the River Course might be the hardest group of par fives on any course in the world. River's 12th hole, not used for the Women's Open, is a sadistic 205-yard par three with a tall tree smack between the elevated tee and the green and a broad river to the right.

But the 18th on the River Course (also 18 on the composite used for the U.S. Women's Open) adds length to the equation, playing 469 yards from the championship tee and 421 for the Women's Open. It's a demanding tee shot with water to the left and a long bunker to the right, with the hazard on the left also guarding the green.

With the playoff tied coming to 18, Pak hooked her drive onto the steep bank of the hazard. If she took a penalty drop, double bogey was a definite possibility with a very long third shot to the green. After taking a long time to consider her options, Pak took off her shoes, stepped in the water, and managed to play the ball down the fairway. From there, she was able to make a comfortable bogey. That was good enough to maintain a tie, as Chuasiriporn, who had holed a 45-foot putt for birdie on the 18th in the final round, ran out of magic and three-putted from long range.

Two holes later, the 20-year-old Pak became the youngest-ever U.S. Women's Open champion by virtue of the championship's highest winning score since 1984.

Opposite, bottom: The durable Se Ri Pak made history in the 1998 U.S. Women's Open at bruising Blackwolf Run.

The name Fazio is synonymous with modern-day golf-course design. Tom Fazio, creator of courses such as Wild Dunes in South Carolina, Wade Hampton in North Carolina, Shadow Creek in Las Vegas, and Black Diamond Ranch in Florida, and the man entrusted with the most recent facelifts of Augusta National, is among the most respected designers in the world. But the Fazio golf-course design dynasty (Tom has a brother and two nephews in the business) began with his uncle George Fazio.

Born in Norristown, Pennsylvania, in 1912, George Fazio once served as head professional at vaunted Pine Valley. A five-time Philadelphia Open champion, he played intermittently on the professional circuit from the 1930s through the 1950s, and won the Canadian Open in 1946 (Fazio actually came within a stroke of winning the 1950 U.S. Open, only to lose in a three-way playoff to sentimental favorite Ben Hogan).

But George Fazio's legacy will be the courses he designed on his own and with his nephew Tom. Although he entered the profession blindly (a friend asked him to help route a course design), George excelled from the start. One of his earlier courses, Moselem Springs in Fleetwood, Pennsylvania, hosted the U.S. Women's Open just four years after it opened. Jupiter Hills in Florida, Fazio's masterful paean to Pine Valley, was a nearly instant addition to top 100 rankings. Before his death in 1986, his deft touch for redesign had been felt at architectural treasures such as Augusta National, Atlanta Athletic Club, Winged Foot, Aronimink, Southern Hills, and Oak Hill.

But Butler National may be Fazio's best known and toughest test of golf. He was hired in June of 1971 with orders to build a "strong" golf course. From the very beginning, the plan was for the new club to host the Western Open. In *Butler National Golf Club, The First Twenty-Five Years,* golf historian Cal Brown writes: "The call for a stern test of golf to satisfy the requirements of the Western Open seemed to fit neatly the concept of a stag club, whose members would be less likely to complain about a rugged, demanding golf course and whose gender is more inclined to exhibit pride in belonging to a 'tough' course and be more willing to subject themselves to the difficulties, even the humiliations, of the game."

Opened in 1974, the course immediately landed the Western, the oldest and one of the most prestigious stops on the PGA Tour. Ironically, the event left Butler National after the 1990 Western in response to the club's male-only membership policies. During its time in the spotlight, particularly the early years when under-par totals for 72 holes were rare, Butler National distinguished itself as a tough course in a tough town.

It may have been *too* tough in its 1974 debut, when Butler National was still raw. Billy Casper came into that event with four Western Open wins in the previous nine years, coming on historic courses Tam O'Shanter, Medinah, and Midlothian (twice). Reflecting on the difficulty of Butler National, Casper recently told the *Chicago Sun-Times,* "The first time we went to Butler, I had six balls in my golf bag and lost them all in eight holes."

The 18th hole is a 464-yard par-four puzzler. The tree-lined tee shot plays across one of Salt Creek's many tributaries. Water also comes into play on both sides of the hole.

George Fazio, designer of vaunted Butler National and patriarch of the Fazio design dynasty.

"Number 18 is a very difficult driving hole," says head professional Bruce Patterson. "On the right there is a little inlet from the creek that goes out about 260. Oaks and elms guard the right. On the left there are more trees. There's a big oak tree out on the corner so you really have to pinch your drive."

The approach to the green—assuming you've avoided the rough, the trees, and the water on your tee ball—must avoid the trees on the left and carry a bend in the creek that snakes menacingly in front of, around, and behind a slightly raised green. And, patrolling the middle of the fairway, blocking the view to the green, is a notorious large tree that's a living testament to flamboyant founder Paul Butler's arboreal predilections. There simply is no room for error on this hole.

"To have a good angle into the green you have to go down the right side, but that's where so much of the trouble is," says

Ben Crenshaw in Brown's thorough club history. "Then you must hit an honest approach to find the green. In all the Western Opens I played at Butler National, no one was ever safe coming into 18, even with a two-shot lead."

In 1988, Peter Jacobsen came to 18 with a one-shot lead but left it with a one-shot deficit and a runner-up finish. He flew a 6-iron off the back of the green and into the creek for a double bogey.

As tough as the hole played throughout its Western Open era—and as tough as it plays today—this hole still has toughness in reserve: In the 17 years that Butler National hosted the Western Open, the Tour players never even used the back tees at several holes, including No. 18. That may have been a good thing, said Hale Irwin, who won at Butler in 1975: "If we played this course all the way back, some guys wouldn't finish."

Don't let the term "demilitarized" fool you. The 248-kilometer-long and 4-kilometer wide corridor that serves as border between North Korea and South Korea is the most dangerous, most suspicion-filled place in the world.

Only an hour or so north of Seoul, it came into existence at the end of the Korean War in 1953, but it serves as a constant reminder of the war that was, the cold war that is, and the fighting war that one day could be. On either side of the "truce village" of Panmunjom, heightened alert is a fact of life. Armed troops patrol barbed wire fences, binoculars are in constant use, land mines await the slightest intrusion, and tanks, artillery, and infantry stand at the ready 24 hours a day, 365 days a year. North and South are technically still at war, functioning under a cease-fire, not a treaty.

Although it can seem absurd—like an exaggerated 21st century version of the Hatfields and McCoys—the DMZ is real. Visitors are required to sign a release warning that "a visit to the Joint Security Area at Panmunjom will entail entry into a hostile area and the possibility of injury or death. Although incidents are not anticipated, the United Nations Command, the United States of America, and the Republic of Korea cannot guarantee the safety of visitors and may not be held accountable in the event of a hostile enemy act."

The release goes on to prohibit speaking or communicating in any way with North Korean soldiers. Gestures such as waving or insulting are forbidden for fear that they may ignite an international incident. From the other side, however, the North Koreans use loudspeakers to blare propaganda over the border.

That a golf hole (and there is only one hole) exists here at all is oddly reassuring and a tribute to Colonel John Patrick, the man who conceived it. The nondescript 192-yard par-three, roughly hewn from an unforgiving slope, is really only recognizable as a golf hole in that it has a pin standing in a cup in a well-worn green, admittedly constructed of artificial turf. And while most greens are surrounded by bunkers or water, this hole was once bounded on three sides by minefields. A sign welcoming players to the hole still reads: "DANGER! Do Not Retrieve Balls From The Rough. Live Mine Fields."

Sports Illustrated featured the hole in 1988 and dubbed it "the most dangerous hole in golf." Legend has it that at least one shank has detonated a land mine. One game that is sometimes played on this hole is "combat golf." Each of four players is armed with a laser-mounted M4 rifle. One player plays while his teammate protects him from the two opposing "snipers." Members of the offensive unit make their way to the hole as the defenders try to "kill" them. The number of strokes is added to the elapsed time from tee to hole. Lowest score wins. The DMZ soldiers went years sharing one set of clubs until 2001 when the State of Indiana sent thousands of golf balls and dozens of sets of clubs to the camp.

On a recent visit to entertain troops, sitcom star (and former Marine) Drew Carey and USO President Ned Powell put the new equipment to good, if unauthorized, use. They each launched golf balls with American flag logos deep into North Korea. Carey followed his shot with an internationally understood gesture of disfavor. No report on his score.

Opposite: Like most things in the so-called "truce village" of Panmunjom, even golf is fraught with danger.

Carnoustie is an unforgiving town. A small gray burgh of some 11,000 resilient souls hard on the shores of the North Sea, Carnoustie is home to a golf course that well reflects its surroundings. The word "bleak" comes to mind.

Still, those characteristics help make Carnoustie the golf course it is. Little is forgiven here, particularly at the 578-yard (from the championship tee) sixth hole. While some will argue that Carnoustie's famous finishing stretch presents more challenging hazards, no hole on the course provokes more thought nor asks more strategic questions than this par five, nicknamed "Long."

On the tee the player has choices to make. He can attempt to carry the brace of bunkers staring balefully at him from the middle of the fairway, he can flirt with the narrow gap between the sand and the out-of-bounds fence on the left, or he can tack safely to the right, hoping to avoid the one bunker down that side.

In 1953, in his only appearance at a British Open, Ben Hogan each day chose the second option, smashing his famous fade down the boundary fence and into the narrow gap, which instantly and obviously became "Hogan's Alley." From there, the legendary Texan hit his four-wood just short of the green (the hole played 521 yards in those days) and in the final two rounds chipped and putted for birdies. He won the title by four shots.

Another fader of the ball, Jack Nicklaus, was less accurate. Fifteen years after Hogan's visit, the Golden Bear stood on the tee vying for the Open title with South Africa's Gary Player. One uncharacteristic hook later, Nicklaus was out of bounds and on his way to a double bogey seven. Player later won the title by those same two shots.

The sixth is not merely a tough driving hole. More danger awaits the unwary up the right side on the second shot in the form of "Jocky's Burn," a thin and largely unseen tributary of the Barry Burn that later weaves through the course's closing holes. Between "Jocky's" and the omnipresent out-of-bounds fence on the left is a gap of just over 20 yards.

In that gap, the ideal line is left of center, leaving a pitch to a shallow, angled green protected front, back, and right by more pernicious bunkering.

Par is hard earned, as it was the day in the 1995 Scottish Open when Colin Montgomerie, in a westerly gale, required two drivers and a 1-iron to reach the putting surface. Bedraggled and windblown, Monty slumped into a chair after the trying round. A foolhardy journalist asked if the wind was a factor at the sixth hole. Monty, incredulous, exploded. "Long" can do that to a man.

In his only British Open appearance, Ben Hogan charted a course through "Hogan's Alley" and won.

Carnoustie Golf Club, Carnoustie, Scotland ~ *18*th hole

Simply stated, there is no tougher finishing stretch to a golf course than the final three holes at Carnoustie. Nos. 16, 17 and 18 are, to quote one European Tour professional, "hard, bloody hard, and hard." This crucible of difficulty has produced some of the greatest and most bewildering finishes in Open Championship history.

While "the gowf" had been played in the region for 300 years, Carnoustie Golf Club proper was founded in 1850. Allan Robertson was retained to design a 10-hole course, and Robertson's course was later expanded to 18 holes by Old Tom Morris in 1870. The course we know today, one that has become a rite of passage for any good player, took shape in 1926 with work by James Braid and his rarely credited associate John R. Stutt. Still, it was felt the finishing stretch wasn't that strong, and a local man, James Wright, redesigned the final three holes in 1937, creating a trio of holes that strike fear into golfer's hearts.

The 16th is a 245-yard par three, and as if it isn't hard enough to hit the distant target with a three-wood, the green falls off on both sides. When he won the 1975 British Open here, Tom Watson failed to make a par in five tries, including a playoff against Jack Newton.

The 433-yard 17th is called "Island" because the Barry Burn crosses the fairway twice and the landing zone for the drive is the area between the two crossings. Scotland's own Paul Lawrie birdied this hole to propel himself to victory in a playoff over Jean Van de Velde (more on him in a minute) and Justin Leonard.

The notorious Barry Burn again snakes across the fairway on the 444-yard 18th, which heads back in the opposite direction from 17. The burn is at its most devious here. A loop enables it to perform the trick of guarding both the right and left sides of the fairway. After continuing up the left, it makes another turn to flow menacingly in front of the green. Predictably it is here, only 25 yards away from the completion of the round, that the burn, after winding its way through the entire course, is at its widest. Legend has it that during one of Carnoustie's Open Championships some debate ensued about the width of the burn. One contestant bet the others that he could jump the burn on foot. He finished with a soggy dinner jacket and an empty wallet.

The burn may be the most commanding feature of the hole known as "Home," but it is far from the only one. A trio of bunkers stands sentry to the right of the narrow fairway. Thick, moist rough lines both sides and out of bounds extends the entire left side of the hole and curls snugly around the back of the green. Finally there is the wind. A hurting wind can make the green unreachable in two for all but the longest players. Even a so-called helping wind can be a problem. The same breeze that might help the nerve-wracked player carry the burn can send his ball through the green and out of bounds.

The 18th hole has secured the claret jug for some and wrenched the cup from more careless hands. Tom Watson birdied the 18th to earn his spot in the playoff in 1975 and his two-iron approach the next day sealed the championship. But just as some have risen to Home's challenge, others have crumbled before it. Johnny Miller finished one shot back in 1975 when he needed two tries to escape one of the deep fairway bunkers and made a bogey. Justin Leonard hit his approach into the burn in front of the green in both regulation and the playoff in 1999.

But all pales against the madness of Van de Velde at the 72nd hole of the 1999 Open. A full three shots clear of Lawrie and Leonard, the Frenchman inexplicably made a triple bogey. The comedy of errors began with Van de Velde's decision to hit driver.

Carnoustie's omnipresent Barry Burn got the best of Jean Van de Velde in the 1999 British Open.

"There is no easy shot I think," he said later, in a comment that rang true with anyone who has ever played the hole. "Even being three ahead, what do you do? Do you hit a five-iron down the left or do you hit something down the right, or do you try to go as far up as you can? I took that option."

His driver was poorly struck, but he miraculously missed both the burn and the rough, landing in the 17th fairway. His next decision was just as questionable. With 189 yards to carry the green-front portion of the burn, he chose a two-iron. He carried it easily enough, but pushed the shot badly and watched in horror as the ball hit the grandstand, ricocheted back across the burn, and settled in some of the deepest rough on the course. Now Van de Velde had to hit over the burn again, from a terrible lie. "I had to hit it hard," he said.

By his own admission the Frenchman didn't hit it hard enough. After three shots his ball lay at the bottom of the burn. After much consideration, Van de Velde took a drop into another awful lie. His fifth shot landed in the right greenside bunker, from which he made a clutch up-and-down to gain a spot in the playoff. Looking back Van de Velde said, the 18th hole "just came out to be a nightmare."

Countless golfers have had their own nightmares on the same hole. Unfortunately for Van de Velde, his occurred in front of an international television audience.

In 1968, the management of a highly successful sugar mill in this small Dominican town was looking for a way to invest their profits. Once they settled on the idea of a golf course, Pete Dye was brought in to assess the land. The water-starved parcel did little to excite the designer, who asked if there might not be another property worth examining. Yes, it seemed there was a plot on the Caribbean Sea.

"Teeth of the Dog was a once-in-a-lifetime piece of real estate," Dye says. "Land like this may never come up again."

Of the marquee names in the golf-course design business, Dye is probably the most hands-on. Short on paperwork and long on seat-of-the-pants creativity, Dye is as likely to be found atop a bulldozer acting out a design impulse as he is to be studying topographical maps. That characteristic only sharpened in the Caribbean where Dye established a particularly close bond with the land, the local workers, and the broader community. Said Dye in *Cigar Aficionado* magazine 1998: "It was the Dominicans who built this golf course virtually hand by hand. It's got a lot of their soul in it."

Blood, too. The course is built on a bed of limestone covered with countless jagged branches of coral that had to be smoothed out before soil could be laid down. Locals call the coral protrusions "*diente de perro*" or teeth of the dog. Dye had his name for the golf course.

With a name like that and a designer renowned for his testing architecture, the course had better be tough. Don't worry: With a course rating of 74.1, it's all the golf you could want. Gary Koch's oft-repeated quote sums it up: "This course will

come out of nowhere, throw you down, and stomp on your head." Locals make a nice business out of supplying used golf balls to bewildered players in mid-round. And while a golf course next to the sea is bound to have beautiful holes, it also has some examinations.

Many great golf courses have a hole or two that parallel the sea. Dye proudly boasts that seven holes do exactly that at Teeth. The 17th hole plays from west to east on a promontory above the Caribbean. While most coastal locations enjoy a breeze off the water, Dye says the prevailing wind at Teeth of the Dog is actually offshore. "You wouldn't think so, but it really comes off the land," says Dye, "a little from the north-north-east. When you play 17, it's quartering from the left." That means pushing both your tee ball and your approach on this dogleg right 435-yard par four toward the comely trouble on the right. That's a challenge when you consider that the tee shot here (especially from the back tees) must carry a few million gallons of sea.

The long-iron second shot is one of the most precise in golf. It's played into a narrow green guarded by deep rough, bunkers on either side, and the yawning sea to the right. Laying up and chipping on for a one-putt par is not unheard of here. Yet few people make the pilgrimage to Dye's seminal design to play it that way.

In the early days of Teeth of the Dog, one of the hardest parts of the golf course was managing the airport that cut right through the place. In fact, a pulled drive on the ninth hole had to account for the tarmac. The airstrip also bisected the 12th and 18th holes. Timing your shots to avoid the deafening distraction of an accelerating jet, then timing your crossings of the asphalt, just added another degree of danger to a difficult round. When the runway was clear, a bell would ring prompting golf carts to scoot across the runway. But four years ago, a new airport was finally constructed three miles away.

"It was fun for a while," says Dye of the old-time jet-dodging game, "but then the air traffic got so heavy down there it was crazy."

Teeth of the Dog furthered Pete Dye's legend as a designer of challenging courses.

At 7,559-tree-lined yards, Castle Pines was for years the longest course on the PGA Tour until being surpassed by Torrey Pines South. Castle Pines also starts off with one of the Tour's longest holes, a drastically downhill 644-yard par five. All that length makes sense when you consider the fact that the Jack Nicklaus-designed course is majestically situated in the Rocky Mountains at 6,300 feet above sea level. At that altitude, the air over Castle Pines is thinner than Charles Howell's pant leg.

Castle Pines, completed in 1981, was Nicklaus's first design at altitude. Having won the U.S. Amateur at the Broadmoor in Colorado Springs in 1959 and finished second to Arnold Palmer in the 1960 U.S. Open at Cherry Hills in nearby Englewood, Nicklaus had played plenty of mountain golf and was well aware of the effect that thin air has on a golf ball.

"I knew that Denver, at a mile high, added about ten percent to ball flight," wrote the Golden Bear in his 2002 architectural treatise, *Nicklaus By Design*. "With Castle Pines being up a little higher, I figured the effect at about twelve percent."

At that rate, the golf course plays more like 6,700 yards, and it favors the long *and* high hitter because the longer the ball stays in the air, the more it benefits from reduced resistance. No surprise that players such as Ernie Els, Davis Love III, Phil Mickelson, and Greg Norman have had so much success here.

The altitude helps on the 485-yard 10th, but not enough to make it anything other than a tough hole. Elite tournament golf is full of par fives that are temporarily converted into par fours for major championship or PGA Tour play. The 10th at Castle Pines is rare in that it was originally conceived by Nicklaus as a par five, but was permanently converted into a par four (for all players) at founder Jack Vickers's suggestion. Still, as you stand on the tee it feels for all the world like a par five.

The hole plays downhill through deep stands of pine and oak, and it happens to be among the course's prettiest holes. Both the famed Castle Rock and the even more famous Pike's Peak are visible on the endless horizon.

"When you get on the tee and you look down, it's just a pretty sight," says Els.

But pretty and tough come together to create a hole that played .49 strokes above par in the 2002 International. Hitting the narrow fairway is a must if you plan to have a go at the green, which is guarded by water at the right-front and bunkers in the rear. The second shot is crucial, coming from about 200 yards out (the last 30 over the water).

As tough as Castle Pines can play, there's always a reward in the end. The lavishly appointed clubhouse claims to serve the best milkshakes in the game. About 2,000 milkshakes are served to contestants and their families during tournament week in flavors ranging from vanilla, chocolate, and banana to fresh berry and butterscotch. An international player once asked for a fig milkshake . . . and got one.

Davis Love III is one of a number of long hitters to find happiness in the thin air (and thick milkshakes) of Castle Pines.

For most of the 20th century the island of Lanai was known primarily as a pineapple farm. The Dole Company controlled the island, the economy of which derived entirely from agriculture. That all changed in 1985 when Dole's parent company ceased farming the site and converted the island's economy from agriculture to tourism.

A small island, Lanai lies just west of Maui and south of Molokai. Because it's located in its neighbors' "rain shadow," Lanai gets far less rain than the other two islands. The ground here looks less like the tropics and more like the mainland. The views, however, are pure paradise, a fact that was not lost on the grateful designer of the Challenge at Manele. Overlooking Hulopoe Bay and affording endless vistas of the Pacific Ocean, the location for the Jack Nicklaus-designed course is the kind of site that players, architects, and developers dream about but rarely realize.

"Several things make for a great par three," says Nicklaus. "Foremost among them is the setting." That theory, espoused in Nicklaus's 2002 book *Nicklaus By Design,* is proven in what may be the most stunning golf hole he has ever created: the 12th at the Challenge at Manele.

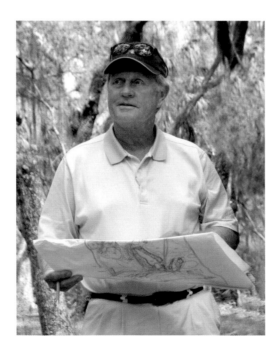

Setting is everything on this majestic par three, as it is with all of Lanai. The island is a volcanic cone whose peak, Lanaihale, rises up approximately 3,400 feet. Much of the coastline is composed of steep cliffs interspersed with spectacular white sand beaches. Along these promontories at the southern edge of the island sits the 12th hole. Measuring 202 yards from the back "Nicklaus" tees (the course has five sets of tees), the 12th plays from a cliff 150 feet above the crashing surf, across a yawning chasm of roiling sea. Laid out in, say, Ohio, the hole itself is not that tough. It is a long par three, but it offers oodles of bail-out room to the right, and the prevailing winds at the player's back can be extremely generous. But played in context—with the stirring view of the Pacific to your left, with the hollow awe that registers in your stomach when you view the chasm, and with the knowledge that a pulled long iron will travel nearly as far downward as it will forward—this hole becomes for the ten minutes it takes to play it (not including film reloading time) the only golf hole in the world, one on which a par or a birdie will be forever remembered. The effect of the 12th at the Challenge is reminiscent of the 16th hole at Cypress Point: Beauty is simultaneously friend and enemy, heightening aspirations at the same time it distracts.

Not surprisingly, the 12th has become one of the most widely photographed holes in the world, and yet few shots can really capture the magnitude of its beauty. How stunning is it? Imagine you are the richest man in the world and you could arrange to be married anywhere in that world. You'd choose the most beautiful setting imaginable, right? That's exactly what Bill Gates did when he got married in 1994. Of all the places that they could have selected, Gates and his bride Melinda chose to exchange their wedding vows on the 12th tee at the Challenge.

Designer Jack Nicklaus was given an unmatched setting for the 12th hole at the Challenge at Manele.

As stand-alone golf-course designers, Dick Wilson and Joe Lee each had plenty of credentials. As a team, which is how they worked from the mid-1950s to early 1960s, they were almost interchangeable. Where Wilson's influence ended and Lee's began is a mystery. But while their exact contributions are indecipherable, the fruits of their collaboration are obvious. Wilson and Lee were among the most respected design teams of the post–World War II era. Together they worked on courses such as Bay Hill, Doral's Blue Monster, and La Costa.

But no Wilson/Lee design has been quite so successful on quite so many levels as Cog Hill Golf and Country Club. In the early 1960s Cog Hill's founder, the late Joe Jemsek, earned a reputation as the father of public golf for his commitment to bringing private-club conditions and amenities to the daily-fee player. Cog Hill is the manifestation of that vision. Beautifully maintained, and operated with an emphasis on old-fashioned service (Joe himself was likely to greet you on the first tee), Jemsek's four 18-hole courses in Lemont, Illinois, represent the soul of Chicagoland public golf.

"Joe wanted to provide the public-course golfer who did not have access to a country club a chance to play a championship course with great conditioning and some, if not all, country-club amenities," says Ed Sherman, sportswriter for the *Chicago Tribune*. "He was a big fan of Olympia Fields, and he wanted to bring that kind of country-club experience to the masses."

The No. 4 Course, also known as Dubsdread, was the last of the four courses built by Jemsek, but it quickly emerged as the flagship of the operation. Opened in 1964, the course was almost immediately added to various golf-course rankings (in *Golf Digest's* most recent rankings, "Dubs," as the locals call it, was ranked 60th in the nation). Eventually, the professionals found a home here. The oldest event on the PGA Tour—the Western Open—relocated from nearby Butler National to Cog Hill in 1991 and has since crowned notable champions such as Tiger Woods (three times), Nick Price, and Ben Crenshaw. And while the atmosphere fostered by Jemsek is notable for its home-spun hospitality (what other PGA Tour players' lounge serves homemade meatloaf?), the Dubsdread layout has a less gracious streak. Holes such as the sixth, 13th, and 16th have been downright rude to Western fields.

But over time no hole has been tougher than the 18th. Played into the prevailing wind, this par four has recently been lengthened to 480 yards from the blue tees. The drive is played downhill between a long fairway bunker on the left and a three-bunker complex on the right, creating a sandy bottleneck. The green is a difficult target for the approach shot of about 200 yards, as it slopes hard from right to left and is guarded closely on the left by a pond. Two bunkers on the right provide conscience to those trying to avoid the water. A shot from either bunker must still contend with the water, because a thinned bunker shot will almost certainly drown.

Even Tiger Woods, who has dominated the Western in recent years, has struggled with the Dubs 18th. In 2003, he led the field by 10 shots after 63 holes. Still, as though bowing to the reputation of the home hole, he closed with a bogey on the 72nd and won by five.

In the 1994 Western, unheralded Greg Kraft could have forced a playoff with a par on the home hole or even won the title outright with a birdie. He reached a greenside bunker in two, blasted out to 25 feet past the hole, and two-putted for bogey. At about 8:30 that night, as darkness crept over Chicago, a dozen or so sportswriters attempted Kraft's bunker shot. Not one got closer than 25 feet.

"Dick Wilson was famous for creating tough first holes," says Frank Jemsek, who took over the reins at Cog Hill after his father's death in 2002, "but the 18th at Dubsdread makes the first hole look simple."

Even Tiger Woods has been humbled by the design work of Dick Wilson and Joe Lee at Cog Hill.

Many courses have black tees. Many courses have blue tees. But you know you're in for a long day when you find yourself playing from the "Black & Blues."

That the tips at Colbert Hills go by such a bruising moniker gives you some indication of the singular vision behind this golf course. Jeffrey Brauer, the Dallas-based designer who teamed up with Champions Tour legend and the course's namesake Jim Colbert to design this muscular track, says, "It was supposed to be hard, and it worked."

Dating back to 1994, Colbert, an alumnus of Kansas State University, had expressed interest in helping the university develop a multi-purpose golf facility—one that would not only provide a home course for the Wildcat golf team and offer opportunities in turf research, but permit daily-fee play and organized youth programs.

The site, 300 acres of cow pasture on the northwest edge of Manhattan, was donated by a fellow Kansas State alum. Colbert anted up a half million dollars to get the ball rolling and collaborated with Brauer, a former president of the American Society of Golf Course Architects, to lay out the course, which opened in 2000. Final cost: $11 million.

The result is a sprawling facility that plays at 7,525 yards from the Black & Blues. To those who envision Kansas as one massive featureless prairie: You're not in Kansas anymore. Colbert Hills offers rolling hills with startling changes in elevation, as much as 100 feet in places, a feature for which Colbert shares the credit with the land's original developer.

"God built about fourteen of the holes, and we built about four of them," says Colbert. "I hope you can't tell the difference."

Hell holes abound, "There's a few of them out there," says Brauer. While the No. 1 handicap hole is the 462-yard (from the tips) par-four ninth, most players familiar with the course will tell you it's the par-three 11th hole that tries the soul. From the White tees and the Purple tees, the hole plays only about 145 yards. But from the Black & Blue tees, the hole measures about 230 yards—and that's before you figure in the Kansas wind.

The 11th was among the last holes added to the routing of Colbert Hills. The ground was so rocky that the architects toured the property by helicopter in order to spare their ankles. The course was largely routed when, says Brauer, "we determined from the air that we could squeeze a par-three into this little wooded area that we hadn't really considered before." The setting was so right for the hole that the architects had little to do. "I don't think we even imported any dirt for the green," Brauer says. "We just pretty much shaped it around what we had.

"The hole plays about due west, and the wind blows from the southwest, so most days the wind is in your face and quartering just a little. It's not unusual for the collegiate players to hit driver. It's kind of hard."

Kind of? The green is very shallow for such a long shot—maybe 20 paces deep—and angled at about 45 degrees to the line of play. A stream and two deep bunkers guard the front of the green, while the rear of the putting surface drops off a cliff into another stream. "It was a small area that we fit the green into, so naturally that it begat a small green," says Brauer.

A high fade is the proper shot. The front left does offer a stingy bailout area, but the further left you go, the more likely you are to find water or marsh. The further right, the greater the distance you need to carry to the putting surface. On top of all that, add in prairie wind. And you thought Dorothy had it bad. "Tee it high and stop it quick," advises Brauer.

Jim Colbert was the driving force behind his alma mater's challenging golf course.

Ask any golf historian or a player who's been around the PGA Tour for any length of time about Colonial Country Club's place in the game. It's right there alongside architectural treasures such as Augusta National and Winged Foot. "It's one of the great golf courses of the world," says Curtis Strange. Certainly the specter of Ben Hogan—the personification of Colonial—infuses the club with a sense of history and gravitas, but it goes deeper than that. As Hogan might say, it's in the dirt.

Colonial was created in 1936 by John Bredemus. Taking into account the superb golf course he designed, and the sparse attention he has since received, Bredemus may be the most overlooked and underrated golf-course designer of all time. He is also one of the more interesting personalities in a profession full of colorful characters. Unlike many designers of the era, Bredemus stood out not for his flamboyance but for his athleticism. A 1912 graduate of Princeton, Bredemus earned his varsity letter in football and was a world-class track and field man. In 1908, he won the Amateur Athletic Union (AAU) National All-Around championship. In 1912, he finished second in the Nationals to none other than Jim Thorpe. When in 1913 Thorpe was stripped of his AAU medals for having violated his amateur status (he had played professional baseball), Bredemus was awarded the All-Around gold.

Bredemus was born in Michigan, but spent much of his adult life in Texas. In fact, one reason his golf-course design work has received such little recognition is that all of his designs can be found in Texas or Mexico. He never worked anywhere else.

Many casual golf fans simply assume that Hogan, Colonial's most famous member, designed the course. Although Hogan was not responsible for the layout, it's hard to say which came first: Hogan's reputation for cool diligence or Colonial's reputation for toughness. Either way Colonial never fails to remind you that you're walking in the footsteps of the immortal Ice Man, who won the Colonial National Invitation Tournament five times after its inception in 1946.

The fifth hole is a mixture of everything that makes Colonial special. At 470 yards, it's long. It's got the grace of tradition. It's stern—intimidating from both the tee box and the fairway. It's tough, annually ranking among the toughest par fours on the PGA Tour. A dogleg right, it is guarded on that side not only by an imposing wall of trees that runs the length of the fairway, but by the Trinity River which is out of bounds behind the trees. Also guarded by trees, the left side helps to add a touch of claustrophobia to the long approach shot. To the left of the bunkerless fairway, near the outside of the bend, is a small treeless spot. When Annika Sorenstam riveted the golf world by playing against the men in the 2003 Bank of America Colonial, she put her 271-yard first-round drive in this little pocket. She then drew her second shot (a low four-iron) around the trees lining the left side of the hole and, 199 yards later, reached the right side of the green in two. Deft as her approach was, she still faced a 63-foot putt.

Sorenstam ultimately bogeyed the hole—the first of her brief PGA Tour career. She would go on to bogey the hole again in round two, this time putting her drive into the trees on the right. "That is the hardest golf hole I've ever played," says Sorenstam. "Every day I would dread coming to that tee." CBS announcer Peter Oosterhuis got it right when he said that Annika had nothing to be ashamed of, that "the fifth hole has been challenging great players since the 1930s."

Annika Sorenstam celebrates after recording her first birdie on the PGA Tour on the 13th hole at Colonial in 2003. She would give the shot back on the tough fifth hole with her first bogey (she played the back nine first in her opening round).

It has been called "The City in The Country." About 90 minutes north of Manhattan in the Catskill Mountains stands a series of resort hotels that have been catering to the 20-million plus population of the New York metropolitan area for more than a century. And while the area's popularity has ebbed some in recent years, the glory days were just that.

In 1932, Jeris hair-tonic inventor Arthur Winarick bought the Concord Plaza, a struggling hotel in Kiamesha Lake. Like most developers in the region, Winarick promised a resort bigger and better than anything (and certainly bigger and better than the archrival Grossinger's). Through the years, the Concord grew famous for top-shelf entertainment. A-list celebrities—from Ed Sullivan to Lucille Ball to Sammy Davis, Jr. and Muhammad Ali—appeared at the Concord.

In at least one respect, the bigness of Winarick's dream lives today. By 1964 the Concord Resort had two golf courses, the 18-hole International Course and the nine-hole Challenger course, both designed 13 years earlier by Alfred Tull. Still, the resort's next owner Ray Parker was on a mission. Legend has it that Parker was snubbed at (or "barred from") a social function at Grossinger's, a resort that prided itself on its golf courses. In retaliation, Parker summoned golf-course architect Joe Finger and told him exactly what he was looking for in the golf course he planned to build: "I want a golf course that Arnold Palmer and Jack Nicklaus can't chop up."

The point was not lost on Finger, an engineer with degrees from both Rice and MIT. The result is one of the great muscle courses in the game. Working with former major champions Jimmy Demaret and Jack Burke, Jr. as consultants, Finger cooked up the Monster (its official name).

Any course built out of spite is destined to be tough, and the Monster is no exception. While it's a test from any tees (the Whites measure 6,989 yards), it's the Blue tees that have earned the course its fitting nickname. The Monster tees measure 7,650 yards and carry a course rating of 76.8 and a slope of 137.

The Monster lives up to its name. Only one par four plays under 400 yards. There's just one par four on the front nine shorter than 454 yards. No. 18 is a 484-yard par four. The fourth hole, a 632-yard par five with water running down the left and then cutting back into the fairway, is the one that earned the course its moniker. Seems Gene Sarazen played the hole shortly after it was built and said, "This is a monster of a hole."

In fact, the course is so tough that back in the glory days of the Catskills, the Concord offered this deal: Pay your green fee, and if you break par on the Monster you win $1,000.

The toughest hole on the course today is the 248-yard par-three seventh. The tee shot plays even longer because the green is elevated; what's more, the left edge of the green drops off precipitously to plummet 30 feet. The drop is so drastic that a stone wall was put in place to bolster the green. Pull your tee shot (likely a three-wood or driver) and triple bogey confidently enters the picture. Bunkers also guard the front, right, and rear of the green. The rear bunker features a nasty combination of sand and willowy fescue reminiscent of the British Isles.

"Even the best players are forced to hit woods here," says Mike Stoltz, professional at the Concord. "And because they're hitting long clubs into an uphill green, a lot of balls end up in the sand."

Just how tough is it? "My son is a pretty good player," says Stoltz. "He just played in the New York State Open at Bethpage Black. He says there's not a par three there that compares to the Monster's No. 7. And I believe him."

The Concord was dubbed "the Monster" by the diminutive Gene Sarazen.

Throughout its existence, Congressional Country Club has been a place for supreme Washington insiders to meet, mingle, and recreate. For the first few years, however, despite all the power and wealth aligned behind the creation of the club, the membership's only real concern was survival: Congressional, which opened in 1924, nearly folded with the onset of the Great Depression.

The club continued to founder until World War II, when the nascent Office of Strategic Services (forerunner of today's CIA) rented the club's grounds as a training facility for spies. The revenue gave Congressional a new lease on life and the club began to focus on its place in championship golf.

In 1949 Congressional hosted its first national championship, the U.S. Junior, won by 17-year-old Gay Brewer. The membership's thirst for national recognition only increased. By 1957 Congressional had hired the "Open Doctor" Robert Trent Jones to add a new nine holes, and in 1959 the club hosted the U.S. Women's Amateur.

In pursuit of the U.S. Open, Congressional let Jones have at nine holes of Devereaux Emmet's original course. Jones's own nine and the redesigned Emmet nine were merged and became known as the Blue Course. (The remaining Emmet nine was dubbed the Gold Course, and it became an 18-hole course in 1975 when George and Tom Fazio added the club's final nine holes).

Congressional, of course, did land the 1964 U.S. Open and produced the most dramatic human-interest story in U.S. Open history when Ken Venturi, stricken with heat exhaustion, staggered to a four-shot victory over Tommy Jacobs in the last 36-hole final ever played in the Open. In 1976 the club hosted the PGA Championship won by Dave Stockton, and in the 1980s it lent its stature to the PGA Tour by hosting seven Kemper Opens. Throughout this golden era, the club was continually lauded as a serious test of skill.

But by the time that club leaders had made the decision to abandon the annual PGA Tour grind in hopes of landing more prestigious and less frequent national championships, equipment improvements had taken away some of the Blue Course's challenge. Trent Jones's son Rees, who had begun to develop his own portfolio of U.S. Open makeovers (Hazeltine and Brookline), was called in, and he performed a large-scale makeover. Holes were lengthened. Landing areas were reshaped and reconfigured. Greens were lowered and recanted. Bunkers were remodeled. Green contours were dramatically improved. The 1964 Open was played at 7,053 yards, then the longest Open course in history. Thirty-three years later, after Rees Jones's redesign, Congressional's Open course measured 7,213, which was also the longest course in U.S. Open history up to that time.

Congressional's Blue Course ends uniquely for a major championship golf course in that the home hole is a par three. Because officials of the USGA, PGA of America, and PGA Tour were long uncomfortable with the idea of ending an important championship on a par three, a composite course was set up. This championship course borrowed two holes from the Gold Course so that tournaments could end on the Blue's exciting 17th, a long par four with a peninsula green. This practice was eliminated for the 1997 U.S. Open, when the club's 18th was used as the finishing hole. As it worked out, No. 17 still stole the show. (The days are numbered for the 18th, though. It will soon be redesigned, with the positions for the tee and green reversed, to become the 10th hole, so that what is now the 17th will be the 18th both for major championships—the 2011 U.S. Open is scheduled for Congressional—and regular play.)

Today's 17th is much more difficult than the hole with which golf fans grew familiar during the 1980s. Back then, long hitters such as Kemper Open champions Craig Stadler, Fred Couples, and Greg Norman routinely airmailed a crest in the fairway and caught the downslope, leaving them with a short-iron shot into the peninsula green. In preparation for the 1997 Open, Jones moved the tees back 40 yards. The 480-yard par four was now demanding and dramatic, and with a pin placement only a few paces from the water, it would ultimately prove decisive.

Four men—Ernie Els, Tom Lehman, Jeff Maggert, and Colin Montgomerie—came down the backstretch of the 1997 Open with a chance of winning. All but Els would be undone by No. 17. Maggert, two behind by that point, bowed out after missing the green and three-putting for double bogey. Lehman, one back, pulled his 187-yard approach shot into the water. ("I would give anything in the world for a mulligan," Lehman said after the round.)

Moments earlier, Montgomerie missed the green at 17 and after chipping to within five feet of the hole missed his par putt. Of the final four, only Els mastered the 17th. His brilliant 212-yard five-iron to 12 feet and the resulting par on a hole that had devoured other contenders all but clinched the championship.

"Monty kind of bailed out," says Jones. "He had to either play it into the fat of the green on the right or try to hit the little tongue of the green on the left. He decided to go for the fat of the green and he left it a little short. That's why he lost the Open. Els really dared to go for it, and he won the championship."

Opposite, bottom: Ernie Els's gutsy play at Congressional's intimidating 17th hole clinched his second U.S. Open title.

The Country Club, *Brookline, Massachusetts ~ 17th hole*

With six holes laid out in 1893, The Country Club wasn't the first golf course in North America, but a year later—by then expanded to nine holes—it helped midwife the modern stateside game. That's when The Country Club joined four other American clubs—Newport Country Club, St. Andrews (N.Y.), Shinnecock Hills, and Chicago Golf Club to create the Amateur Golf Association of the United States, forerunner of the USGA.

By 1913, golf was being enjoyed across the country but still in small numbers. It was then that an unheralded 20-year-old local amateur named Francis Ouimet startled the old and new worlds by turning back British standouts Ted Ray and Harry Vardon in a U.S. Open playoff staged on the golf course across the street from Ouimet's childhood Brookline home. This, the seminal moment in the popularity of U.S. golf, will forever link The Country Club with the growth of the American game.

Since 1913 TCC has hosted two more Opens, five U.S. Amateurs, two Walker Cups, and the most spine-tingling, if controversial, moment in Ryder Cup history. The course has the look and feel of a living museum.

"There's not too many places where, when you get out to the grounds, you know you're in a special place," says 1999 Ryder Cup captain Ben Crenshaw, himself a golf history buff. "The Country Club is one of those places."

The Country Club is wonderfully schizophrenic in that it can alternate between being a stern physical test and a supreme mental exam. Often one hole acts in both capacities. This may reflect the fact that the course is not the work of one man, but

rather a patchwork. Five years after Scotsman Willie Campbell added his three holes in 1894, the club added another nine holes to create a full 18-hole test (this is the golf course over which Ouimet won the Open). In the years since, the course has been remodeled, renovated, added to, or updated by William Flynn (who added the Primrose nine in 1927), Geoffrey Cornish, William G. Robinson, and most recently Rees Jones, who worked on the course in advance of the 1988 Open and the 1999 Ryder Cup. In fact, Jones's work at Brookline spurred the trend of remodeling old golf courses.

"We went in and took out all of the changes that had been made in the previous 20 or 30 years that had no resemblance to the original design," says Jones. "And so we restored the entire golf course in style."

No hole crystallizes both the history and difficulty of the modern-day Country Club better than the 17th. (Note: the last two Opens and Ryder Cup were played on a Composite Course made up of holes from all three nines. This hole is the 17th on both the Composite Course and the 1913 course.) A short par four, the 17th seems a creampuff, but therein lies the problem. Its deceptive appearance has proven decisive over the years.

The 17th is a 385-yard downhill dogleg left with heavy rough on the left and two fairway bunkers that today's players can easily fly. The better player will hit no more than a long iron or fairway wood off the tee. Those who play it safe and push it will find trees on the right. But the essence of the hole is the green, which Jones completely rebuilt and redesigned prior

to the 1988 U.S. Open. When Clyde Street—on which Ouimet grew up and which the 17th hole abuts—was widened, the club built a diagonal green that had little resemblance to any of the other greens on the golf course.

"We basically took the green back to the original size that it was when Ouimet won," says Jones. Today's 17th is—like all greens at Brookline—small. Surrounded by five bunkers, its surface features three levels, a lower portion, a slight terrace middle right, and a more definitive terrace on the back. Classic chocolate-drop mounding protects the right side. Finally, for those who go over the green, an abrupt wall of rhododendron awaits. "You're dead if you go over the green," says Jones. "In the '88 Open and '99 Ryder Cup, the pros used the rear terrace as a backstop so they could pull it back when the hole was up front. But," says Jones, "if they went over, they basically could not recover *to* that back terrace when the hole was in back." With a back-left hole location in the final round in 1988, the hole played as the toughest on the course.

In both its old and new forms, the 17th has a rich history of crowning champions and crushing contenders.

~ In the final round of the 1913 Open, Ouimet birdied the 17th to tie Vardon and Ray and force the playoff in which he prevailed.
~ In 1963, Jacky Cupit had the championship in hand until he double-bogeyed the 17th. He fell into a three-way playoff

with eventual champion Julius Boros and an under-the-weather Arnold Palmer (Ouimet himself refereed that playoff).
~ In the final round of the 1988 Open, Curtis Strange came to the 17th hole with a one-shot lead over Nick Faldo. Strange was 15 feet from the hole, but he had a downhill putt on that precarious back shelf and he ended up three-putting. Matching pars at 18 forced the playoff ultimately won by Strange.
~ In 1999, with the weight of the Ryder Cup on his shoulders, Justin Leonard holed an indescribably unlikely 45-foot putt to all but assure the American victory. Leonard's putt, the most momentous in the event's history, was nearly impossible. "He really went through two transitions," says Jones. "First was a sidehill to the first tier, and then an uphill transition to the back tier. Give him 100 tries and he might get it close a few times." The chaos that ensued—players, wives, and caddies rushing the green and celebrating with Leonard—neglected the fact that Olazabal still had a chance to tie the hole (he would miss) and elicited global complaints about boorish American behavior.

As Crenshaw says, the sense of history at Brookline is palpable. However at the 17th hole, it's barely manageable.

Opposite: The 17th hole at The Country Club is better known for this joyous birdie celebration by the U.S.team at the 1999 Ryder Cup than for a century's worth of bogeys.

The most difficult part of playing the 11th hole at the Country Club of Charleston may be the anticipation. Throughout the first 10 holes, the focus is on going as low as possible before the inevitable. When you step on the 11th tee, savvy club members offer this unsettling advice: Take your medicine and hope to recover.

The 11th is only a par three, what could be so difficult? Just read what some of the game's better players have said about the hole: "It's the only par three where I can tee off while the group ahead is still on the green," says two-time U.S. Amateur and three-time Mid-Amateur champion Jay Sigel, who has since joined the Champions Tour.

Ben Hogan, who left behind more "favorite" holes than a wildcatter, has been quoted as saying, "It's one of my favorite holes . . . to hate."

Homegrown LPGA Hall of Famer Beth Daniel once wrote a letter to the club suggesting a redesign of the 11th. "The hole," she wrote, "should remain difficult but fair, good shots should be rewarded, and that is not happening now."

The list of gripes runs nearly as long as the club's history. By 1925 course architect Seth Raynor, an engineer by training, had emerged from the shadow of his better-known collaborator C. B. Macdonald. Macdonald had firsthand experience with and a deep appreciation for the great links courses of Scotland and Great Britain. That affinity rubbed off on Raynor, who reprised the Redan in sadistic fashion at Charleston's 187-yard par-three 11th. The hole features no water, no white stakes, no island trickery, just man, ball, club, and gravity.

"Clearly the most difficult hole I have played where there are no obvious penalties," says habitual club champion and six-time Azalea Amateur champion, Frank Ford III.

The tee shot is played from the course's highest elevation (approximately 22 feet above sea level) to a putting surface that is elevated over the intervening terrain. The green is set at a diagonal and slopes away in such a way that only a brave heart would dare target a left or even a middle pin. The first twenty paces of the green constitute a false front, which also serves as a deflector for high tee shots, a speed bump for low runners, or a bank for the chip shots that await Sigel disciples who lay up off the tee.

For tee shots that are even a touch too strong, the deep, vertical-faced greenside bunker at the back left is doom. An anonymous quote from the club's rich lore suggests, if you land in that back bunker, "Just bury your ball and put up a grave marker. Your score is history."

A weak push, block, or slice, and an even deeper bunker, a twelve-foot vertical drop, leaves a completely blind sand shot to an elusive strip of green that slopes dangerously away.

In 1989 Hurricane Hugo descended on Charleston. The Country Club lost 1,000 trees, mostly pines. A redesign team was brought in to rehabilitate the clubhouse and the course, specifically No. 11. A few more years of too much top-dressing compounded the damage done by remodeling shortcuts, and the 11th became virtually unplayable. The edges of the green sloped away from the center to leave the par three with a nearly unputtable surface.

"We had some small events where three-fourths of the field wouldn't even post a score on the 11th out of embarrassment," says Ford. "I witnessed double digits, and one year we had the Azalea field averaging 4.5 strokes, a full stroke and a half over par. That's when enough was enough."

In 1999, Ford personally oversaw the re-restoration of No. 11.

"Today it is a much more playable par three, with the original shape and depth I think Mr. Raynor had in mind," says Ford. "Oh, it's still a good test and strikes fear into any player posting a medal score."

The hole remains a landmark in South Carolina golf, despite Ben Hogan's sentiments. In 1959 he wrote to the Country Club, "Your greens are beautiful, but what you need for that 11th hole is about five sticks of dynamite."

Charleston native Beth Daniel is only the latest in a long line of well-regarded players to file a grievance over the infamous 11th hole at the Country Club of Charleston.

Crooked Stick *Golf Club, Carmel, Indiana ~ 14th hole*

It was 1966 and even though the front nine of his new course was open for play, Pete Dye and the other founders had yet to settle on a name. As Dye was walking the property with another charter member, the architect picked up a crooked, knobby stick and swung it at a stone. Thus the name Crooked Stick was born.

The fact that Crooked Stick was born out of a whack should surprise no one. Dye has been beating up on PGA Tour players for years. Crooked Stick was not his first design, but it's one of the first that he specifically designed as a serious test for the accomplished player. "Alice and I felt the Indianapolis area could use a bold new golf club to seriously challenge the better players of the day," writes Dye in his autobiography, *Bury Me in a Pot Bunker.*

The result was Crooked Stick, an early example of Dye's devilish creativity and a course that in 1991 would unknowingly usher in the Era of Extraordinary Length. With all 18 holes completed in 1967, this 7,000-yard golf course seemed more than long enough to contain even the biggest hitters of the day. In fact, Dye took added measures to combat long hitters, such as building inclines into the landing areas to diminish bounce and roll.

Enter John Daly. The unheralded alternate demolished Dye's golf course, which by then had been lengthened to 7,295 yards. For the championship, the 18th played the hardest hole for the field. On Friday, Daly hit driver, seven-iron to five feet on that hole and made the putt. Afterward he said sincerely, "What a great golf hole. That's the toughest 18th hole I've ever played."

Today Dye believes the 468-yard, par-four 14th is the toughest hole at his home course. It's not only a long par four, but it's a very sharply angled dogleg left. A creek crosses the fairway, runs up the left side, makes a sharp left turn at the dogleg, and then runs the length of the left side of the hole. (The hole began as a par-five homage to the 13th at Augusta, but Dye ran out of room.) Long hitters have plenty of opportunity to let the shaft out without driving through the dogleg, but they don't gain an advantage by doing so. Thanks to the hole's sharp turn, shorter hitters won't have much greater yardage left for their second shot.

At least that's the way it was *supposed* to work. While building the course, Dye summoned the longest-hitting members of the club and had them drive ball after ball on the shortcut over the creek, and positioned the tee far enough back that they couldn't carry it.

Amazingly, the resulting 265-yard carry was kid stuff for Daly. "He carried the dogleg off the tee and had a landing area the size of a football field, and he was hitting half-wedges [actually short irons] into the green," says Dye. The designer has since changed the hole so that today's merry band of long drivers can no longer belittle the hole, "but," says Dye, "God only knows what equipment and the ball might be doing in a few years."

John Daly's major championship career was forged in the crucible of Crooked Stick.

The 16th at Cypress Point, in all its craggy, seascaped grace, is as hard to describe as it is easy to embrace. Its beauty verges on the primal: What's not to love about crashing surf and hunched cypress trees? The amazing thing about the 16th hole, however, is that for 75 years her idolaters' praise has gone largely unrequited: She remains as unrelenting as she is lovely. To borrow Leon Uris's description of Ireland, the 16th hole truly is a "terrible beauty."

The credit for this most beguiling of golf holes goes to Alister MacKenzie, a British-born physician who served in the Boer War as a surgeon. During his time in South Africa, MacKenzie was impressed by the Boers' expertise in camouflage. Returning to his hometown of Leeds, MacKenzie is believed to have tinkered with golf-course design in the form of models. Two developments pushed him onto the global design stage. First, in 1907, acclaimed designer H. S. Colt took him on as a consultant in the design of Alwoodley Golf Club, where MacKenzie was a founding member. MacKenzie's second break came in 1914 when he entered a contest in which *Country Life* Magazine (published by C. B. Macdonald) asked readers to submit a design for a par four. MacKenzie's design won.

MacKenzie's impact on golf-course design is inestimable. While not as prolific as, say, Donald Ross, he demonstrates remarkable quality in his portfolio, and his thinking on golf-course design, published in his 1920 book *Golf Architecture,* is still instructive today. MacKenzie's stature is such that when Bobby Jones was dreaming up Augusta National he could have hired any designer in the world. MacKenzie got the job.

While MacKenzie and his on-site sounding board Robert Hunter have been credited with the design of Cypress Point's No. 16, it's probable that the hole was first conceived by Seth Raynor, who was hired by Marion Hollins in the early 1920s to design Cypress and several other courses in the area. In fact, Raynor had completed a routing that featured the current peninsula green, but he died in 1926 before he could see his plan realized. Ultimately the credit for all of Cypress Point goes to Mother Nature. The setting cried out for a golf course.

The 16th hole is the *ne plus ultra* of golf-course design. On a basic aesthetic level, its raw, seemingly untouched beauty is dumbfounding. But the inner beauty of the hole is its strategic brilliance: While its reputation and appearance tempt even the most conservative player, the 16th offers options. The shot to the green 233 yards away is *all* carry, often against wind, fog,

squalls, and whatever else the Pacific can serve up. Most players are forced to use driver or risk falling short into the ocean. Driver makes sense because even a long ball, and they are rare here, will be saved by bunkers in back of the green.

Any miss to the right will find the ocean, because the carry is longer in that direction and the drop-off to the right offers no mercy. It's a bit safer to play towards the left. On that side, there is a sandy beach from which one is welcome to play to the green. Too far left, though, and, as Jimmy Demaret once said, "There is no relief. The only place you can drop the ball over your shoulder is in Honolulu." Not that the beach is a bastion of safety. In the 1959 Bing Crosby Pro-Am, Hans Merrell hit his tee shot there, had more than a little trouble escaping, and ended up making a 19.

The safe route, followed by short hitters and truly conservative, disciplined players (the kind who can walk calmly past a plate of warm cookies) is to lay up, hitting a mid-to-short iron over 140 or so yards of majestic cliffs and rocky beach, toward the now decrepit trademark cypress tree (two new trees have been planted beside it). From there they'll hope for a pitch-and-putt par (and what's more, they'll probably win the hole).

Graced by MacKenzie's trademark bunkering, and it is some of the most striking bunker work in his portfolio, the green complex is virtually unchanged from its original design. Two rear bunkers subtly frame the green. Companion bunkers guard the more heavily trafficked front right and front left.

The miracle of Cypress is not that Hollins, MacKenzie, Hunter, or Raynor saw the possibilities. The true mystery of the course, and the 16th hole in particular, was summed up by Pat Ward-Thomas, Herbert Warren Wind, Charles Price, and Peter Thomson in their book *The World Atlas of Golf.* "The real wonder of Cypress," they wrote, "is that anybody can keep his mind on playing golf over it."

Opposite: In his 16th at Cypress Point, Alister MacKenzie may have designed the ultimate par three.

How many golf courses are so well known, so well ensconced in the psyche of the golfing public, that they have a nickname? Such is the relationship that the Blue Course at Doral Golf Resort and Spa has developed with Tour players, amateurs, and arm-chair players alike. Unlike most nicknames, however, the appellation is not based on intimacy. The name "Blue Monster" is born of respect.

Since it began hosting the PGA Tour's Miami stop in 1962, Doral's legendary Blue Course has basked in a reputation for toughness. The Blue was originally the work of golf-course architect Dick Wilson. Over the last 30 years the layout has been tweaked by various designers ranging from the team of Robert von Hagge and Bruce Devlin in 1971 to PGA Tour great Raymond Floyd in 1996 to renowned instructor Jim McLean in 1999 and 2003. Floyd was brought in to toughen a golf course that had been weakened by modern equipment. McLean was then summoned first to undo some of Floyd's sinister bunkering, which was tough for resort guests to handle, and then to

add even more length than Floyd's redesign did as driving distance on the Tour continued to escalate. Still, even with all the tinkering, Doral has always retained Wilson's basic vision: a tough, long, wind-riddled, heavily bunkered golf course with water either visible or in play on every hole.

No single hole embodies Wilson's vision better than the famed 18th, one of the most feared finishing holes on the PGA Tour. Recently lengthened to play 467 yards, the 18th presents a cornucopia of challenges. First is the water. Several holes at Doral offer aesthetic water, meaning it's visible but largely out of play. But the water hazard that runs the entire length of the 18th hole is vehemently *in* play not only off the tee, but on the approach and even on a greenside chip. Second is the bunkering. Bunkers have played a huge role in earning the Blue Course its reputation as a monster. Seven bunkers grace the 18th hole, all on the right side. The third factor is the wind. The prevailing wind at Doral ranges from directly into the player's face to a quartering wind left-to-right and hurting.

Moving the tee back restored fear to the drive, which had become easier as players were able to drive past the tightest part of the fairway into a wider area where the water wasn't much of a factor. Now they must steer between water left and bunkers, rough, and trees on the right. Bogey is almost assured to the right, especially since it's a longer second shot from there, but going too far left is even worse.

The approach shot demands precision as well. The wind is likely to exacerbate a pull or push and bring both the greenside water (left) and the rough and bunkers (right) into play. While the water can drown a player's chances, the right side again is no bargain. The green, which slopes toward the left, demands an exquisite touch on any chip from the right side.

"It is a very, very dangerous hole," says Steve Elkington, who won at Doral in 1997 and again in 1999. "It is the hardest tee shot we play. The water is obviously down the left, the hole goes to the left, and you don't want to go right. The player almost has to curve the ball right-to-left to get it in the fairway. Then if you mishit your second shot, you are going to go in the water."

In the 43 years the PGA Tour has been playing at Doral, only two players have ever birdied the 18th hole to win (Ben Crenshaw in 1988, Jim Furyk in 2000). That's why it was so stunning when Australian Craig Parry eagled the hole with his 176-yard six-iron approach to defeat Scott Verplank on the first hole of a playoff in 2004. He did it on a newly-lengthened hole that played as the hardest on the PGA Tour all year and, according to PGA Tour player Briny Baird, is "as tough a hole as you could ever imagine playing."

Opposite: In 2004, Craig Parry demonstrated that the best way to avoid trouble on the famed 18th at Doral's Blue Monster is to drain your approach shot.

Strangely, for a country that has produced so many great players over the years—Ernie Els, Bobby Locke, and Gary Player to name but three—South Africa is not a land blessed with many great golf courses. Only the Durban Country Club is currently ranked in *Golf Magazine*'s top 100 courses in the world.

DCC, however, is one to treasure. Designed in 1922 by George Waterman and transplanted Scotsman Laurie Waters (Waters was an apprentice to Old Tom Morris before emigrating and becoming four-time South African champion), the course is a delightful mix of links and inland features. Home to the first of Player's 13 South African Open wins, this is a course of great beauty dotted with holes to match those anywhere in the world. The most demanding among them is the 513-yard third.

Built in a natural valley amid dunes fronting the Indian Ocean, this rumpled par five is shielded from the sandy beach by thick bushes, giving it an impression of seclusion which only adds to its atmosphere.

That said, the drive must be struck from an elevated tee that affords a birds-eye view of all that lies ahead—both good and bad. The fairway is edged on the left by the dunes and on the right by bushes. Neither is a desirable spot for golf balls, at least those owned by players whose desire is to make par. Only a straight drive will do here—no easy task given the almost ever-present breeze off the water and the infancy of the round. Mental intimidation is an ever-present problem. Too often a golfer's last thought here involves a "don't."

While it's true the green can be reached in two shots, the hole throws up its toughest defenses against those who try to do so. The large bunker up the left side is reachable only by the long hitter, so going for the green in two requires a particularly accurate drive. The golfing gorilla must be as accurate with his approach as he was with his drive if he wants to get home in fewer than three shots. Unhelpfully, the green is slightly raised, so running the ball on is unlikely; a high, brave shot is required. Anything left or right is likely to be lost in the African bush.

Durban's third hole also challenges the less powerful. Bunkers left and right and nearly fifty yards from the front of the putting surface force even the cautious to be wary. The pitch to the green is no bargain. Up to an elevated surface, it is a strict test of distance control and feel. Par is always a good score here.

Gary Player won the first of his 13 South African Open titles on the famed Waterman-Waters design of Durban Country Club.

East Lake is without a doubt the toughest golf course in the world. No, it's not the most difficult layout in the game (although, as we'll see, it certainly has its moments), but given its long, turbulent life—its rise, fall, and resurrection—genteel East Lake stands as the most resilient, most durable club extant. It's the course that wouldn't die.

Ten years after its formation in 1898, the Atlanta Athletic Club opened its first golf course, designed by Tom Bendelow and built on the shores of East Lake in a well-to-do section of Atlanta. Five years later, in 1913, the club hired Donald Ross to redesign Bendelow's course (later referred to as the No. 1 Course). As most golf fans know, it was here that a youngster named Robert Tyre Jones, Jr. learned the game at the feet of club professional Stewart Maiden.

In 1925, a fire destroyed the club's Tudor-style clubhouse (a similarly destructive fire had struck in 1914). In 1928, Ross was again hired, this time to build a second 18 (the No. 2 Course). With two great golf courses in the East Lake community and a legitimate claim to the rearing of Bobby Jones, Atlanta Athletic Club gained an international reputation for golfing excellence. While that reputation was indelible, some of its veneer would eventually fade.

By the mid-1960s, the neighborhood, located a few miles southeast of Atlanta, had seen a rapid decline. The club sold the No. 2 Course to a developer. In 1967, most of the members migrated to the Atlanta Athletic Club's new (and current) location in Duluth, Georgia. Meanwhile, the No. 1 Course, which had hosted the 1963 Ryder Cup, was acquired by a group of members who were determined to sustain their club even in the face of an overwhelming cultural shift. By 1970, public housing had replaced the No. 2 Course site and the once-elegant neighborhood surrounding No. 1 slid into poverty and despair. Through the 1980s, drug abuse, serious crime, and violence grew so rampant in East Lake that the once elegant community became known as "Little Vietnam."

In 1993, a charitable foundation inspired by Atlanta real estate executive and philanthropist Tom Cousins acquired what remained of the East Lake area. With corporate donations, Cousins revitalized not only the golf course and clubhouse, but the entire community, building grade-A housing, a new school, and even a Rees Jones-designed, executive-length public golf course. Cousins's plan, which seemed quixotic at best, actually worked. In 1994 Rees Jones was brought in to remodel the old No. 1 Course, and soon thereafter the legendary club was hosting the PGA Tour's elite Tour Championship and the 2001 U.S. Amateur Championship.

The tenuous years of the 1960s, 1970s, and 1980s seem to have had a vulcanizing effect on the course, ensuring that this swatch of golf history would emerge stronger and better than ever. Today's 16th hole surely reflects that tempering. A long and pretty par four (481 yards from the tournament tees), it begins with a memorable view of the Atlanta skyline. The tee shot must be forced into a narrow, sloped landing area. Even well-struck drives can wind up in the rough. From the fairway a mid- to long-iron is needed to reach the green, with two large bunkers awaiting any errant approaches to a large and receptive putting surface that slopes from back to front. As he does on all his work, Jones paid special attention to this green's contours.

"If you miss the green on the right side and the pin is on the right, it's pretty hard to recover," says Jones. "And that's where they tend to miss that green, on the right."

In the 1998 Tour Championship, the 16th hole surrendered only three birdies over four rounds. While that tournament will be remembered for Hal Sutton's playoff win over Vijay Singh, Singh's yeoman save on No. 16 preserved his chance at a playoff.

As ever, tough and East Lake go hand in hand.

Opposite, bottom: Hal Sutton prevailed in the Tour Championship's debut at East Lake in 1998.

If it's true that in business success breeds success, then it may hold true that in golf-course design difficulty breeds difficulty. Consider the problems that designer Jack Nicklaus encountered in the creation of English Turn and you can begin to understand the venom that infuses the course's home hole. Simply put: Until the tournament moved to the new TPC of Louisiana in 2005, year-in, year-out, there was no harder hole on the entire PGA Tour.

The difficulty of English Turn is rooted in the land itself. Nicklaus and his client USF&G were looking for a location that would not only serve as the new home for the PGA Tour's New Orleans stop (in 1989 the course replaced Lakewood Country Club, which had hosted the Tour since 1963), but one that could also double as a real estate development. "Rather than going out of town and buying high ground, we stayed in town and built the course on land that was nine feet below sea level," says Nicklaus. In fact, the Mississippi River ran right by the mucky property and actually stood above the site.

The site was so low that it cost the developers $11 million just to get the land up to a level where they could even think about building and sustaining a golf course. Next, because the site consisted of heavy clay-like soil and therefore would not drain as quickly or effectively as a golf course requires, Nicklaus and the developers "plated" the entire site with a two-foot layer of sand that allows the water to "percolate" or trickle away from the grass surface and helps the course recover quickly from heavy rains or even regular watering.

Of course, the existing mucky surface meant that the heavy equipment that's rolled on to most other sites would have bogged down here, so all the heavy work—the cutting and filling of land—was done entirely with draglines. An additional $5 million later, the course was finished.

The 18th hole is nearly as difficult to play as it was to build. For starters, it comes directly after the challenging 17th hole. Then, at 471 yards from the tips, its length is an issue. Like the rest of the golf course, water also abounds on 18 (there is at least one water hazard on every single hole at English Turn). The lake that guards the entire left side of the hole and the beach-like bunker that parallels it are to say the least, eye-catching distractions. Nearly as distracting is a patch of deep bunkers that guards the right side of the fairway. They are fully in play for anyone who drives the ball anywhere from 240 to 300 yards. Between the beach and the bunkers lies a landing area less than 30 yards wide.

Even the biggest, most accurate drivers will be faced with at least 170 yards into the green. But most players will have an approach of anywhere from 190 to 200 yards to a narrow space that appears to have been spun about 45 degrees to the left. Well protected by the water on the left and copious amounts of sand immediately in front, Sunday's left-side hole location became a favorite of PGA Tour fans and a nightmare for its players.

The greenside sand didn't bother David Frost in 1990. The South African holed a bunker shot for a birdie on the 72nd hole to join the list of players who beat Greg Norman by sinking a shot from off the green on the final hole.

It's only fitting that the term English Turn is derived from a 1699 battle between the French and English for a nearby section of the Mississippi River. The French, who were actually out-manned, convinced the enemy that the English troops were in fact outnumbered. The English turned and retreated. Three hundred years later, as you stand on the 18th tee, that doesn't seem like such a bad idea.

David Frost conquered English Turn's 18th—and Greg Norman—in 1990.

Firestone was founded in 1929 by Harvey Firestone, scion of the eponymous tire company. However, it wasn't until a quarter century later, in 1954, that Firestone began to make a name for itself as host to world-class championship golf. Certainly some of that status derives from the fact that Firestone and its leadership never shied away from a little exposure. In fact, in 1973, Firestone Country Club became the only course in the world to host three televised tournaments—the American Golf Classic, the World Series of Golf, and the CBS Golf Classic—in the same calendar year. But Firestone's reputation goes beyond TV. It earned its place in golf history the hard way: by consistently beating up the game's best players.

After settling in Cleveland, little-known Bert Way, a Brit who quit elementary school to work as an assistant to Royal North Devon's legendary Willie Dunn and who once served as personal golf professional to John D. Rockefeller, designed the original South Course for Mr. Firestone. Envisioned as a gift for Firestone employees, the Way-designed course was relatively docile. It was Robert Trent Jones who thoroughly revamped the course in 1959 and gave the South Course the teeth on which it would stake its reputation. The remodeled South hosted the 1960 PGA Championship. That week a muscular 30-year-old named Arnold Palmer triple bogeyed a hole and referred to it as a "monster." The nickname stuck. In fact, the entire golf course became known as "The Monster."

The hole was the 625-yard 16th.

The PGA Championship returned to Firestone in 1975, and it looked like another of the game's legends, Jack Nicklaus, might be headed for a triple bogey on the 16th in the third round. Leading the championship, he hit his drive into an unplayable lie on the left, took a penalty drop, and knocked his next shot through the fairway and into the trees on the right side. From there, though, he lofted an eight-iron over a tree to 20 feet, sank the putt for an unlikely par, and was never challenged on the way to the title.

Nicklaus redesigned the hole in 1986, doing nothing to ease its agony. Playing largely downhill it came through the years to offer the longest hitters a dim shot at eagle if they could somehow negotiate a one-iron or three-wood shot from a downhill lie over or around a green-front pond that was actually enlarged by the Golden Bear. When the hole was lengthened by 42 yards in 2003, to measure 667 yards, it staved off technology's march and again became virtually untouchable in two and reinstated itself as the most formidable par five on Tour.

The added length has not been universally lauded, particularly among long hitters who have now seen bogey re-enter the picture. No less than Tiger Woods has succumbed to 16. In the 2003 WGC-NEC Invitational, Woods was one shot off the lead

in the second round when he came to "The Monster." To add insult to injury, the hole was playing into a brisk wind. Woods drove into the right rough, and then caught the face of a fairway bunker on his second, leaving him little choice but to play his third short of the pond. His fourth sailed over the green, and his 20-foot putt barely prevented a double-bogey. (Woods was in good company: there were 86 bogeys, 21 doubles, and 12 triples or worse on the 16th hole that year.)

Says Woods, "You can make seven there so fast. It's so easy to do because if you lay up short of that bunker, you're faced with a pretty tough shot to a pin where you have no green to work with, and you've got water and gusty winds. It makes for a really tough shot."

One of the reasons the hole is so befuddling to Tour players is that they are used to handling par fives rather easily. Of the top 21 most difficult holes on the 2003 PGA Tour, only Firestone's 16th, which averaged .388 strokes over par, was a par five.

"It is brutal," says Darren Clarke, who won that tournament. "If you miss your tee shot there at all it turns into a very, very tough hole."

Clarke didn't miss his drive in the first round, hitting a colossal smash that left him with 276 yards to the front of the green. "I had a real, real chance at going for it," he said, "only the ball was laying on the slight downslope. I had the three-wood out and put it back in the bag again, and I had it out and I put it back in the bag again. I had it in and out three times."

He laid up, and eventually won. Not everybody is intimidated by the green-front pond. Lon Hinkle found a new way to navigate the hazard. In 1979 he intentionally skipped his approach across the surface of the water with his third shot from the right rough en route to his only World Series of Golf title.

Opposite: Jack Nicklaus made a miracle par in 1975 and later did design work on the 16th at Firestone.

When architect Jeff Brauer was asked to do a second course for Giants Ridge, he was determined that it would be different from his Legends course. The difference began with site selection. Whereas the first course is laid out in a typical northwoods setting, the second course is built on a defunct quarry.

The second course is also different in temperament.

"The first course was playable and everybody seemed to like it," says Brauer, "but the better players were looking for a little more of a challenge. So that's what we tried to do. We knew it was going to be more difficult to start with, but when I saw the quarry site—those abrupt changes and deep pits—that made it happen."

The 478-yard (from the tips) par-four eighth is typical of the course's demanding genius. Very reminiscent of Pine Valley, the hole plays slightly uphill, particularly on the second shot. The old quarry is visibly present on both sides of the fairway. The strategy of the hole is that you try to carry a diagonal waste bunker that pinches the right side of the fairway. The further you carry the ball, the better your view of the green through a little gap in some spoil mounds.

"The fearsome part of the hole," says Brauer, "is what happens if you try to carry it and you miss."

That fairway bunker has a very steep bank that measures about eight to ten feet deep. "Basically, if you hit that sand, you've made the hole a par five," says Brauer. "It's quite the architectural dilemma."

Even perfectly placed drives leave the golfer with a difficult approach. The shot of 200-plus yards is played into an old-fashioned green that can be accessed by bouncing a shot in from the left. Shots to the right are likely to be repelled by steep contouring. Many of the pars made here are of the chip-and-a-putt variety.

While the quarries have been inactive since the 1970s, their legacy lives on in Brauer's Quarry Course design. Fittingly enough, when the quarry was in operation it was called the Embarrass Mine.

Only open for play since July 2003, the course is still making a name for itself. And while it has yet to host the world's best players, it has been visited by *Golf Digest*'s Ron Whitten. In his review, he wrote that the Quarry "is as fine a set of golf holes as has been produced thus far in the 21st century. . .It is already hands-down the finest course in Minnesota. Hazeltine National looks like a cornfield next to it, Interlachen like a quaint museum artifact. In the national arena, this Quarry will swallow up all Quarries before it, from Florida to California. It's a combination of Pebble Beach, Pine Valley, Merion, and Tobacco Road, with a bit of architectural Tabasco sauce sprinkled in for the occasional jolt. . . It is the rarest of courses, 18 holes without a single lackluster feature."

Architect Jeff Brauer made the second course at Giants Ridge a test for better players.

In the mid-1970s, not long after the completion of Muirfield Village, Jack Nicklaus was asked by the president of the Royal Canadian Golf Association to design a golf course that would serve as the permanent home for the Canadian Open. "They had the site all set in Oakville, Ontario," writes Nicklaus in *Nicklaus By Design*. "In fact, there was an old golf course there. Aside from a stream that ran through a limited low section of the land, it was a pretty bland piece of property on which we could do nearly anything we wanted."

Nicklaus recalls his work at Glen Abbey for two features, both breakthroughs for spectators. The first is his vision for creating a spoke-and-wheel layout, positioning the clubhouse so the holes run out and back from that central hub a few times. This way, reasoned Nicklaus, more people could see more golf shots with less walking.

The other feature was stadium golf. Both at Glen Abbey and at Muirfield Village, Nicklaus was an early devotee of stadium mounding. While Pete Dye became known as the father of the spectator mound, Dye himself admits that Nicklaus was the innovator.

Glen Abbey hosted the Canadian Open from the course's opening in 1977 through 1979, again from 1981 through 1996, and again in 1998, 1999, 2000, and 2004. Over that time the course has consistently showcased exciting golf, particularly down the stretch where two potential eagles lie in the last three holes. But the par-four 14th is the most difficult hole on the course. Canadian-born Dick Zokol has played in several Canadian Opens and has recorded dozens of rounds on Nicklaus's course. He says No. 14 is the kind of hole that can keep a guy up nights.

"The 14th is a particularly difficult driving hole," says Zokol, who explains that there are two forces to contend with on the drive. "First is the dogleg right. Then Sixteen Mile Creek runs left to right diagonally. So the farther right you want to go in an attempt to shorten the hole, the longer your carry over the creek must be. The hole favors a left to right shot, which is obviously part of Nicklaus's strategy."

The green design is also difficult because of a horseshoe-shaped ledge that Nicklaus installed. "You have to be very precise on your second shot to get to the quadrant of the pin location for that day," says Zokol. "It's very demanding. It's the kind of hole that's in your mind," he says. "When you're going to the course, you say, I've got to deal with No. 14 today."

Nicklaus says 14 is not the best hole at Glen Abbey but concedes that it is the most difficult. "It's very deceptive in its design," he says. "Plus, it sets up awkwardly for most players. They just can't get comfortable."

Nicklaus himself has felt the sting of the hole. The Canadian Open is the most significant tournament he never won in his career, but he appeared ready to rectify that in 1984 when he took the lead with a birdie on the 13th hole in the final round. He promptly hit his tee shot into the water on 14, made a bogey, and ended up losing to Greg Norman.

Jack Nicklaus's best chance for a Canadian Open title was undone by his own design at Glen Abbey.

Hallbrook *Country Club, Leawood, Kansas ~ 7th hole*

Tom Fazio is not known for building particularly difficult golf holes. Sure, he's designed and remodeled courses that test the best players—Butler National, on which he worked with his uncle George comes to mind, as does his remodeling work at Oak Hill in 1979 and Augusta National in recent years. But Fazio has made his name designing beautiful golf courses that provide enough challenge and more than enough visual delight to keep members both busy and happy.

So it's surprising that the hardest golf course in Kansas, and one of the most difficult in the country, is a Fazio design. From the championship tees, Hallbrook Country Club measures 6,862 yards and boasts a slope of 151 and a course rating of 75.0. This is Fazio? A little history is in order.

If the 1970s will be remembered for disco, then the 1980s should be remembered for hard golf courses. As *Golf Digest* architecture editor Ron Whitten says, "In the 1980s—PGA West through Koolau—everybody wanted the toughest golf course." The peak came shortly after 1983–1984 when the USGA came out with its slope ratings. Suddenly, says Whitten, "every developer wanted the toughest course in the world; it was a badge of honor."

Hallbrook was built for Don Hall, longtime chairman of Hallmark Cards, on the Hall family farm. The year was 1988, smack dab in the era of what Fazio himself describes as "strong golf."

A contributor to the trend, says Fazio, was the increasing influence of media, marketing, and communications; an emphasis on the best new golf courses, the best this, the best that, the top 100, cover-girl golf holes. "People would go play a new course, and someone would ask, how did you like that new course, and the guy would say, there were a couple of weak holes. Well, every great old golf course in the world has a couple

of weak holes," says Fazio. "That doesn't hurt the old courses. But if you've got a brand new course and there's a couple of holes that don't look dramatic or play hard, then the raters are going to give it an average rating."

Compounding the toughness trend was an increasingly demanding and sophisticated golf travel market. Whether it be Hilton Head, Palm Beach County, Scottsdale, or Palm Springs, people were selecting vacation destinations on the strength of the new golf courses. Fazio remembers one marketing consultant involved with the Hallbrook project: "He said, 'Tom, what people want is the same kind of quality, the same kind of strength that they go and find at these other places. That's an important part of what people want. You can't *not* give them that because of the expectation level.'"

Within those parameters, Fazio created what is among the hardest holes in his portfolio. The seventh at Hallbrook is a 454-yard (from the tips) par four with trees right and a creek left. Like the rest of the golf course, the fairway here is wide, but if you miss fairways and greens the course is extremely penal. The second shot is a difficult one off a downhill lie into a triple-tier green that's guarded in front by a creek.

"There are three strengths to the golf hole," says Fazio. "The Midwest, of course, always has wind blowing. So when you're on the tee and you're playing a strong golf hole, you've got to deal with the wind. Now you get into the fairway landing area, and the contour of the land has a lot to do with it. Where is the ball hitting and rolling? Then comes the putting surface."

When you combine the difficulty of the tee shot, the length, the contour of the fairway, the second-shot approach, the angle of the green, the putting surface, and the ever-present Midwestern wind, you end up with a severely difficult hole.

"You could take the same length golf hole," says Fazio, "the same square footage of sand that's in the bunkers, take the same square footage of green, and build a very easy golf hole. It's just a matter of the twists, the turns, the angle, and the details that allow you to go from a very easy hole to an extremely difficult hole."

Opposite, bottom: Hallbrook Country Club, says designer Tom Fazio (shown standing on the course's 18th hole), is a product of the 1980s, the era of "strong golf."

Although many assume that golf immigrated to America via the Northeast, the fact is that the first designated golfing ground on American soil was Harleston's Green in Charleston. It was there that members of the South Carolina Golf Club, founded in 1786, played over an unknown number of holes in what is now downtown.

Harleston's Green is long gone, succeeded by its descendant club, the Country Club of Charleston. But the fact that the game has such deep roots in the Palmetto State is fitting because it is in modern-day South Carolina, 90 miles south of Charleston, where the game's past and future commingle every spring. In a state where the game is more than 200 years old, the greatest players of the 21st century compete on a world-renowned course designed by one of the art's true revolutionaries and co-designed by the greatest player of all time. There's a reason the PGA Tour event played there is called the Heritage.

Charles Fraser, the man who converted Hilton Head Island from low-country swamp to a thriving resort town, had as keen an eye for the future as he did for the past. As Pete Dye, who co-designed Harbour Town with Jack Nicklaus, writes in his autobiography, "Fraser had the most imagination of any developer I've ever known. He took a little desolate island that did not even have a bridge to it and convinced his skeptics that he could develop a multifaceted resort that would captivate the world."

Fraser was convinced that the key to developing a successful golf resort was luring a PGA Tour event to the Carolina coast. He knew that in order to draw the attention of Tour officials and a world rich in golf resorts, his resort would not only have to strive for quality, but for what the advertising industry calls "a point of difference." The team of Dye, who was fairly new to the trade but had exhibited an independent streak, and Nicklaus, who had already established himself as the greatest golfer since Bobby Jones and who wanted to dip his toes into golf-course design, was a no-brainer.

Even Fraser was surprised by what he got. In the mid-to-late 1960s, American golf-course architects were increasingly relying on length and enlarged greens to challenge golfers. At Harbour Town, Dye and Nicklaus went completely in the opposite direction. The course became famous for the fact that while short in length (6,655 yards in its original form; 6,916 today), it tested the best players by demanding and rewarding accuracy both off the tee and with the irons. A drive to the correct spot in the fairway has always been more useful at Harbour Town than a mindlessly long bomb. Fairways here have always been considerably wider than at other Tour stops. Bunkers, mostly with low lips, are used judiciously, leaving trees and the ever-present wind to dictate strategy. The fairways mirror the flatness of a site where only six feet separates the highest point from the lowest. The greens, still among the smallest on the PGA Tour, are relatively mild in contour, particularly after a 2000 remodeling overseen by Dye. Ever since its 1969 opening (the first round ever played on the course was the opening round of that year's Heritage Classic), Harbour Town has succeeded in one of the game's toughest balancing acts: challenging world-class fields and pleasing vacation-minded tourists alike.

Hal Sutton says, "It's fun to play when there's a premium on accuracy. Here you can be in the fairway and it still might not be very good."

Harbour Town's eighth hole is an excellent example. The dogleg left par four, which originally played at 433 yards, now measures 470 from the Heritage tees. Nicklaus's oft-cited philosophy of "playing" a hole mentally from green to tee is useful here. The small green is hard against a bunker and water hazard that run parallel for the last 100 yards of the hole. Given the dogleg left, the green can only be accessed from the right side of the fairway. Furthermore, the fairway widens invitingly to the right and encourages players to hit driver. A drive to the left is not challenged by anything but trees and good sense.

Phil Mickelson, one of the best in the game today at shaping shots, agrees. "Driving on this golf course is critical," he says. "This is probably one of the best shotmakers' golf courses out here. You've got to fit the ball all the way. You can't just get up there on any tee and hit it straight. You've got to fade it or draw it, and the second shot is also either a fade or a draw. The wind just makes it that much more difficult.

"I love to be creative. And the great thing about this golf course that goes unnoticed is that the fairways are really twice as wide as the actual landing area, meaning the part that you're hitting to is half the fairway width. If you miss that part, you have to be creative to hit a left-to-right or right-to-left shot around trees. But because you're in the fairway, you have the opportunity to do that."

Praise for Harbour Town, pre- and post-remodeling, is one of the constants in modern golf. So much so, it's hard to believe that a course universally loved today was nearly thrown on the scrap heap after its grand opening. The course was so raw in its Tour debut that Dye was still touching up bunkers as the field began to tee off, and the early reviews were not good.

Grumblings about trickiness and unfairness, compounded by high scores, seeped into the press tent during the early part of the first round. Then Jim Colbert came in with a surprise 69 and diverted sportswriters by comparing the course favorably to Pine Valley. Three days later, when Arnold Palmer broke a 14-month slump by winning the Heritage Classic, Harbour Town had a place in golf history. As Dye states in his autobiography, "Jim Colbert and Arnold Palmer may have grabbed the headlines in that first year, but the Links proved that 7,000-yard-plus golf courses weren't needed to challenge the top professionals."

Opposite: Designer Pete Dye was making changes right up to the start of the first Heritage Classic, which marked the course opening.

In his 27-year career, Dave Hill's statistics read as follows: 13 wins, $1.1 million in earnings, and at least one practice-range fistfight. But among golf fans in Minnesota, Hill will likely be remembered as a pioneer in the art of golf-course criticism.

It was 1970, in the days when Tour players usually found something nice to say about a host course. The congenitally candid Hill, who had just carded a second-round 69, was asked to meet with the media. Lubricated with no fewer than four vodka tonics, Hill agreed.

"How did you find the course?" he was asked.

"Hell," groused Hill, "I'm still looking for it. If I had to play this course every day for fun, I'd find me another game. Just because you cut the grass and put up flags doesn't mean you have a golf course."

"What does it lack?" asked the reporter.

"Eighty acres of corn and a few cows," said Hill.

"What do you recommend they do with it?"

"Plow it up and start over again," growled Hill. "The man who designed this course had the blueprints upside down."

Hill was only the most outspoken critic of the golf course (despite the fact that he eventually finished second to Tony Jacklin). Hazeltine made few friends that week. In fact, the course as it played in 1970 was probably the most disliked Open venue of all time. Hill only said, albeit with a little more flair,

what was on nearly every contestant's mind—that the Robert Trent Jones-designed golf course, with its blind tee shots and sharp doglegs, was not up to hosting the National Open.

In the wake of that criticism, an embarrassed Hazeltine went back to the drawing board. By 1988, 12 of its 18 holes had been significantly redesigned, the most dramatic changes coming on Nos. 16 and 17, both of which were virtually scrapped and designed from scratch. No. 16 went from being a par three with a backdrop of water to a par four with water very much in play on both shots. And the 344-yard par-four 17th was replaced by a 182-yard par three.

The USGA returned in 1991, and the Open title won by the late Payne Stewart was largely decided on the two brand new holes. Eleven years later, the PGA of America staged the 2002 PGA Championship at Hazeltine. Again, No.16 played a pivotal role as unlikely victor Rich Beem birdied it to stave off a Sunday charge from Tiger Woods. Both championships produced thrilling, colorful finishes, and Hazeltine finally carved out its place among America's great championship tests.

No hole has done more for Hazeltine's image rehabilitation than the 16th. It's still far from the professionals' favorite; in fact, Fuzzy Zoeller says, "It just doesn't work as a golf hole." But whether players love it or hate it, the 16th has earned its reputation as a championship test of nerves and skill.

"Next to the 12th hole at Augusta, it's the most terrifying hole in golf," says Nick Price.

Measuring only 396 yards—in fact, it's one of the shorter par fours on the course—the 16th is all about wind and water. It's the only hole on the course that brings the winds coming off Lake Hazeltine directly into play, and the tee shot requires a carry of some 200 yards over lake and marsh. The narrow strip of fairway is guarded on the left by a four-foot-wide brook, courtesy of Rees Jones. During his touch-up for the 1991 Open, Jones discovered a drainage ditch in the left rough. Certain that there would be some dispute during the Open as to whether the ditch was actually a hazard, Jones removed the doubt by widening it to four feet. But the USGA's thick rough often kept balls from finding the new hazard. In 2002 the PGA shifted the fairway cut so that the brook, which now runs up the left side about three-quarters the length of the hole, is clearly in play on the tee shot.

Hazeltine National's challenging 16th hole made the difference in the 1991 U.S. Open playoff for Payne Stewart, shown celebrating his birdie, and Scott Simpson, who bogeyed.

On the right, the lakefront stretches the entire length of the hole. For an extra measure of aquaphobia, the lake loops around the peninsula green to guard the back as well. The green is slightly raised and encourages an approach from the left side of the fairway.

"It's a great little hole," says Minnesota native Tom Lehman. "It's a very scary hole, especially the fact that the wind almost always blows in some form or another, usually in your face and across. It requires a great tee shot, a great second shot. It takes a lot of courage to play."

Another Minnesotan, Tim Herron, says: "A lot of disaster can happen on that hole." And happen it has. Take the 1991 Open. Like lemmings into the lake, players such as Billy Andrade, Mark Calcavecchia, John Inman, Jodie Mudd, Andy North, and Chris Perry all came to the 16th hole in contention and left in sodden distress. At the 2002 PGA, John Daly penciled in a soggy 11 in the first round after putting a total of four shots in the water. The 16th harassed the field that year for an average score of 4.496.

Stewart forged his 1991 Open championship on the 16th hole, tying Scott Simpson for the lead there on Sunday and sealing the deal with a birdie on Monday. Conversely, the 16th is where Simpson lost it. During the four rounds of regulation play Simpson carded nine bogeys, three of them on the 16th hole.

In the Monday playoff, Simpson bogeyed it again, giving Stewart the lead.

On the eve of the final round of the 2002 PGA Championship, Rich Beem seemingly anticipated his coming showdown with the 16th. "If I have a one- or two-stroke lead going into 16, that will be probably one of the hardest shots I've ever hit."

He did have the lead and it was a test. Beem came to the 16th with a four-stroke margin, but Woods, in the group ahead of him, was about to make the second of four consecutive birdies to finish the round.

"I was probably as committed to that shot as I've been to any shot that I've ever hit," says Beem of his tee shot. "I hit a beautiful little 7-wood out there, and that's when I got a little bit nervous. I felt really pumped up, and I was afraid I was going to hit my nine-iron (second) too far. I had 148 and I felt that, you know, if I really go after this, and I hit it solid, it's going to go long. So I tried to back off a little bit, and I pushed it, and I honestly didn't know if it was going to clear the hazard or not. Luckily, it did."

Beem's putt from 35 feet was true. He would go on to win his first major championship, and not only had the 16th hole taken its rightful place in golf history, but the restoration of Hazeltine's pride was complete.

In the annals of golf-course design, the tandem of Colt and Alison is akin to Hollywood's Hope and Crosby or television's Burns and Allen. Lasting success has bound the names for eternity.

Both British-born partners abandoned successful non-golf careers to pursue the burgeoning field of golf-course design. Harry S. Colt practiced law until 1905 when his successful redesign of Sunningdale Golf Club outside London suggested a new career. Among his designs was Stoke Poges Golf Club, also near London. C. H. "Hugh" Alison was a journalist-turned-club secretary of Stoke Poges. His assistance to Colt on that course's design spurred a historic and prolific partnership that would last from 1908 until Colt's death in 1951.

The partnership brought innovation to golf-course architecture and did so at a time when the game was expanding well beyond the British Isles. Colt was the first golf-course designer to utilize blueprints. Alison was the first truly global golf-course designer. While the men shared credit on dozens of projects, Colt and Alison rarely worked together. Colt oversaw the team's work in the U.K. and Europe. North America and the Far East were Alison's domain.

In the early 1930s Alison undertook an extensive survey of the Far East. At the time Japan was still undergoing a Westernization, though it would soon turn away from it. Among the many new ideas and pastimes filtering into the culture was golf. Alison took advantage of the game's nascent popularity and designed Hirono Golf Club in the port city of Kobe on the island of Honshu.

Hirono is not only one of the finest golf courses in Japan—it is routinely ranked among the 100 greatest courses in the world—but it is also among the toughest. In fact, many of Japan's most respected critics say the par-three 180-yard 13th hole is the hardest hole in this golf-crazed region.

A wide creek guards the green, as do typically broad and fluidly designed bunkers. In fact, Alison's bunkering at Hirono was so distinctive and had such an influence on Japanese golf-course design that to this day the Japanese often refer to bunkers as "arisons." But Ken Yamada, one of Japan's leading TV golf analysts, says that, like another world-class par three, wind is the real issue here.

"There are three different wind directions, always," says Yamada, two-time Japan Amateur Champion and successful touring professional. "One is on the teeing ground, then on the pond, and again on the green." No surprise, therefore, that Yamada and others liken the hole's difficulty to that of the challenging 12th at Augusta National.

"That makes for very difficult distance and direction judgment," says Yamada. "You feel side-wind on your cheek, but the flag shows a different direction. Then the wind on the pond adds one more element, which makes for big confusion."

In the course of Japan's late-20th-century golf boom, classic design was not always the priority. Many of the country's modern courses are short on subtlety and long on overt toughness. Hirono, says Yamada, is the real thing—classic and tough.

C.H. Alison's bunkering at Hirono made such an impression on the Japanese people that his surname has entered the national golf vernacular. Alison is shown here on the site of what would become the famous 13th hole.

Hell hath no fury like a millionaire scorned.

In the early 1950s, Bert Suprenant was a fast-rising and hard-edged entrepreneur. As Suprenant Wire & Cable Corporation, a manufacturing company based in Clinton, Massachusetts, continued to grow, Suprenant slowly and by some accounts reluctantly began trading in his blue-collar background for a white-collar lifestyle, but he never lost his rough, earthy edge.

One story has it that this model of New England independence was denied membership at the exclusive Worcester Country Club. The other is that Suprenant, who was a member of nearby Wachusett Country Club, had a falling out with the owner of Wachusett and reacted by building his own golf course, one that in Suprenant's mind would put Worcester, Wachusett, and other area clubs to shame. His course would be better than anything around. For Suprenant, better meant bigger and brawnier.

Exactly what it was that riled Suprenant may never be known, but what's certain is that in 1953 he acquired Runaway Brook Golf Club, a nearby nine-holer, and soon hired Geoffrey Cornish to design his first solo 18-hole design over 325 beautifully forested acres. With input from a variety of local experts, including 1913 U.S. Open champion Francis Ouimet and long-time PGA Tour player Paul Harney, Cornish ended up building what was at the time the longest golf course in the world. Harney won seven times on the PGA Tour and was known as a long hitter. His role in the design was to stand on a proposed tee box and hit a drive as far as he could. Suprenant told Cornish to place a bunker wherever the ball landed.

The White tees measure 6,547 yards, the Blue run 7,138 yards, and the world-famous Tiger tees (named long before Eldrick Woods was born) step off at a tongue-lolling 8,325 yards—nearly five miles of golf course. And length is only part of the Pines Course's madness. The greens are enormous and loaded with movement. The bunkering, toned down in a 1972 Robert Trent Jones renovation, was sinister and is now merely brutal. From the Tiger tees, the course carries a slope rating of 154 and a course rating of 77.

Suprenant's ire is most palpable in the course's signature hole, the 715-yard par-six fifth. That's right, par six from the Tiger tees (it's a mere 607-yard par-five from the Blues). Par sixes—and there are a few in the game—are often regarded as gimmick holes, contraventions of decorum, if not USGA Rules. But par six holes are totally legitimate, says Marty Parkes, senior director of communications for the USGA. "We do acknowledge them," says Parkes. "We do rate them, and they are figured into our handicapping system."

International's par six is a dogleg left . . . eventually. Playing from the Tiger tees you'll need to cover approximately 570 yards (250 just to reach the fairway) before you can even get a glimpse of the green. The long hitter (and who else would play the Tiger tees?) had better cover most of those 570 yards in two shots in order not to be blocked out from going for the green in three, because the first eighty percent of the hole is a straight, tree-lined corridor. There are not even any bunkers until after the dogleg, the final 150 yards into the hole.

The fifth's green alone is a lesson in land management, measuring 29,000 square feet, more than two-thirds of an acre, in size. Suprenant is said to have asked Cornish to name the biggest green he had ever seen, and then ordered one that was bigger. The resulting surface is 89 yards deep and about 35 yards wide. Says Mike Daron, head professional, "If one of the maintenance guys pulls fifth-hole duty, he knows he's done something wrong."

The size of the green is one thing, the movement is another. The radical undulations make it look more like an Easter Island megalith than a putting surface. Putts of 50, 60, and 70 yards are common. In fact, the greens at the International's Pines course are so large and boast so much contour that superintendent Ron Milenski tries to keep them at moderate speeds (9 to 11 on the Stimpmeter). "Otherwise," he says, "you couldn't keep the ball on the green, and a round of golf would take six hours."

Although the par-six Tiger tees get the most attention, the fifth hole unquestionably plays harder as a 607-yard par five than it does as a 715-yard par six (regardless of tee selection, the fifth is the No.1 handicap hole from all the men's tees).

"The par is irrelevant," says Daron. "All you're really trying to do is shoot the lowest possible score. From the Tiger tees, if you get on in three, you have an eagle putt. It's easiest as a par six. If you play it as a 607-yard par five and you make a birdie or a par, now that's substantial."

Opposite, bottom: In 1956, architect Geoffrey Cornish laid out what was then the longest golf course in the world at the International.

Tom Fazio has been working on and designing golf courses since he was a 16-year-old, tagging along with his uncle, course designer George Fazio. After 42 years in golf-course design, Fazio has come to the following conclusion: "All kids hit it long."

Fazio has some first-hand experience with long shots, not only playing with his own children, but in designing a golf course for Oklahoma State University. He isn't complaining, and he's not arguing to scale back the ball, he's simply stating a truism of golf-course design in the 21st century.

"We can say isn't it a shame that there are no Corey Pavins and Ben Crenshaws anymore," says Fazio, "but that's like saying isn't it a shame that we don't have any Johnny Unitas-sized quarterbacks anymore. That's life, that's the way it is." And while he concedes that equipment and golf balls have clearly boosted 21st-century distance, he has no concerns that golf is getting too easy. "For the rest of us," he says, "for the normal people, there are plenty of hard golf courses out there."

Karsten Creek is one of them. It better be. It's not only the home course of the national powerhouse Oklahoma State golf team, but while Fazio was working on the course—which measures 7,095 yards from the tips, with a 74.9 course rating and healthy 142 slope rating—legendary OSU golf coach Mike Holder approached him to say "I don't think it's hard enough for my kids, I've got future tour players here, I want a strong golf course."

Holder got one. One local sportswriter put it this way: "Karsten Creek is Holder's Quantico, a training ground for champions in the making."

Any collegiate practice facility in which covered stalls face south in order to blunt biting northerly winter winds and on which outdoor tee boxes create an enormous circle that allows players to work directly into the wind when they choose has been created with future Charles Howell IIIs in mind. (The long-hitting Howell is one of several former OSU players on the PGA Tour.)

Something's working: The Oklahoma State Cowboys have won two national championships since the course opened in 1994. Furthermore, Karsten Creek hosted the NCAA Championships in 2003. Ron Whitten, the noted golf-course critic, wrote in a recent review of the course: "Karsten Creek . . . is worthy of a U.S. Open, but nobody seems to mention it in the same sentence with Bethpage Black, Torrey Pines South, or Cog Hill No. 4."

The course is both difficult and handsome. Its beauty derives from its natural appearance (only about 130,000 cubic yards of earth were moved here). The difficulty comes from a variety of factors, particularly on No. 17. Survivors insist that this is the hardest hole on the course. A par four, it's listed as 464 yards on the card but it plays directly into what is usually a 20-mile-per-hour (or more) wind. Depending on the severity of the wind, the effective playing length of the hole is anywhere from 470 to 500 yards. A straightaway design, there's water to carry off the tee, water left for the entire length of the hole, and deep woods on the right.

"You've got to hit it straight," says staff professional Wes Graff. "If you miss the fairway on either side, it's either going to be a lost ball in the water or a lost ball in the woods. From the tee box it makes your knees shake."

For shorter hitters the fairway looks forever away. You'll need to clear about 130 yards of water from the regular tees. From the back, it's about 215 yards. Fazio might have figured that the tee shot was hard enough, so the only bunkers on the hole are short and left of the green (they can actually prevent some hooked shots from ending up in the water).

The better player will still face an approach of about 180 yards, again into the wind. The water awaits anything left. The green is elevated and slopes severely from back to front, with eight feet of elevation change. If you putt from the top level, you probably won't hold this slick green. (Holder likes to maintain the greens at 11.5 to 13 on the Stimpmeter. That's U.S. Open speed.)

In the NCAA Championships won by Clemson (the individual title was captured by Arizona State freshman Alejandro Canizares), the 17th was the toughest hole for the week. The rough, which had been overseeded with ryegrass, measured about six-and-a-half inches on the last day. "Guys were losing balls in the rough before they even got a chance to go into the woods," says Graff. It took the field so long to get through the penultimate round that NCAA officials actually had to institute a cut, axing out the last 10 teams prior to the last day's play. At that point in the proceedings San Diego State was already 101 over par.

Opposite: Arizona State's Alejandro Canizares, who won the individual title, lines up a putt during the 2003 NCAA Championships at Karsten Creek. The course has been described as "a training ground for champions in the making."

At the top of New Zealand's North Island, where the Pacific Ocean meets the Tasman Sea, the coastline is jagged and dramatic. A series of tiny islands dot the coast, and windswept beaches remain largely unpeopled. On a nearby 4,000-acre farm, Kauri Cliffs, a luxury resort and golf course, sits perched on cliffs above the shore. Nature handed the course's architect, Florida-based David Harman, a sloping plot of land that allowed him to create sea views from 17 holes.

The front nine, which begins by sweeping inland away from the clubhouse, eventually arrives at the southern coastal edge of the course at the par-three seventh. Named Cavalli after the group of islands that lie off the coast, the hole stretches northward and is played from one headland to another—with nothing but a 350-foot drop between the tee and the two bunkers that stretch across the front of the 6,200-square-foot green.

Harman says the seventh was one of several holes on the striking property that didn't require any landscaping. "We made minor modifications to create the green and the tees," he says, "but the hole is as natural an oceanside hole as I have seen anywhere in the world. We took great care to leave the cliff faces undisturbed."

New Zealand-born touring professional Michael Campbell fell in love with the course when he played it soon after its opening in 1998. He believes that visitors shouldn't let the challenge of the hole overshadow its beauty (easy for him to say). "All amateurs," he says, "should hit from the front tees. Just give yourself a chance at par and walk away with a memory that will last a lifetime."

The hole can be played from any of four tee boxes ranging from 105 to 220 yards, so it's not necessarily distance that makes the hole a daunting proposition. It's the prevailing wind from the southwest (downwind and across) that coaxes shots toward the sea, and rattles the nerves. Without any fairway and with such little room for error, the player's difficulty is not only picking the right club, but also allowing for the crosswind. Harman says the angle of the hole makes it difficult for a right-handed player who tries to cut or fade the ball, particularly because downwind gusts can make it difficult to hold the green. In that sense, a shot into the front bunkers is a reasonable play.

The alternative is even more challenging. "When the weather changes," says Harman, "the wind comes from the east-northeast and off the ocean. This direction completely changes the hole because the wind is directly in the player's face. I have seen players hit everything from a 5-iron to a driver depending upon the conditions."

Since the course's opening, visitors have been learning that the seventh can humble the best of them.

Native New Zealander Michael Campbell fell in love with Kauri Cliffs at first sight, but recommends that amateurs play No. 7 from the front tees.

Kingston Heath *Golf Club, Cheltenham, Australia ~1st hole*

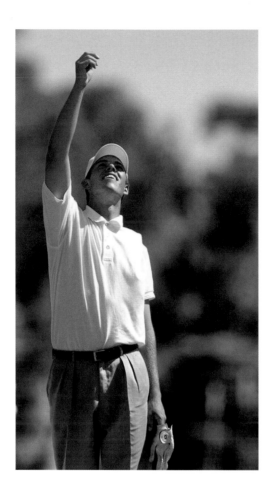

Few people on earth are as lucky as those in Melbourne when it comes to golf. The famed Sand Belt has any number of inviting tests from Royal Melbourne on down. You don't have to descend too far on that list to find Kingston Heath.

Ranked number two in Australia behind Royal Melbourne, Kingston Heath has hosted many of the biggest events in the country, including the Australian Open. Originally designed by Sydney-based professional Dan Soutar in 1923, the course subsequently gained many bunkers added by Alister Mackenzie during his trip down under four years later. Those additions have inevitably created some similarities to Royal Melbourne, but Kingston Heath is flatter and more heavily wooded. It's longer and tighter, too. In 1933 the course measured 6,845 yards, making it one of the longest in the world at the time.

Kingston Heath is a test right from the first tee. The first hole is a 465-yard par four (originally a short par five), and the tee shot must be played up and over a hill with bunkers dramatically cut into its right side. The wind is nearly always a factor at Kingston Heath, and this hole is no exception. Because the fairway runs east to west, any breeze is across the play rather than down or into it.

The left side is the safer play from the tee, but that side gives a more difficult angle of approach. There is, in fact, plenty of room on the left. An important factor in any opening hole, even one as tricky as this, is that there is a bailout for the cautious player.

So, while the better player has a smaller target for his ideal drive off the first tee at Kingston Heath, the less-skilled can play the hole safely for a five. You can go for it aggressively or play safe. The undulating green has typical Sand Belt bunkering, cut close to the very edge of the putting surface. The cautious approach, to the front of the sizeable green, will always leave a relatively easy shot, whether putt or chip. Pin-high or beyond, however, and the third shot is markedly more difficult. Whether a putt or a chip, the player is in for an early and strict test of touch.

One who failed such an examination—albeit en route to ultimate victory—was Aaron Baddeley. Leading the 2000 Australian Open by four strokes with a round to play, the defending champion began the final day with a double bogey six, courtesy of four putts on the first green. Suddenly his lead was two and Kingston Heath had given him a rude awakening.

Aaron Baddeley nearly derailed his bid for the 2000 Australian Open with a double bogey on the fearsome first at Kingston Heath.

Koolau *Golf Club, Kaneohe, Oahu, Hawaii ~18th hole*

It's little surprise that so many of the toughest 100 holes in the world have played host to significant championships. They have been tested repeatedly by the best players in the world and have both history and statistics to back up their inclusion. Koolau, on the Hawaiian Island of Oahu, has never hosted a major championship, and it's safe to say due to its location that it never will.

Still, Koolau is probably the hardest golf course in America and could very well be the toughest golf course ever built. No, there are no PGA Tour stats to offer into evidence, no anecdotes from the U.S. Open files. Few greats have even played it, but according to the USGA, Koolau has earned the highest slope rating of any golf course in the country. (The slope rating measures how much harder a course plays for a "bogey" golfer than a scratch player and is generally an indication of difficulty.)

When the course opened in 1992, Koolau was awarded a slope rating of 152. At the time, Dean Knuth was senior director of handicapping for the USGA. He oversaw all course-rating operations. In fact, Knuth is the man who invented the slope system. When he saw that Koolau had been designated a 152 (the slope rating scale starts at 55 and tops out at 155), he had to see it for himself.

"I didn't believe it," says Knuth. "I'd played all the highest-rated courses in the country and 152 just didn't seem possible." So Knuth, a solid six-handicapper, played the course. He was right, the course had been misrated: 152 was *too low*. Knuth ordered another rating. At 162 (gold tees) the new slope rating was literally off the charts (158 from the blues, 154 from the whites, and 143 from the reds). Because the slope rating system does not allow for a rating higher than 155, both the gold and blue ratings were reduced to 155.

Standard advice for first-time visitors to Koolau is to bring at least as many balls as you have strokes in your handicap. You'll need them. But you may want to bring a camera, too. This public course, designed by Dick Nugent and Jack Tuthill, is a four-hour lesson in the rugged topography and variable climates of Oahu.

At 7,300 yards long, Koolau wends its way over, around, and through serpentine rock-walled ravines and cascading waterfalls and affords jaw-dropping views of Kaneohe Bay. The course also undertakes extreme changes in elevation; in fact, 18 holes at Koolau will take you through three distinct climatic zones. The surrounding jungle is so dense that during construction of the golf course (which reportedly cost $100 million) workers found a military plane that had been missing since World War II, skeletons included.

Every hole at Koolau is tough, but to most anyone who has played the course the most malevolent hole is the dogleg-right 18th. At 476 yards from the gold tees (448 from the blue), the 18th was described by one visitor as "a par five disguised as a par four." The drive is a 150- to 200-yard carry (depending on tees) into the prevailing wind, over a waste bunker, and across a bottomless gorge to a fiendishly small landing area. Once you're safely in the fairway, the approach to the green requires carrying the same bottomless gorge and, for most, at least 200 uphill yards to the green. A stand of trees that is nearly impossible to clear with a long iron guards the left side of the green, suggesting a lay-up and a sand-wedge third into a narrow contoured green that is surrounded by roughly a dozen man-sized bunkers. A two-putt bogey here, with majestic Mt. Pali towering over you, is something to write home about.

Just in case the vistas have you daydreaming, there is an alternate route to the 18th green. Those who can carry the ball 290 yards (no kidding) can stand virtually sideways on the tee, cut the corner of the dogleg, and land within a wedge of the green. Good luck.

After his fact-finding trip to Koolau, Knuth's lasting impression was "that this is a golf course I would only want to play once. It's beautiful but it's extremely difficult." He made a return visit recently and confirmed that while the other 17 holes are now a tad more manageable, "The 18th is still one of toughest holes I've ever seen."

The home hole at Koolau is off-the-charts hard.

It is one of the curiosities of golf in Scotland that, while the home of golf is not short on first-class links, it suffers a dearth of comparable inland courses. The majesty of Gleneagles springs immediately to mind, as does the lovely Rosemount course at Blairgowrie. Downfield in Dundee has many proponents. But thereafter the roster of inland courses become spotty.

At least until late in the 20th century. It was then that former British Open champion Tom Weiskopf and his then-partner Jay Morrish were commissioned to design and build the first course on the peerlessly picturesque banks of Loch Lomond.

"I was immediately captivated by the place," says Weiskopf. "I knew right away that this was surely the best piece of land I would ever be given the opportunity to work with. It has everything: natural and subtle changes in elevation, trees, and, of course, wonderful scenery. It was an honor to work on it."

There were some initial financial hiccups—the first owners went bankrupt and the Bank of Scotland had no interest in the place—and it wasn't until American tycoon Lyle Anderson took over that Loch Lomond began to realize its true potential. While some would question the existence of such a high-end enterprise in such an egalitarian golfing environment as Scotland, there is no doubting the quality of Weiskopf's layout.

As home to the Scottish Open, the course has produced a winner's roll of the highest quality—Thomas Bjorn, Ernie Els, Retief Goosen, Tom Lehman, and Colin Montgomerie have all won on the "bonnie banks"—and has been praised long and loudly. Six-time major champion Nick Faldo has called it "the best inland course in Europe."

Loch Lomond's toughest test is the closing hole, a 430-yard right-to-left beauty that swings around a tributary of the loch. With the water left and bunkers right, the player is forced to thread the needle off the tee. To do so is only half the job. The approach shot to the slightly elevated and undulating green is just as tricky. Only the most precise of shots will yield the chance of a closing birdie.

In the 2000 Scottish Open, three men—Els, Lehman, and Montgomerie—arrived on the final tee tied for the lead. None of them, as it turned out, played the hole in an orthodox manner. And only one, Els, could make his par, courtesy of a splendid explosion shot from the front-right bunker.

Lehman was first to flounder. The American's tee shot was hooked and found a watery grave. The five he made was one shot too many. Likewise, Montgomerie's problems were from the tee. The Scot missed the fairway to the right, dumped his second in Els's bunker, and failed to get up and down.

At Loch Lomond's 18th only the very best will do. That's what Thomas Levet provided in 2004 when he smacked a daring drive over the corner of the water, hit an eight-iron to four feet, and made the putt for a birdie, a 29 on the back nine, and a one-stroke victory.

Opposite, bottom: Thomas Levet relied on cool precision to birdie the stern 72nd hole at Loch Lomond in 2004.

If you didn't already know that Medinah Country Club was founded by the Ancient Arabic Order of Nobles of the Mystic Shrine—better known as Shriners—the clubhouse could be a bit of giveaway. The elaborate Moorish structure with its distinctive dome has become, like the golf course beneath it, a landmark in golf history.

Founded in the early 1920s as a country retreat, the club has three golf courses, simply referred to as No. 1, No. 2, and No. 3. Each was designed by Tom Bendelow in the mid-1920s. Over time, the No. 3 Course, which has hosted Western Opens, U.S. Opens, and PGA Championships, has earned a reputation as one of the most difficult courses in the game. That's a far cry from its rather meek origins. When the three courses were originally laid out, No. 3 was supposed to be the women's course.

Things changed drastically in 1931 when members saw the potential and brought back Bendelow to extensively redesign No. 3. From then on, the course has been increasingly regarded as a killer—a long, disciplined trek. Over its proud history the club has hosted virtually every great player. Winners at Medinah include such golf legends as Billy Casper, "Lighthorse" Harry Cooper, Hale Irwin, Dr. Cary Middlecoff, Byron Nelson, Gary Player, Gene Sarazen, and Tiger Woods. In addition, major champions Tommy Armour and Ralph Guldahl have served as head professionals at the club.

In short, the club is steeped in difficulty and history. "It's a combination, maybe, of Winged Foot, Oakland Hills, and Oakmont," says Jay Haas. "You don't have a lot of water hazards, but the ones you do have are right there. The second hole, the 13th hole—they make you hit good shots. You can't get away with an indifferent one."

During the 1999 PGA Championship, memorable for Tiger Woods's win and Sergio Garcia's ebullient final round charge, No. 3 played roughly 7,400 yards to become the longest major championship course ever played at sea-level.

The course does "have some formidable par fives, but length on the golf course is distributed well," says Ben Crenshaw. "Obviously there are three long par-threes on which we hit long irons, but the par fives are, many times, three full shots anyway. So the 7,400 yards is a little bit misleading."

In recent years the course has grown more difficult under the hand of Rees Jones, who has tweaked it in advance of the 2006 PGA. One of the notable par threes referenced by both Haas and Crenshaw, the 13th hole, is now a fiercely demanding 245-yarder almost 30 yards longer than it was in 1999. The 2006 PGA field will see a significantly different and harder hole than the one they saw in 1999.

"We added another tee and rebuilt the green," says Jones. "The green is very well bunkered in the front, but if you go over, you're going to get in the high rough." And given that a 245-yard par three with water in front will force players to use long irons or even woods, there's a very good chance they *will* go over.

"I think that's one of those holes where they'll be glad to just get out of there with a par," says Jones.

Even at its shorter length, the 13th played a dramatic role in the 1999 PGA. Garcia had been nibbling at Woods's lead when he birdied the hole to pull within three shots. Playing immediately in front of the leader, Garcia looked back at the tee and gestured as if to send a message.

"I wanted Tiger to know that I was still there," says Garcia, "I was kind of telling him: If you want to win, you have to play well."

Woods double-bogeyed the hole, but went on to beat Garcia by one shot.

Before a 1980s redesign of the course, this hole played as the 17th, and it cost a couple of prominent players U.S. Opens. In 1949, Sam Snead was questioned for using a putter from the long fringe when he bogeyed 17 and lost to Middlecoff by one. In 1975, Crenshaw's two-iron tee shot found the water, leading to a double bogey and ultimately missing a playoff by one shot.

Opposite, bottom: Ben Crenshaw's two-iron tee shot at Medinah's 13th (then the 17th) might have cost him the 1975 U.S. Open.

Rare indeed is the uphill hole that inspires affection in the soul of any golfer. The combination of climbing and facing a semi-blind shot (or two) is hardly the stuff of which friendships are made.

But there are exceptions to any rule, none more consternating than the 191-yard 13th hole at Scotland's Muirfield, home of the Honourable Company of Edinburgh Golfers. This par three breaks almost every rule. Not only does the long, narrow, and devilishly fast green sit above the level of the tee, the hole runs straight down the prevailing west wind—even more so now that the tee has been moved to the right so that the player hits straight down the green, rather than slightly across it as before. The combination makes it hard to hit a soft-landing shot.

But what makes this a great and difficult hole is neither the strength or direction of the wind nor the placement of the starting point. As with Muirfield in general, it is the bunkering that makes this hole. Both left and right, the putting surface is jealously guarded by what can only be described as diabolically deep pits.

The green, too, is no bargain. The slope from back to front, especially in the fast-running conditions so beloved by the membership, is one to be respected. Any putt from above the hole is a potential disaster. One tale, possibly apocryphal, has Walter Hagen deliberately hitting into one of the bunkers during the 1929 Open in order to avoid a putt from above the cup.

Faced with a difficult stance and lie in the second of the left-hand bunkers in 2002, Ernie Els exploded to within two feet of the cup and saved par. Ten holes later (including a five-hole play-off), the South African was the winner of the Open Championship. And four months after that, his stroke of genius at Muirfield's 13th was voted shot of the year on the European Tour.

Others have, however, been less fortunate than the Big Easy. Three decades before Els arrived on the tee, Tony Jacklin plugged his tee shot in the same bunker, blasted out over the green, and took two tries to escape a deep bunker on the right, making a triple bogey. Two days later, he lost the Open by two strokes to an inspired Lee Trevino.

Less well known is the tale of a now long-ago final in the East Lothian County Cup, a foursomes event for all of the clubs in Muirfield's immediate area. At the 13th, the match was close and had attracted a crowd of perhaps 200. Hitting first, the man from Dunbar Castle stuck his partner in one of the deep bunkers. Their opponents hit the green. As the crowd made its way up the slope to the putting surface, the caddies left the bags at the tee, because the next hole runs back in the opposite direction. One hesitated, however. Should he take his man's sand wedge with him in case his partner failed to escape from the bunker?

Sure enough, the ball almost made it to the top of the steep face, but fell back into the bunker. As 200 faces turned to the caddie, all thinking he would have to run back down the hill, he straight-facedly handed the wedge to his man. Even the unsuccessful escapee had to laugh.

For amateurs and professionals alike, Muirfield's 13th demands respect.

Opposite, bottom: Ernie Els staged a miraculous escape from this greenside bunker on Muirfield's 13th hole on the way to the 2002 Open Championship.

During the week of April 5, 1966, Jack Nicklaus was ensconced in a rented home in Augusta, Georgia. In town for the Masters, Nicklaus and his wife Barbara were relaxing in the company of their longtime friends, Ivor and Carol Young. The discussion turned toward the uniqueness of Augusta National and the Masters tournament. "We were saying how great it would be to do something like what Bobby Jones did there, but to do it in Columbus, Ohio, where I grew up," Nicklaus says. "The idea was not so much to repeat Augusta National the golf course as it was to replicate Augusta National the experience."

Shortly thereafter Nicklaus began scouting sites, ultimately accumulating 1,600 acres of gently rolling terrain rich with streams and a variable topography that weaved between woodlands, wetlands, and pastures. At the time, Nicklaus was partnered with iconoclastic designer Desmond Muirhead. This odd couple of golf-course architecture created the plan for what would become the crown jewel of Nicklaus's design legacy.

A key element of the design, and revolutionary for its time, was Muirfield's stadium golf concept, with mounds and greenside amphitheaters designed specifically for spectators. The essence of Muirfield Village Golf Club is tournament golf.

Three decades after Muirfield Village opened its doors, the course remains on virtually every magazine's ranking of top golf courses in the United States, even the world. Nicklaus, a disciple of Jones, has succeeded in his mission to transplant the experience of Augusta National to Dublin, Ohio. And the Memorial Tournament has secured its place among the most prestigious tournaments in professional golf.

The 18th hole has played a leading role in the dramas that have forged reputations for both the golf course and the tournament. A 444-yard dogleg-right par four, it starts with a tee shot that is challenging despite a generous fairway. Bunkers and trees guard the right corner of the dogleg. A drive hit too far and left will find a creek that was recently rerouted by Nicklaus to come more closely into play. Even if a ball avoids the creek, the approach to the green from the far left side is still impeded by a cluster of black walnut trees. The approach shot—the shot on which Nicklaus the designer places the most importance, and the shot with which Nicklaus the competitor sealed many of his major championships—plays decidedly uphill across a large swale to an ample two-tiered contoured green that is heavily bunkered.

"A player is forced to decide whether he wants to risk blasting up to where the stream bounds the left side of the fairway," says Nicklaus. "If he's successful, he's got a shortish iron into the green. The other option is to play it safe, short of where the stream comes into play, but then he's left with a longer iron into the green. To my mind, such decisions are what the game is all about."

Muirfield Village—in particular the 18th hole—has served as the stage for more than its share of history. In the inaugural Memorial in 1976, Hale Irwin found tree trouble off the 18th tee during his playoff with Roger Maltbie. In 1993, Paul Azinger hit one of the great bunker shots in PGA Tour history, holing out on the 72nd hole from the front left greenside bunker to beat Payne Stewart. Few will forget Tom Watson's resurrection in 1996 when, at the age of 46, after battling the yips for several seasons and going nine years with out a PGA Tour title, he beat David Duval by two shots.

Back in 1977, the Golden Bear himself had his own great moment on 18. In the third round, Nicklaus holed out from a right greenside bunker to take the lead. He would go on to win by two shots over Hubert Green. The victory, which tied together an amalgam of childhood memories, a love for the game, an unceasing admiration for Jones, and his own competitive success, was among the most meaningful of Nicklaus's illustrious career.

"I've had a lot of accomplishments in the game of golf," he said to the gallery that ringed the 18th green in 1977. "I don't think there's any greater than this one. And nothing's given me a bigger thrill."

Opposite, bottom: Paul Azinger memorably secured his 1993 Memorial Tournament title by holing out from a greenside bunker on the 18th hole.

In the dusty sunlight of summer, the grounds are evocative of another era. The yellow clapboard clubhouse stands solidly in the nineteenth century. Horses canter about the well-worn sandy paths with worry-free riders on top. Farmland merges with rocky forest and gives way to a golf course as pure and as puritanically unforgiving as any in the world.

Dozens of golf courses have hosted the U.S. Open. But there are Open courses and then there are Open courses: Oakland Hills, Oakmont, Shinnecock Hills, and Bethpage Black. Myopia played tougher then any of them. In fact, the highest winning 72-hole score in the history of major championship golf was carded by Willie Anderson at Myopia in 1901. He shot a 331 (by comparison, the highest winning score in a major championship in the last 50 years was the 293 carded by Julius Boros in the 1963 U.S. Open).

That's just for starters. Myopia also holds Open records for highest score, highest first-round score, highest second-round score, highest third-round score, highest second round by a winner, highest third round by a winner, highest final round by a winner, and highest course average. In fact, four of the five highest winning scores in Open history were recorded at Myopia.

Sure, the equipment of the era had some role in this misery, but so did the designer. The fiend behind Myopia was Herbert Corey Leeds. A Harvard football star (Leeds scored the Crimson's first points in the inaugural Harvard-Yale football game) and lifelong bachelor, Leeds was a true turn-of-the-century sportsman. He was not only a gifted golfer, but an accomplished sailor and bridge player (he authored books on both topics). After taking up golf at about 40 years old, he quickly won back-to-back club championships (1893, 1894) at The Country Club in Brookline.

While Leeds was blossoming as a competitor, the sport was growing in the United States. Myopia, established in 1879 (on another site), had long been an equestrian center, but in 1894 the master of the hounds overcame (or ignored) the horsemen's con-

cerns and plotted a nine-hole golf course. In June of that year, an invited guest won the first-ever golf tournament held by Myopia. His name was Herbert Corey Leeds.

Leeds ultimately became a member at Myopia. Since he had already designed the Kebo Valley Club in Bar Harbor, Maine, he was asked to redesign the nine holes at Myopia. According to the club's history, Leeds pursued the assignment with "the determination to make Myopia links as testing as the lay of the land permitted and never settle for a level putting surface when undulations or a slope were available."

Leeds's first nine holes at Myopia opened in 1896 and measured 2,928 yards, one of the longest nine-holers in the country at the time. Three years later he added a second nine to complete his tortuous signature 18-hole design. He felt that the stone walls that criss-crossed the site were an unfair hazard, so he had them torn down. No, Leeds was not going soft. He had the rocks gathered into five- and ten-foot piles at strategic points around the golf course and then grew grass over them. These "chocolate-drop" mounds are a Leeds trademark that exist to this day.

Myopia is a cornucopia of classic golf-course design elements, but Leeds's calling card was and is his bunkering. He would regularly walk the golf course with small white chips in his pocket. When a particularly long or skilled player sliced or hooked a drive, Leeds would mark the spot. Within days a new bunker would appear. Virtually all the bunkers are low-profile "pot" bunkers that lack the raised lips of typical modern bunkers.

A round at Myopia is delightfully painful. For example, the first hole is utterly unique. A par four, it measures only 275 yards, but every one of them is almost vertically uphill. A 253-yard par three, the third, is the longest, toughest, and most magnificently bunkered par three in the Bay State. It played particularly tough during qualifying for the 1996 Massachusetts Amateur. It seems a contestant pulled his tee shot into one of the club's paddocks. "Practice swings were no problem," says Bill Safrin, the amiable head professional, "but each time the guy began his full swing he was charged by a territorial horse."

But the 12th hole is the toughest hole on the toughest course in Open history. A 447-yard par four, it was originally designed as a par five. The tee is set high on the property and offers a magnificent New England view. But even the view can't soften

the hole. Guarded on the left by thick woods, the hole features a large rock on the right that blocks the view of the landing area. Given that the fairway slopes from right to left, a fade off the tee is the best way to stay in the fairway. But miss the fairway to the right, and all you can do is hope.

"It's very penal rough down there," says Safrin. "Miss the fairway even by a foot and you may very well have trouble finding your ball."

The approach is played to (what else?) a small, crowned green that slopes away from the player.

One can argue that Myopia's four Opens were staged in American golf's dark ages and that equipment and skill must have caught up with the course's devious ways. After all, at only 6,500 yards Myopia must be a pushover by now. Not quite. Myopia is so unlike any other course and so punishing, that even in the Titanium Age she exudes Brahmin superiority.

The highest winning 72-hole score in U.S. Open history belongs to Willie Anderson, a 331 total in 1901. The course was Myopia.

In 1974, the uncle-nephew design team of George and Tom Fazio was hitting its stride. Twenty-nine-year-old Tom had just become a full partner in the business when they were called in by Canadian developer Gil Blechman to erase an existing golf course and replace it with a top-shelf one.

"Gil bought this existing course and wanted to know how we could redo it," says Tom Fazio. "We did all these plans and went back to Gil and said we just don't have enough land to do what you want. We can upgrade the course, but it won't meet the criteria of building the best possible course unless you can get more land."

Fortunately for Canadian golfers, Blechman got the land. The new course, the National Golf Club of Canada, was completed in 1976 and quickly achieved status as the most challenging golf course in the country.

PGA Tour veteran Dick Zokol, one of the finest players Canada has produced, is clear in his view of the National. "It is no doubt the toughest golf course in Canada," he says. "It's notorious—extremely demanding."

Ask anyone who's ever played the course, and they'll be certain to tell you that it is among the toughest, if not *the* toughest, they've ever played, and that No. 7 is the hardest of the hard.

From the back tees, the par four measures 463 yards. The first order of business is carrying an 80-yard-wide and 40-foot-deep gorge. From the back tee, it requires a minimum carry of 215 yards. The landing area—bentgrass bordered by bluegrass rough—demands accuracy. The area is narrowed further by grass bunkers on the left and two large fairway bunkers on the right. Even those whose drives clear the gorge are soon confronted with crossing it themselves. There is no bridge. It's crossed on foot, down and up through the rough.

Once you catch your breath, the second shot plays about 200 yards. While the fairway ribbons up and then down, it is a fairly level shot. That's small solace when you need to negotiate a steep hill on the left that slopes away from the fairway into deep fescue followed by trees. A large collection bunker sits on the left side of the green, and two bunkers guard the right, one in front, one in back.

The green is somewhat kidney-shaped and bends around the left bunker on the front. Everything drops off to the left into a continuation of the gorge that borders the entire left side of the hole. Even the putting surface cants from right to left. The green, reminiscent of a sideways saddle, is constructed of three distinct sections. The front slopes toward the player and left, the back slopes away and left, and the middle slopes left. Both in terms of speed and conditioning, the greens at the National are unrivaled among Canadian courses.

The National became widely known in 1979 when Lee Trevino shot 67 to win the Canadian PGA Championship, establishing a course record which still stands. Over the years, the course has been considered as a host for the Canadian Open, but according to distinguished Canadian golf writer Lorne Rubenstein, the layout has been deemed too confining. And now, under current regulations, the all-male National couldn't host a PGA Tour event anyway—a shame given the challenge it presents.

In the end, it shouldn't really come as a surprise that a golf course built on this location should be so tough. The name of the original course that stood here and was removed by Blechman? Pine Valley.

Opposite, bottom: Lee Trevino carded a course record 67 at the National on his way to winning the 1979 Canadian PGA. Twenty-six years later, the record stands as a monument to the course's difficulty.

New South Wales *Golf Club, La Perouse, Australia ~*6*th hole*

If the greatness of a hole is determined by the number of photographs in which it has been featured, the sixth at the New South Wales Golf Club, in La Perouse just outside Sydney, is in a class almost by itself. Measuring 193 yards across a rocky, exposed peninsula flanked on the left side by the crashing breakers of the Pacific Ocean, this is a hole to rank alongside those at Cypress Point or Royal County Down.

Originally credited to the great Alister MacKenzie, who designed the course during his sole trip down under in the late 1920s, the sixth is now thought to have been the work of an Australian, Eric Apperly, in the years immediately following World War II.

Still, the influence of MacKenzie, who designed the famous 16th at Cypress Point, is clear from the exhilarating tee shot to the cleverly contoured putting surface. Apperly did a wonderful job in preserving or emulating the risk and reward philosophy that pervades so much of MacKenzie's work.

This hole can be played safely for a bogey or challenged for a birdie. Whatever else can be said about it, it is not boring. It is a tribute to Apperly, in fact, that the hole sits so naturally in its spectacular locale. Quite simply, it looks right.

The influence of the ever-present wind, sweeping in off Botany Bay, cannot be denied. Playing anywhere from a medium iron to a fairway metal depending on the direction and force of the breeze, the tee shot is an intimidating one, especially for those prone to the pulls. Simply getting to the tee box is a spectacle. The player must walk across a bridge to a little island with Botany Bay to port and the Tasman Sea aft and starboard—and the foreboding remnants of a shipwreck just below the tee. It is a truly dramatic setting.

From the tee, the obvious shot is one drawn off the right side into the middle of the green. Right is safe—or at least dry—but leaves either a difficult pitch to a green that runs away from the player, or an equally difficult sand shot from one of the two bunkers guarding that side. Short, too, is better than pin-high.

The green itself, generous enough in size, slopes from back to front and from right to left. It is effective without being overtly severe.

When the ANZ Championship was played here, one European Tour professional said that "if you took away the view and the water there is nothing remarkable about the hole." But until those features are permanently subtracted from this gem, it will remain one of the toughest tests in the hemisphere.

Paul Casey kept his head in the game on the beautiful sixth hole at New South Wales and walked away with the 2003 ANZ Championship.

In the mid-1920s, after the nascent Oak Hill Country Club had agreed to swap sites with the nearby University of Rochester, Donald Ross completed both the East and West course designs on the new location. It was then that Dr. John R. Williams, a locally respected physician, went to work. A botanist by hobby, Williams was confident that the addition of trees would complement, even complete, Ross's treeless ground. It was God's plan to have trees at Oak Hill, argued Williams, who proceeded to plant 75,000 seedlings, most of them oaks.

To some Ross purists, Williams's crusade reeked of blasphemy. To others, Williams's arboreal corridors are a visual delight. But to golfers—most recently the battered and bruised 2003 PGA Championship field—Oak Hill's trees are just another complicating factor in what can be a serious major championship examination. Unlike say, Pine Valley, Bethpage Black, or Oak Tree, Oak Hill is not a monumentally hard golf course under ordinary conditions. But under PGA Championship conditions, which have been rivaling U.S. Open conditions in recent years, the course was extremely severe. However, a remarkable number of players insisted that it was fair nonetheless.

"Oak Hill is the best, fairest, and toughest championship golf course I've ever played in all my years as a tour professional. It is totally awesome," says Ernie Els.

Tiger Woods strikes a similar tone. "It's the hardest, fairest golf course we've ever played," he says. "Carnoustie wasn't fair that year [1999]. But this is by far the hardest."

Oak Hill is an old hand at staging major championships. It hosted the 1956, 1968, and 1989 U.S. Opens won respectively by Ben Hogan, Lee Trevino, and Curtis Strange. In 1980, Jack Nicklaus won the PGA Championship here. The 1995 Ryder Cup Matches, memorable for Europe's upset win over the U.S., were contested here, as were the 1949 and 1998 U.S. Amateur Championships.

Before the 1956 Open, Ben Hogan declared that the East Course was too easy to host the national championship. After finishing second to Cary Middlecoff, Hogan changed his tune and pronounced the first hole the toughest opener he had ever faced. But the East has undergone numerous face-lifts since 1956. Robert Trent Jones made changes twice, in 1956 and again in 1967. George and Tom Fazio did extensive work in 1979. Most recently, long-time Tom Fazio associate Tom Marzolf tweaked the course for the 2003 PGA.

That week, and under these conditions—deep rough, greens running 12½ on the Stimpmeter, 7,134 yards of golf course, and an average fairway width of 23 yards—the course was treacherous. Of the rough that week, veteran Jay Haas said, "It's just

so thick, you can't get a club through it. I had one just over the green on No. 12, and I could hardly identify it. The marshal said it was mine, but who knows. Half a dozen balls are still up there."

On this horribly hard course, the final two holes ranked first and third in difficulty for the week. Giving up only 17 birdies while racking up 205 bogeys, the 17th was the most excruciating major championship hole in recent memory. It's a par five for the members, but in the 2003 PGA it was a 495-yard par four. The field was required to drive the ball up the hill at least 280 yards to reach the dogleg to the right. But players who bombed their drives down the middle could go through the fairway and into the left rough, so longer hitters had no choice but to fade the ball around the corner. Shorter hitters did not have to be so crafty but faced a longer shot into the green. For everyone it was find the fairway or kiss birdie, and often par, good-bye.

"If you miss the fairway there, there's absolutely no chance in the world of hitting the green," said two-time U.S. Open champion, Lee Janzen. "Most of the holes, you can't hit the green, but you can at least advance up near the green. That one, you are probably hitting out to where you have 130-yard shot in. That's got to be the toughest hole on the course."

While the 2003 PGA will always be remembered for Shaun Micheel's approach to within two inches of the hole for a clinching birdie on the 18th, it came after he bogeyed No. 17 to cut his lead to one. Was the 17th set up too tough up for the PGA? If it was over the top, it's because Oak Hill has its sights set on landing another U.S. Open. Even long-time Oak Hill club pro Craig Harmon, who as the son of legendary Claude Harmon grew up on a steady diet of Winged Foot, says the newly lengthened hole was too long. But then again, he adds, "What's wrong with a touring pro actually having to hit a long iron into a par four?"

Opposite: Shaun Micheel's stunning birdie on the final hole distracted from his and his fellow competitors' struggles with No. 17 at Oak Hill East.

Just after completing his revolutionary work on Harbour Town and while wrapping up his design of Casa de Campo's Teeth of the Dog in the Dominican Republic, Pete Dye was approached by two former touring professionals turned golf real estate developers about a project they were planning for their home state of Oklahoma.

It was the early 1970s, and Ernie Vossler and Joe Walser had already built a course with Dye (Cardinal Golf Club in Greensboro, North Carolina); now they were determined to build a golf course that could rival Oklahoma's Southern Hills both in its difficulty and its ability to attract serious players and major championships. Dye's only concern upon viewing the relatively featureless and wind-riddled 1,300-acre site was its remote location: While he knew he could maximize the site's features, he questioned whether anyone would ever bother to see or play a course 30 miles north of Oklahoma City.

That was Vossler and Walser's problem. If you build it they will come, was the duo's mantra. The charge to Dye was simple: "Build us a championship golf course, one with no compromise." In fact, Dye often has said that when he was working on Oak Tree the only comment Ernie and Joe made was "Can't you make it any harder?"

The course is 100 per cent Dye, yet it holds true to one of the prime tenets of Dye role model Alister MacKenzie. In Dye's severely dog-eared copy of MacKenzie's landmark book *Golf Architecture,* the author writes: "The chief object of every golf-course architect or greenskeeper worth his salt is to imitate the beauties of nature so closely as to make his work indistinguishable from nature itself."

And while Dye carved a visual masterpiece from this Oklahoma ground, he also devised an all-out test. According to one reviewer, Oak Tree "is Pete Dye unchained." As Dye worked on the design, Vossler and Walser began to consider names. One candidate would have underscored the expectations for difficulty: Waterloo. Ultimately, the course was dubbed Oak Tree in recognition of the trees that line the inward nine.

The course quickly rose to prominence. Only eight years after opening, it hosted the 1984 U.S. Amateur. Not surprisingly, that championship was won by Scott Verplank, a four-time All-American at nearby collegiate golf powerhouse Oklahoma State.

By the time the 1988 PGA Championship came to town, the par-71 golf course had been stamped with a course rating of 76.9, then the highest in the United States. Officials eased up on the course set-up because they feared making it too hard,

especially considering that wind is a near-constant factor in Oklahoma, but that week the weather took a tranquil turn. Stunningly, Oak Tree, promoted as one of the world's most demanding tests, turned in near record-low scoring. A windless tournament took the bite out of Oak Tree's bark, at least for that week.

Sure, there were horror stories. Seve Ballesteros triple-bogeyed the 13th hole after finding himself in the creek behind the green. Jack Nicklaus carded a dread quad when he lost two balls on one hole (the 16th), the first and only time that has happened to him in his entire career. Both players missed the cut.

The decisive hole in 1988 was the fifth, where eventual champion Jeff Sluman holed a 115-yard wedge for eagle. But the hardest hole on the golf course, says Dye, is the ninth. Played as No. 18 in the PGA Championship because it made for a more dramatic finish, the hole employs more than a little Dye trickery. Even in the calm of 1988 it played as the hardest hole of the week, averaging 4.29 shots per player.

A lot of the difficulty on the ninth comes from an optical illusion. Off the tee the hole dips down, then up to the fairway, and then down and up to the green. Physically the hole plays about 40 feet uphill, but because of the series of ups and downs the actual extent of the elevation is very hard to assess. The three-tiered green is heavily contoured and protected in front by Dye's version of St. Andrews's Valley of Sin.

Oak Tree will finally get back into the limelight when it plays host to the 2006 Senior PGA Championship. With recent remodeling work done by Dye and former PGA Tour player Mark Hayes, the course now measures more than 7,400 yards from the tips (it won't stretch quite that far for the seniors), but some of the severe slopes on the greens have been softened to allow for more hole locations.

Opposite: Jeff Sluman shot a brilliant final-round 65 at Pete Dye torture chamber Oak Tree to win his first and only major championship.

Oakland Hills Country Club is not the oldest club in America. In fact, the South Course was only opened in 1918. It is not the most exclusive golf club in the country; it was founded not by robber barons or corporate titans but by an accountant and a printer. Still, Oakland Hills and its South Course are entrenched in major championship lore. Host to six U.S. Opens, two PGA Championships (with another scheduled for 2008), two Senior Opens, a U.S. Amateur, and a Ryder Cup in 2004, Oakland Hills is infused with history. Oakland Hills's first club professional was none other than Walter Hagen, himself an Open champion at the time of his hire. The list of victors at Oakland Hills includes Ralph Guldahl, Ben Hogan, Gene Littler, Jack Nicklaus, Arnold Palmer, and Gary Player. The list of runners-up—T. C. Chen, Ben Crenshaw, Bobby Jones, Davis Love III, and Sam Snead—is equally colorful and a testament to the course's severity.

Like so many major championship venues, the South Course was designed by the legendary Donald Ross. The Scottish-born son of a stonemason, Ross came to the United States in 1899 and promptly changed the face of golf-course architecture, raising it from a teaching pro's sideline into a stand-alone profession.

Ross's design for the South Course remained virtually untouched until 1950 when Oakland Hills brought in Robert Trent Jones to prepare the South for the 1951 U.S. Open. Jones's goal: to give the best players in the world what he described as "the shock treatment." Jones wanted to make definitive landing areas on each par four and par five—one per fairway and one per green. To emphasize these targets he went on a bunker-building binge. By the time the remodeling was complete, 120 bunkers containing 400 tons of sand had constricted the South Course's fairways and fortified her greens. A new era in golf-course architecture—one that fully exploited modern earth-moving technology—had been ushered in.

Jones's work elicited the shock he had hoped for, but it also laid the foundation for a little awe. Hogan, the defending champion, struggled at first with Jones's target strategy. After scores of 76, 73, and 71, Hogan carded one of the great rounds in golf history. Frequently opting for fairway woods off the tee in order to avoid Jones's new hazards, Hogan recorded a 67. He successfully defended his Open title while scoring the lowest round (by two) on the remodeled course.

Fittingly, Hogan capped off his defense with a birdie on the mighty 18th hole, which, for its day, was a massive 459 yards. Playing at 494 yards for the 2004 Ryder Cup, the 18th is a par five for members, but it earns a spot in the 100 Toughest Holes as a par four. A downhill tee shot, the slight dogleg right is guarded by three bunkers on the inside of the bend. The fairway slopes from right to left, and the left side of the bend is guarded by a bunker that, while small, has a healthy appetite. Further left is out of bounds. In recent years, a large bunker has been added on the left to reign in the long hitters, who can go through the fairway and into this bunker if they don't fade the ball off the tee. That's what happened to Tom Lehman in the 1996 U.S. Open, and he made a bogey to lose by one stroke.

The approach is one of the most daunting in major championship golf: approximately 200 yards severely uphill to a small green that slopes dramatically from back to front. Players will feel compelled to take an extra club here, but those who go over the green will be hoping for bogey as they're forced to chip out of Open-style rough to a slick downhill surface. When Andy North won his second Open at Oakland Hills in 1985, he laid up on this, his 72nd hole, and two-putted for bogey. In the final round of the 1996 Open, Davis Love III came to the 18th tee tied for the lead with Lehman and Steve Jones, who were playing behind him. Love's three-wood tee shot put him in the first cut of rough. His six-iron approach flew directly over the pin, but came to rest 20 torturous downhill feet from the hole. He three-putted the final green, and Jones, a qualifier, went on to win.

In *The World Atlas of Golf,* written by the veritable blue ribbon panel of Pat Ward-Thomas, Herbert Warren Wind, Charles Price, and Peter Thomson, the 18th is described as "the kind of hole where tournaments are far more often lost than won."

Opposite, bottom: Qualifier Steve Jones capitalized on Davis Love III's and Tom Lehman's inability to manage the brutish 72nd hole and walked away with the 1996 U.S. Open at Oakland Hills.

First holes are odd animals. Whether it's the start of a weekend four-ball or the first round of a major championship, a first hole is a breeding ground for the jitters. As a result, most golf-course architects make their first holes fairly simple and straightforward. Then there's the first at Oakmont.

This hole is anything but forgiving and brings opening-tee jitters to a new level. It's an appropriate start for a golf course that many consider (weather aside) the toughest test of championship golf in the world.

Oakmont owes its creation to Henry C. Fownes and his son William C. Fownes. In the hundred years since its founding, Oakmont has reinforced its reputation for toughness by hosting seven U.S. Opens, three PGA Championships, a Women's Open, and five U.S. Amateurs (Oakmont will also host the 2007 U.S. Open).

"Reinforced" is the operative word, because long before ground was broken for Oakmont, father and son were committed to a tough golf course. In fact, the senior Fownes pledged brazenly from the outset that the course he and his son were designing would be the toughest in the world. This goal may have been fine for the Fowneses, both of whom were skilled players, but it has since humbled generations of able competitors.

In 1911, the son, then head of the greens committee, conspired with longtime superintendent Emil "Dutch" Loeffler to follow through on his father's bold pledge. They increased the number of bunkers. They created special heavy rakes that plowed deep furrows into the sand, increasing the chances of a bad lie. They installed ditches that dot the golf course, serving as both hazard and drainage. William Fownes and Loeffler also concocted what are still reputed to be the fastest greens in captivity. "That probably is true on a day-to-day basis," says John Zimmers, Oakmont's superintendent. One rumor, propagated for so long that it has been largely accepted as fact, is that Oak- mont actually slows its greens down in preparation for a major. "Let's put it this way," says Zimmers, "when an Open comes around we don't have to do much to get the speed they're looking for." The design of the greens only makes things harder. Many of Oakmont's greens slope away from the fairway and toward the back, meaning that approach shots have not only to be precise but soft.

The first hole at Oakmont embodies all the hallmarks of the Fownes's appetite for humiliation. At 467 yards from the championship tees (444 from the middle) it is longish and fairly well bunkered. A ditch in the left rough will trap a pulled tee ball. Third-round leader Ernie Els wasn't quite that far left in the final round of the 1994 U.S. Open, but he was in deep rough. An erroneous ruling allowed him a drop because of interference from a television crane, even though the crane was movable. Els dropped into a much better lie and hit the green with his second shot, but made bogey anyway when he took three putts. He finished regulation tied with Loren Roberts and Colin Montgomerie, then won an 18-hole playoff—after hooking his drive on the first hole left of the ditch and making a bogey.

The key shot here is usually the approach. From the fairway landing area the green is considerably downhill and rivals the greens on Nos. 2 and 10 as the most severe on the golf course. The front of the green is canted aggressively toward the fairway while the back half coaxes even well-hit balls to run through. The entire green slopes precipitously from right to left at the standard Oakmont clip of 11-$\frac{1}{2}$ to 12 on the Stimpmeter. "You can't even think about landing a ball on that green," says Zimmers, Oakmont's Marquis de Sod.

Putting enters an entirely new dimension at Oakmont, where the putting surfaces are comprised of Poa Annua grass. While extremely difficult to maintain, "po" unquestionably provides the fastest putting surface in the game. With the slope of the green and the severity of the speed, there is no shame in three-putting No. 1.

The first hole at Oakmont can ruin a round fast. Greg Norman began the 1983 Open by missing the first fairway at Oakmont. He carded a triple-bogey seven and went on to miss the cut. Somewhere a Fownes was smiling.

Opposite, bottom: Eventual champion Ernie Els was aided by a fortunate ruling on the first hole of the final round in the 1994 U.S. Open at Oakmont.

Since the Ryder Cup's inaugural matches at Worcester Country Club in 1927, a total of 29 golf courses have hosted this international competition. Most of them—courses such as Royal Lytham and St. Annes, East Lake, Muirfield, Pinehurst, Scioto, and Ridgewood—have hosted other important championships, so the Ryder Cup Matches are but another jewel in their respective crowns.

It's safe to say that no host course's identity is as closely tied to the Ryder Cup as the Ocean Course at Kiawah Island. A confluence of political, cultural, and historical factors made it so: Nationalism inspired by the fall of communism, patriotism inspired by the first Gulf War, and embarrassment brought on by the fact that the United States had seen its Ryder Cup dominance begin to fade, made the American people particularly hungry for a win in 1991.

The final factor in the inexorable bond between Kiawah and the Cup is the fact that the duneland course essentially debuted at the 1991 Ryder Cup.

The Pete Dye-designed course is *sui generis*. It is not a true links course, but it's a far cry from the inland courses of Muirfield Village, PGA National, The Greenbrier, and Laurel Valley, the immediately preceding American venues. This question of identity left both teams claiming disadvantage.

"We did not do ourselves any favors," said U.S. team member Hale Irwin of the course selection. "I don't think there is any home-course advantage."

Likewise, European team captain Bernard Gallacher dismissed suggestions that the links-like feel of Kiawah would favor his squad. "There is no course in Europe that is anything like this. It doesn't resemble any of the Scottish or Irish links courses."

The only thing that timeless links courses and Kiawah had in common was uncommon beauty and unforgiving wind. At Alice Dye's suggestion, six feet of sand was used to elevate several fairways and afford players a stunning water view. This alteration not only made the course far prettier, but, by raising the course's profile, brought the wind more aggressively into play.

When discussing tough holes at Kiawah, most people recall the wreckage that piled up at 17 during the 1991 Ryder Cup and assume it's the toughest hole. But No. 2 has been described by Pete Dye as the "most diabolical thing on the whole golf course." He's right. Wind, waste area, and marsh combine to make this a hellacious par five even at the seemingly manageable distance of 528 yards from the tips (501 championship, 490 regular).

A lot of the second hole's difficulty stems from the wind. First of all, a three-shot par five gives the wind three cracks at your ball flight. Secondly, as Ocean Course head pro Brian Gerrard points out, the wind can hurt you coming and going. "You don't really know how a so-called 'helping wind' will affect your ball, it may lift and carry the ball, it may drop it down."

The hole is a double dogleg, favoring a draw off the tee and suggesting a fade into the green. Two decisions need to be made after the drive. First is whether or not to go for the green in two. Very few players even attempted the shot in 1991, and only Davis Love III pulled it off when the course hosted the World Cup in 1997. Go for it and you're on your own, as marsh and waste area await an errant shot.

Assuming you lay up, the next question is whether to lay up before the cross hazard, leaving a 125- to 140-yard shot, or lay up past that hazard leaving as little as a sand-wedge shot into a long green. Dye heightens the drama by pulling a huge waste area in close to the right side of the green, or so it appears as you stand over your approach. Upon closer inspection there is about 20 yards of chipping area between the sand and the green.

"No. 2 is one of the toughest par fives I've ever seen," says Gerrard, "I would put it up against any par five out there."

It can certainly scuttle a round. In the Sunday singles in 1991, Spain's Seve Ballesteros carded a double bogey here to *win* the hole for Europe. His opponent, Wayne Levi, had a triple-bogey eight.

Opposite, bottom: Seve Ballesteros's double bogey was good enough to win the second hole at the Ocean Course in his 1991 Ryder Cup singles match against Wayne Levi.

In golf, there is "The King" and then there are the kings. The former, Arnold Palmer, was crowned for his dominance of the sport in the late 1950s and early 1960s. No one suggests stripping the title from Palmer, but history also owes a nod to three real monarchs who shaped the future of the game. In 1123, it was King David I of Scotland who deeded the linksland in and around St. Andrews to the people of this seaside village. Three hundred years later, golf in the region had become so popular that it was tempting young men away from military training, so King James II of Scotland outlawed the game. The restriction lasted for 45 years until James IV, the patron of golfers worldwide, lifted the ban and actually took up the game himself.

The short-lived ban notwithstanding, golf has been at the heart and soul of Scotland's identity for roughly 500 years, and the heart and soul of Scottish golf is unquestionably the Old Course at St. Andrews. As the home of the Royal and Ancient Golf Club, founded in 1754, St. Andrews serves as the world's flagship golf club and the earliest arbiter of the Rules of Golf. The course's sandy linksland serves as the model for, the very definition of, true links golf, and the course, created almost entirely by nature, is the game's most celebrated masterpiece.

All that hagiography aside, this is a golf course that, like haggis and whiskey, is an acquired taste. What some see as the most sanctified altar in the game, other see as a rumpled, browned-out pasture. Even the game's most astute observers struggle to digest the Old Course. David Fay, longtime executive director of the USGA has said, "Anyone who raves about the Old Course after just one or two rounds there is either a liar or a fool."

First-time visitors often have a hard time discerning where to aim on a seemingly featureless landscape, where many of the bunkers are hidden from view. It also takes several rounds, preferably with the wind coming from various directions, to appreciate all of the strategic decisions that go into playing the Old Course.

Normally you don't think of a par three as being a particularly strategic hole, but that's not the case with the 11th at the Old Course, which can accurately be described as the mother of all par threes. While it measures a moderate 172 yards, that distance is misleading. It doesn't take into account the ferocious winds that capriciously blow off the Firth, nor the draconian back-to-front slope of the green, nor the intimidating pair of bunkers, Hill and, guarding the front of the elevated green, the notoriously deep Strath. The primary objective off the tee is to avoid the bunkers, but an extra club could well leave a downhill putt on what just might be the most three-putted green in the game. Peter Thomson once took four putts here from only a few feet away. Simply keeping the first putt on the green is sometimes a worthy goal.

The hole's horror stories are numerous, but none is more cautionary or instructive than that of young Bobby Jones. In 1921, during what biographer O.B. Keeler described as Jones's "lean years," the intemperate 19-year-old entered his first British Open. In the third round, after playing the outward nine in a horrible 10-over-par 46, he promptly doubled No. 10. From the tee at No.11, his ball came to rest deep in the bowels of Hill bunker. After taking three strokes to escape the bunker, Jones impetuously picked up his ball and withdrew from the championship. Jones later described his performance as the "most inglorious failure" of his competitive career. Six years later, in the sweet spot of his career, Jones returned to St. Andrews and won the claret jug.

By 1958 the disease-ridden Jones had clearly acquired the taste. He was awarded the Freedom of the Royal Burgh of St. Andrews, an honor not bestowed on an American since Benjamin Franklin. In his acceptance speech Jones said, "The more I studied the Old Course the more I loved it, and the more I loved it the more I studied it, so I came to feel that it was for me the most favorable meeting ground possible for an important contest. I felt that my knowledge of the course enabled me to play it with patience and restraint until she might exact her toll from my adversary, who might treat her with less respect and understanding." In closing, the 56-year-old Jones added, "I could take out of my life everything except my experiences at St. Andrews and would still have had a rich and full life."

Opposite, bottom: In winning the 1927 British Open at St. Andrews, Bobby Jones (shown here with his father) exorcised the demons of six years earlier with a final-round par on the treacherous 11th hole.

As the most famous hole on the most famous golf course in the world, the Road Hole on the Old Course at St. Andrews needs little introduction. In fact, in the minds of many golf course architecture historians the 17th hole is the first golf hole ever "designed."

In the mid–1800s, Allan Robertson was making a name for himself both as the greenkeeper at St. Andrews and as Scotland's finest player. In his capacity as greenkeeper, he supervised the golf course, which included updating the layout. In 1848, Robertson is credited with widening the fairways of St. Andrews and expanding the putting surfaces into the course's now famous double greens. But during that "re-modeling," Robertson also sited and designed a new green for the Road Hole instead of making a double green with the first hole. The design, featuring a bottomless greenside bunker that Bernard Darwin once described as "eating its way into [the green's] very vitals," permanently changed the complexion of St. Andrews. It seems the first hole ever specifically designed was also the first intentionally difficult hole.

This was still the era when match play was predominant, and long before the concept of par, so the hole's true difficulty was muted. Even when par was first introduced, the 17th was a par five, allowing players some wiggle room. But when par at the Road Hole was officially changed to four in 1964, difficulty had found a new home.

Today the 461-yarder is widely recognized as the toughest hole in all of golf. In British Open play, the Road Hole has cast its spell over the very best. In 1978, Japan's Tommy Nakajima had seemingly tamed the hole when, while in contention during the third round, he hit the elusive green in two shots. Lulled into a false sense of security, Nakajima then putted into the Road bunker. Shot followed excruciating shot until four blasts of sand later he was back on the green. Tommy took a nine, and the bunker has since been nicknamed the "sands of Nakajima."

The devilish qualities of the Road bunker, which tends to collect shots that come anywhere near it (even more so after a 2004 redesign), are only the tail end of the Road Hole's difficulties. The problems begin on the tee, which offers a blind drive over what used to be the black railway sheds, now part of the Old Course Hotel. The shortest route is a drive down the right side of the fairway, but the out of bounds wall awaits the indiscreet. The combination of temptation and intimidation is the perfect blend. The challenge of the tee shot is compounded by the fact that the left side is not as safe as it usually is at St. Andrews. Instead of a double fairway, deep rough awaits those who drive wildly to the left.

Mostly, the locals play the hole as a par four-and-half, shooting down the left side of the fairway off the tee, then short and right with the second to avoid the Road bunker. That leaves a relatively straightforward pitch up the sharply right-to-left sloping putting surface. In 1990, en route to the second of his three Open titles, Nick Faldo played the hole in just such fashion, eliminating the dangers of both the bunker and the eponymous road, which sits hard against the right side of the green.

Where both these bedeviling hazards come into play, of course, is when the player gets greedy with his second shot, trying to reach the middle or back of the green. In the final round of the 1984 Open Championship, Tom Watson, already a five-time winner of the event (but never at St. Andrews), hit a perfect drive. Only a few yards from the wall up the right side, Watson, tied for the lead, had a clear view up the green to the pin. Selecting a two-iron on the advice of his caddie, Watson hit his approach long and too far right. "The wrong shot with the wrong club at the wrong time," remarked the late Dave Marr on the telecast. The ball finished nearly against the wall and Watson took the almost inevitable three shots to get down. (One of the unique features of the hole is that there is no relief from the road, the ball must be played from it.) Watson lost by two shots to Seve Ballesteros of Spain, who birdied the 18th, and became just one more victim of golf's ultimate test of talent and nerve.

The Road Hole is as capricious as it is difficult. Each time he faced it in the first three rounds of the 1960 British Open, Arnold Palmer hit a six-iron second shot to the center of the green, putting himself in birdie or eagle position on what was then a par five, but three-putted every time. In the final round, the King hit a five-iron onto the road, and inexplicably got up and down for birdie. Palmer lost to Kel Nagle by one shot.

Opposite, bottom: A faulty swing with a two-iron on No. 17 at St. Andrews in the final round of the 1984 British Open put Tom Watson on the Road to ruin.

In its fabled 81-year history, the Olympic Club in San Francisco has crowned four U.S. Open champions. In any U.S Open there are more losers than winners, more disappointment than joy. But the losses at Olympic, perhaps better described as near-wins, are legendary for their particularly stinging brand of defeat for some of the game's legends. In 1955, unheralded Jack Fleck derailed sentimental favorite Ben Hogan's march to an unprecedented fifth Open title. Eleven years later the most popular player in the world, Arnold Palmer, stood on the 10th tee with a seven-stroke lead. Through a combination of aggressive mistakes and sloppy play, Palmer was caught from behind by a red-hot Billy Casper. Casper disposed of Palmer in a playoff the next day. Scott Simpson's title in 1987 came at the expense of Tom Watson, whose last-ditch bid to force a playoff came up three agonizing inches short. Finally, Lee Janzen's one-stroke win in 1998 is remembered for the handful of bad breaks that Payne Stewart sustained en route to a second-place finish.

Beyond the frustration they engendered, each of these Olympic Opens had one thing in common: The 17th hole played a significant role. A middling 520-yard par five for the members, the 17th at Olympic is played as a brutal 430- to 470-yard par four in Open play. Sort of like taking all the agony of a marathon and cramming it into a 1,500-meter race. The hole plays uphill all the way. But it is the dramatic left-to-right side slope that really makes the hole devilish because it effectively halves the width of the fairway. There are no water hazards or fairway bunkers on 17 (the entire course has no water and only one fairway bunker), but then again this is a hole where landing in the middle of the fairway could result in a ball that ends up in the right rough. Because of the slope, it's a big advantage to work the ball from right to left.

The uphill shot to the small green must navigate heavy bunkering both left and right. There is a small bounce-in area in front, but even a well-placed shot is forced to contend with the fierce left-to-right and front-to-back slope of the green.

In 1966, Palmer retained his fading final-round lead until the fateful 17th when he found the left rough off the tee and the right rough on his second. Casper drew even with a par.

Pars at 17 were vital for the other three winners at Olympic, too. Fleck birdied two of the last four holes in an unlikely finish to catch Hogan in regulation in 1955 before winning a playoff, but just as important was his par on the toughest hole on the course. In 1987, Scott Simpson played the 17th hole with a one-shot lead on Watson, who was hungry for a major after a five-year drought. After putting his approach in one of the greenside bunkers, Simpson got up and down with Watson watching from the fairway.

Janzen played the 17th in five-over when he won in 1998, going bogey, double bogey, double bogey before finally making a par in the final round to preserve a one-stroke lead that would also be his margin of victory.

Robert Trent Jones redesigned the Olympic Club in advance of the 1955 Open. In his landmark book, *Golf's Magnificent Challenge,* Jones described converting the 17th into a par four in championship play as "an example of man messing with nature."

The USGA played the hole at 461 yards that year, but moved it up to approximately 430 yards for the next two Opens. In 1998, it was back to 468 yards, in part so drives would land on a flatter part of the fairway. Still, the hole played to an average of

4.716, the hardest Open par four between 1986 (when the USGA began keeping such records) and 2004. The whining was constant and particularly shrill. Cries of "tricked up" and "unfair" echoed through the eucalyptus trees. Payne Stewart said he regarded the golf course as a par 71, "because I really feel that's a par five hole." Jack Nicklaus sniffed, "The 17th is just a way to get from the 16th green to the 18th tee."

Not surprisingly, the eventual champion had the most detached view of the issue. "I come to the U.S. Open expecting nothing to be fair," Lee Janzen said in 1998. Yes, the USGA is a nonprofit organization, but no one ever said anything about the courses being charitable.

Opposite: Lee Janzen was five-over par on the 17th when he won the 1998 U.S. open at Olympic.

How difficult is the 17th hole at The Oxfordshire? Consider this. At the end of 1995, Irishman Padraig Harrington turned professional after a distinguished amateur career in which he made three appearances for Great Britain and Ireland in the Walker Cup Matches. After getting his European Tour card, Harrington won in only his sixth start, the Spanish Open of 1996. For one so inexperienced in the ways of the professional game, it was a remarkable achievement.

Then Harrington arrived at The Oxfordshire for the Benson & Hedges International, where he was paired with six-time major champion Nick Faldo. The opening round was uneventful, as was most of the second round until the 17th, a 585-yard par five with split fairways separated by a lake.

Harrington's drive was a good one, leaving him the option of playing safe or going for the distant green in two. He chose the latter and grabbed his three-wood. Splash. After a drop, and from slightly closer range, he then went with his three-iron. Splash. Three-iron again. Splash. Six-iron was next, in a belated attempt to lay up. Splash for a fourth time. It all added up to a 13.

"My only worry was that he was going to run out of balls," said Faldo afterward.

The 17th is that sort of hole. After the drive, there are, in fact, three options: going for the green à la Harrington, laying up to the right, or laying up to the left, albeit with carriage of the water.

The man behind this hole is Rees Jones.

"You like to have the tougher holes at the end of a round rather than at the beginning," he says. "And I think the 17th is the hardest par five I've ever designed." In the 1996 Benson & Hedges, the hole produced every score between a three and a 13.

"Designing a par five that can rank among the toughest holes is a real achievement for an architect," says Jones, "especially in light of today's distances. So it has to be a smallish green, it has to be an elevated green, it has to have decent transitions."

The 17th has all those traits and more. By the way, Harrington's mother, in a display of maternal cheek, has a newspaper chart of his thirteen shots "proudly" displayed on her kitchen wall.

Padraig Harrington earned an unwanted place in European Tour lore—and on his mum's fridge   by making a 13 on the 17th at The Oxfordshire.

Paraparaumu Beach *Golf Club, Paraparaumu Beach, New Zealand ~17th hole*

Alister MacKenzie visited the Antipodes only once in his life, but it was a trip from which golfers have drawn benefit ever since. Not only did MacKenzie leave behind the great Royal Melbourne in Australia, but those lucky enough to learn at the feet of the master took his design philosophy all over Australia and New Zealand.

One such disciple was Alex Russell. A good enough player to have won the Australian Open as an amateur in 1924, Russell executed MacKenzie's plan on the East Course at Royal Melbourne, then designed the West Course himself and continued to spread the great man's word. A couple of decades later, that mission was completed with the last of Russell's courses at Paraparaumu Beach on New Zealand's North Island, perhaps an hour's drive from the city of Wellington.

The 17th at Paraparaumu, a classic links of modest dimensions that draws its difficulty from the almost ever-present breezes off the Cook Strait and Tasman Sea, is the best hole in New Zealand and, many believe, the best hole Russell ever designed. A dogleg right, this 442-yard par four fits beautifully into the available terrain and offers the player a choice, especially when a brisk southerly wind is blowing.

From the tee, the two routes to the distant green are starkly illustrated by the split fairway. The lower and shorter option to the right takes the ridge between the fairways out of play but leaves a much more difficult angle for the approach. From there, the green is very wide but shallow, making it a most elusive target, especially downwind.

On the four occasions he played the hole during the 2002 New Zealand Open—in which he finished tied for sixth—Tiger Woods played to the left-hand fairway all four times, but found the target only once . That said, the right-hand option is most often chosen when the wind is in the player's face, because the drive cannot easily carry the ridge to safety. A headwind then works in the player's favor for the second shot, alleviating to an extent the difficulty of the acute angle that remains.

The upper option is harder to hit and hold, because the drive must first carry the ridge, then stop on the angled fairway. Too far left and the ball disappears down a steep slope—an exacting punishment indeed. Correct execution brings its proper reward, though. A well-placed drive gets its due with an easier second shot. From the top fairway the green is a long and not-too-narrow target. Missing the putting surface is not recommended, however. The left side is especially penal. Down the steep bank on the side is no good at all.

The green itself is a great example of one whose problems lie not in the surface but in the surrounds. Thus, the correct angle for the approach is so important.

Strangely, in the early 1990s the lower fairway was left to grow in and eliminate the alternative from the tee. By the time of that 2002 New Zealand Open and Woods's first visit, however, the hole had been restored to its former glory. And the green proved crucial. It was there that New Zealand native Michael Campbell three-putted from four feet en route to losing the title to Australian Craig Parry.

Opposite, bottom: Michael Campbell's slip-up on the 17th at Paraparaumu Beach cost him the 2002 New Zealand Open.

"Often it is difficult to pinpoint the event, the circumstance, that launches a career or at least accelerates it," states Robert Trent Jones in *Golf's Magnificent Challenge,* his brilliant 1988 book on a life in golf-course design. "For me the moment is relatively easy to determine. Peachtree did it."

Peachtree, for which planning began in 1945 and which opened in 1948, elevated the 39-year-old Jones from solid success to superstardom. Two elements fueled the new course's fame: its brilliant design and Jones's famous, similarly-named client/collaborator, Robert Tyre Jones, Jr. In fact, until the creation of Peachtree, both men went by the name Bobby. During a get-acquainted round of golf at Atlanta's East Lake Golf Club, Jones the player found himself introducing Jones the designer to several friends as Bobby Jones. Afterwards, the player asked the designer, "What are we going to call you?" and the designer responded, "There can only be one Bobby Jones in Atlanta and that's you. From now on, I'll be Trent Jones."

How much of Peachtree is player Jones and how much is designer Jones may never be known, but it's impossible to study Peachtree and not be struck by its visual similarity to Augusta National. Likewise, it's impossible to look at other Trent Jones designs and not see similarities to Peachtree. In fact, if you look at the hallmarks of Trent Jones's portfolio—hard pars and easy bogeys; large, contoured greens; multiple and long tee boxes; strategically and aesthetically placed hazards; a stern test for the better player, but navigable for the average player—Peachtree is the embodiment of his beliefs.

The par-four 12th at Peachtree is the hardest hole on what can be a brutally hard golf course (*Life* Magazine termed the course "a par-buster's nightmare"), and it serves as an excellent example of the Joneses' thinking.

First, there are multiple tee options that allow the roller-coaster dogleg right to play anywhere from 339 yards (women's tees) to 455 yards (gold). From any of those tees, the hole initially plays downhill to a blind landing area. At the bottom of the hill, about 285 yards from the back tee, a creek bisects the fairway on a bias and runs the length of the right side of the hole. From the forward tees (or even the back tees for a big hitter), a thinking player will take a fairway wood or long iron and lay up short of the creek. This shot leaves a long approach—uphill all the way—to a contoured plateau green. As with most of their holes at Peachtree, the Joneses allowed gravity—not fairway bunkers—to punish errant shots on 12 (in fact, on a course that constantly plays up and down valleys, only two holes at Peachtree feature fairway bunkers.)

Jimmy Gabrielsen played on the United States Walker Cup team in 1971 and captained the U.S. squad in 1981 and 1991. Peachtree, of which Gabrielsen is a member, hosted the 1989 Walker Cup.

"It's a very difficult hole," he says. "That's mainly because of the second shot. Today's players, as long as they are, are not going to be able to hit a driver off that tee because of the ditch crossing the fairway. That leaves a medium to long iron into an elevated, small, well-bunkered green. It's just a very hard target to hit. A lot of shots are either short or right, and that hill catches them and sweeps them down into those bunkers."

The "signature hole" concept is a modern marketing fabrication that is anathema to purists, but No. 12 at Peachtree has slowly supplanted the second, fourth, seventh, and 17th holes as the toughest peach in the basket.

The 1948 design of Peachtree marked the true arrival of architect Robert Trent Jones.

While the vast beauty of Pebble Beach makes it an unparalleled place to spend four hours, it doesn't make the golf course any easier. It's as though Mother Nature is dwarfing us, constantly reminding us that while we may be *fortunate* mortals, we are in the end mortal nonetheless.

Pebble Beach, designed in 1919 by local amateurs Jack Neville and Douglas Grant (it is the only course that either would ever create), has any number of holes that could arguably be included in a book about the toughest or the best holes in the game. Two stand out. On their own, the eighth and ninth are remarkable golf holes, but coming as they do one after the other, they create what may be the most difficult and beguiling one-two punch in the game.

The eighth hole is a waterfront par four that measures 418 yards. Around the world there are probably dozens of holes that could be described similarly, but none does such a mind-bending job of tying together the elements at hand—view, wind, elevation change—and mixing them with shot value to create a visually cohesive and strategically ingenious hole.

Once you get past the awe, the tee shot at the eighth is all about placement. From the tee, this dogleg right plays uphill and slightly inland. As if extending a hand to a dazed soul, the eighth offers an aiming rock in the middle of the fairway to help with alignment. A drive of 240 to 250 yards down the right center will put you in good position for your approach. Anything too far to the right fools with the bay below and requires a much more difficult second shot. Anything longer than 250 must be played to the left side of the fairway (Tour professionals usually hit less than a driver off this tee).

Depending on the drive, the second shot can call for a mid-iron, a long iron, or sedation. Standing at the inside edge of the dogleg, you are now facing one of the glorious views and great second-shot tests in golf. The turn in the dogleg is punctuated by an unfenced 100-foot cliff that lords it over Monterey Bay. The shot requires a downhill carry over cliff, chasm, sea, and sand to a small green that is also heavily protected by shoreline. Like most great holes, the eighth presents an option: either go for the green, which means carrying all of the chasm, or lay up. In this case, the designers have offered a large flat expanse of fairway to the left. A short-iron lay-up over the narrow end of the chasm will leave a short-iron third into the green and a chance at par.

Birdies at the eighth are reserved for the brave. The entire green complex slopes sharply from left to right, so the shot into the green is best played center/short. Anything long and left will leave a very difficult downhill chip or bunker shot. Short and right can be buried in rough, on the rocks, or downright drowned. The green itself is small, only 20 to 25 yards deep. In fact, with an average size of 3,500 square feet, Pebble Beach's greens are the smallest greens of any course on the PGA Tour (the average is 6,500 square feet).

The eighth has a way of bringing players down to earth. In the final round of the 1982 U.S. Open, Jack Nicklaus birdied five straight holes starting at the third before making a bogey at the eighth. He would finish second to Tom Watson. Ten years later, a short but glorious chapter in U.S. Open history came to a blustery close here. During the third round, Gil Morgan birdied the seventh hole to go 12-under par for the tournament, the lowest any player had ever gone in Open competition. On the eighth, he drove the ball solidly to the crest of the fairway. Then, aiming for the left side of the green, he pured a six-iron, but the ball came to rest on a downhill lie in the left-hand bunker. Morgan barely got out of the sand, chipped past the pin, and two-putted for a double bogey. Like Icarus, he had flown too close to the sun. He would come crashing down to 13th place.

In 1992 at Pebble Beach, Gil Morgan went further under par than anyone had gone in a U.S. Open before—until he reached the eighth hole in the third round.

Hard on the heels of Pebble's eighth comes the 466-yard par-four ninth. With nearly the same amount of visual drama and almost 50 yards more length, the ninth is arguably the hardest par on this majestic golf course.

"If you could put the tee shot from No. 9 at Pebble onto the approach from No. 8, you would definitively have the hardest golf hole in the world," says Tom Fazio.

At 240 yards off the tee, the first of four left-side bunkers is in play for many players. It would seem the strategy would then be to play to the right. Simple enough? Not exactly. Nearly the entire ninth fairway slopes dramatically from left to right (toward the bay). In order to keep a drive from ending up in the right rough, players are forced to aim down the left side of the fairway, and thus pull the bunker back into play.

For mortals, a solid drive will likely leave an approach shot of anywhere from 200 to 230 yards, less for the pros, to a small green that's reminiscent of the eighth, 24 yards deep, with a cavernous bunker protecting the front left and the vigilant bay standing guard to the right. If that's not enough, the ball will almost certainly lie below the player's feet for this second shot, encouraging a seaward push. Regulars who carry mid to high handicaps will often lay up on their second shot and settle for a bogey rather than risk worse. (The Open is scheduled to return to Pebble Beach in 2010, and the ninth is likely to be lengthened by some 25 yards.)

There are a few instances in this world where an icon and its location make a perfect match. The Statue of Liberty in New York Harbor is one example. Who can imagine the Eiffel Tower anyplace but Paris? Likewise, there is something right about the coupling of Pebble Beach Golf Links and the craggy coastline of Monterey Bay.

"It's the pristine beauty," says Tiger Woods. "There is no other golf course that has cliffs like this that let you overlook the ocean, gorgeous holes, but demanding holes. If you took away the ocean, took away the view, this is still a fantastic golf course. You add in the beauty on top of that, and you have what you have here. It's a wonderful combination."

In a 1972 article in the *San Francisco Chronicle,* Jack Neville contemplated on this beauty more than 50 years after designing the course. "Years before it was built," he said, "I could see this place as a golf links. Nature had intended it to be nothing else."

Tiger Woods, who won the 2000 U.S. Open at Pebble Beach in a runaway, says, "If you took away the ocean, this is still a fantastic golf course."

With more than 400 original designs to his credit and another 100-plus redesigns to his name, Donald Ross was one of the most prolific golf-course designers in history. Amazingly, over a century after he designed his first golf course and over fifty years after his death, the quantity of his work is matched only by its enduring quality.

Ross's work was extraordinarily influential in the global growth of the game in the early 1900s. His trademarks—minimal movement of earth, wide fairways, ball-repelling greens, and heavily contoured putting surfaces—have been studied and imitated by golf-course architects for a century, but his unique touch has rarely been duplicated. Any discussion of great golf courses is likely to reference several Ross designs. Historic layouts such as Seminole, Oakland Hills, and Oak Hill—all original Ross designs—are touchstones in the history of the game and its architecture. Congressional, East Lake, Interlachen, and Inverness are among the courses that have benefited from his deft redesign work.

No Ross course is more celebrated or embodies Ross's philosophy more definitively than Pinehurst No. 2. Remarkably, it was among Ross's first projects. In 1900, one year after immigrating to America, the Scotsman Ross was hired by James W. Tufts, the founder of Pinehurst, to replace the fledgling resort town's rudimentary golf course (one nine designed by Dr. Leroy Culver, the other by John Dunn Tucker) with two 18-hole layouts simply referred to as No.1 and No.2.

It can be argued that no single Ross hole captures the essence of his thinking as well or as sternly as the fifth hole at Pinehurst No. 2. A 483-yard par four from the U.S. Open tees (442 yards from the blues), the fifth is not the longest par four on the course, but it plays that way because it's very much uphill. Although the fairway is generous and bunker-free, a rise off the tee obstructs the fairway landing area from view. In typical Ross fashion, the emphasis here is the very trying second shot.

Even the pros face an approach of around 200 yards here. Positioned diagonally to the fairway, the heavily bunkered green slopes toward the player. The only safe access is from the right side of the fairway. But when it comes to a Donald Ross-designed green, reaching the green is only half the battle. Holding the surface and then successfully putting that surface are the ultimate tests.

"The philosophy of Donald Ross is evident in the way he's structured the greens," says Greg Norman. "He built this as a second-shot golf course. There's not a lot of trouble off the tees. Not a lot of fairway bunkers. But the way these greens are built, they are inverted, basically. The fifth hole is probably an 8,000-square foot green, and it has only 700 square feet of pinnable surface. You think about that, that's 7,300 square feet of movement of the green. So it's a very, very precise second shot."

Combine that movement with the fact that, as Norman says, Ross's green designs are inverted or crowned. This combination can frustrate even the best. In the 1999 U.S. Open, John Daly took two attempts at an uphill putt from off the green on the eighth hole. Both rolled back. As the second attempt came rolling toward him, he knocked it over the green. Including his two-stroke penalty, Daly carded an 11 and a final-round 83.

Some Ross-savvy players like David Duval, who grew up playing Timuquana Country Club, a Ross design in Jacksonville, Florida, have learned to ignore the pins altogether. During the 1999 Open, Duval was asked how he approached the difficult fifth.

"I have a certain target I have picked out behind the green that I'm aiming at regardless of whether the pin is there or not," Duval replied. "So I have very definite places I'm looking. Going into the hole, I think I already know where I'm going to hit the ball. I don't think about anything else, I just try to hit it there."

Phil Mickelson nearly won the Open at Pinehurst, finishing one shot behind the late Payne Stewart. His assessment?

"No. 5 is a brutal hole," he says. "I don't want to say impossible, but it's very close to it. That's a tight area to have a ball end up, 30 feet on a 490-yard par four."

Ultimately, Pinehurst No. 2 and its fifth hole will serve as timeless monuments to the genius of one of the modern game's founding fathers.

Opposite, bottom: Payne Stewart mastered Donald Ross's trademark greens to win a second U.S. Open title at Pinehurst No. 2.

Pine Valley *Golf Club, Pine Valley, New Jersey* ~ *5th hole*

Tommy Armour was one of the great player-teachers in the history of golf. He also published two successful instructional books. In one he wrote: "No single factor affects more golf shots than fear."

It's unknown whether Armour played Pine Valley. To anyone who has ever teed it up on the legendary fifth hole, however, Armour's words ring frightfully true. An exhaustingly uphill par three, the fifth measures 232 yards from the back tees, but it's especially intimidating for the average golfer at a stout 221 yards from the regular tees. Once you account for the slope, the hole plays more like 240 to 250 yards, which means that many people need to pull out a driver. Directly in front of the tee, there's a well-stocked trout pond. The green stands regally, almost unattainable, atop a harshly landscaped mound. It seems the fifth hole can sense a golfer's fear and weakness. The only safe shot is a perfect shot. Anything less is repelled by the hole's steep surrounding grades. As the ball tumbles away from the green complex, it is virtually certain to end up in what Herbert Warren Wind once described as "an anthology of hazards."

Gene Littler has read that anthology. In 1961, the *Shell's Wonderful World of Golf* TV series pitted newly crowned U.S. Open champion Littler against the legendary Byron Nelson in a stroke-play match at Pine Valley. Nelson came into the fifth hole with a one-shot lead. A flurry of sand and grass later, Littler carded a quadruple-bogey seven and went on to lose the match to the retired Nelson by a score of 74 to 76. Afterward he was interviewed by the show's elfin host Gene Sarazen.

"You did a wonderful thing after that tragedy on the fifth hole," said Sarazen. "You played like a true Open champion and you finished with two birdies."

To which Littler replied: "After the fifth hole, I'm just glad I finished."

Littler and countless fellow victims of the fifth hole have only George Arthur Crump to blame. A Philadelphia hotelier and sportsman, Crump was an avid golfer who convinced a group of friends in 1912 to invest in his dream, a golf course in the nearby sand hills of New Jersey. Crump, who died in 1918 at the age of 47, spent the last six years of his life and more than $250,000 of his own money on the project. He decided that despite his lack of experience, he would design the golf course and supervise its construction. While knowledgeable friends and advisors, including everyone from a local golf-loving Catholic priest to the accomplished designer Harry S. Colt, offered their opinions, the blueprint for Pine Valley is still credited to Crump. (There has long been some question as to how much input Colt had. Some sources say he laid out the course, while others credit him only with refining Crump's plan.) When Crump died in 1918, only 14 holes had been completed. The construction of the final four holes (Nos. 12 through 15) was completed over the next four years under the supervision of Hugh Wilson, his brother Alan, and C. H. Alison, partner with Colt in the famed design duo of Colt & Alison.

The end result is one of the most prestigious clubs in the world and one of the most fascinating, punishing, rewarding, creative, strategically ingenious golf courses ever built. In 2000, noted golf writer and historian Jim Finegan published *Pine Valley Golf Club, A Unique Haven of the Game*. In this definitive club history, he poses the salient question facing anyone who has experienced the painful pleasure of playing Pine Valley: How could Crump ever have done it? How could he ever have imagined Pine Valley?

Gene Littler arrived at Pine Valley shortly after winning the U.S. Open, but he was undone in a made-for-TV exhibition by the brutal fifth hole.

Pine Valley is almost impossible to find. You weave a series of lefts and rights through various nondescript townships, down a forgettable road to nowhere, and over some railroad tracks. It's like finding a dacha outside Moscow: The only thing harder than getting in is getting there.

Because Pine Valley is such a private enclave (it has its own fire station, police force, and post office), the course is shrouded in mythology. Each of the 18 holes has enough tales of terror to fill its own book. Maybe it's the story of the club member who played the first four holes in four-under, stopped in the club-house for a nerve-settling libation, and never returned to the course. Maybe it's the baptismal rite of newcomers destined to struggle on the first hole; the countless humiliating stances that a day at Pine Valley requires; the extrication of a ball from the "Devil's Asshole," a hellish green-front bunker on the 10th hole; or doing an archeological dig in No. 7's Hell's Half Acre (named for purposes of alliteration, the bunker actually measures more than an acre). At any rate, Pine Valley is to golf stories what the Library of Congress is to books.

No hole at Pine Valley has built up more mythology than the thyroid-case 15th. Like most holes at Pine Valley, the regular tees aren't all that far ahead of the back tees, which means that while low handicappers are apt to consider the course short (6,656 yards), middle handicappers find it anything but. Not that the 15th is short for anyone, playing at 571 or 590 yards. As integral as length is to No. 15's toughness, the true difficulty of the hole comes through only when combined with these other complicating factors:

~ The Wind. Typical of course designer and founder George Crump's twisted genius, the 15th plays into the prevailing wind, making it play more like 600 yards plus.

~ The Water. The 15th tee is in one of the lowest sections of the property. The water that guards the 14th green stretches out between the 15th tee and the 15th fairway. To carry the water is only about 100 yards from the regular tee location. It just looks a lot longer.

~ The Incline. From the time you clear the water, the hole is an uphill trek. The slope is not that noticeable until you find yourself wheezing over your third shot. Don't worry, you'll catch your breath in time for your third putt.

~ The Grade. The farther that the 15th hole progresses up the hill, the more the fairway cants to the right. Any second shot that lands center or right of the fairway inexorably finds its way into the rough on the right (or worse). Shots pulled too far left will end up in a sinister combination of bushes, trees, roots, sand, and earthen ledges.

~ Encroachments. While the landing area off the tee is generous, the fairway gets stingier with every step. By the time a weary player has staggered to within 30 yards of the green, the throat of the fairway measures about 20 feet wide, sloping uphill and hard to the right.

~ The Sand. There are 20 bunkers on the hole, very few of which can be seen from the tee.

~ The Green. Humiliating. Approach shots missed to the right drop down into a chipping Neverland. The green is sloped noticeably from back to front. A false front means that a ball must carry at least 30 feet onto this green or risk rolling off and down into the throat of the fairway. In his rich history of Pine Valley, Jim Finegan writes about trying to keep the ball on the 15th green. "For pure perversity, this moment is almost in a class with the downhill putt on the fifth."

It is believed that since the course's opening in 1922, the 15th green has been reached in two shots only five times. The first to accomplish this Olympian feat was Gary Groh in 1985. Groh, who is now the head professional at Bob O'Link Country Club in Highland Park, Illinois, played the PGA Tour from 1971 to 1979. Winner of the 1975 Hawaiian Open, he was one of the big hitters of the late persimmon era. Groh had played Pine Valley prior to his historic round and was well aware of the 15th hole's history. After driving into the right side of the fairway, he was left with 270 yards, uphill. He selected a three-wood.

"The guys in the group said it sounded different," says Groh as he recalls the epic meeting of club and ball. "It sounded a little harder." The ball hit just short of the green, bounced up to the right side of the putting surface, and held. Groh two-putted for birdie.

Crump took one crack at golf-course design and created the art's definitive masterpiece. If he were alive today, would he be surprised at the legend he wrought? "I don't think so," says historian Finegan, who maintains that even though Crump saw only 14 holes completed, the feedback he received was extraordinarily positive from the beginning. In fact, it verged on gushing.

"Pine Valley has remained at the pinnacle of golf courses for ninety years because that's where it started," says Finegan. If the by-all-reports modest Crump could ever be informed that his golf course was widely regarded as the best test in the world, Finegan imagines this phlegmatic response: "Where else would it be?"

Opposite: In 1985, former PGA Tour player Gary Groh became the first to reach the "unreachable" 15th green at Pine Valley in two shots.

Anyone thinking about building a golf facility would do well to take a few pages out of the Pumpkin Ridge story. In 1996, when the 36-hole facility was only four years old, the developers landed the U.S. Amateur. Not just any U.S. Amateur, but the occasion of Tiger Woods's historic win over Steve Scott, giving Woods a third straight U.S. Amateur title. The drama of the contest was matched only by the natural beauty of the course and its surroundings, and a star (or two) was born.

The USGA has since returned several times to the still-young venue. In 1997, Witch Hollow (the private course; the other course, Ghost Creek, is semi-private) hosted the U.S. Women's Open. The facility simultaneously hosted the 2000 Junior Amateur and the 2000 Girls' Junior. Then in 2003 the Women's Open returned with stunning results. Hilary Lunke, a virtual unknown, turned back Kelly Robbins and Angela Stanford in an 18-hole Monday playoff after the best player in the women's game, Annika Sorenstam, blew her chance at the 72nd hole. Lunke became the first qualifier ever to win the Women's Open.

The architectural mastermind behind both Pumpkin Ridge layouts is the highly regarded Bob Cupp. A former designer at Nicklaus Design who assisted the Golden Bear on courses such as Castle Pines and Muirfield Village, Cupp founded his current practice in 1988.

The extent of Witch Hollow's visual appeal and the quality of the course's routing and strategy come as no surprise when you consider that Cupp is a trained artist (he holds a Masters in Fine Art from the University of Alaska); that he was once a good enough player himself to consider competing professionally; and that his assistant in Cupp Design was John Fought, 1979 PGA Tour Rookie of the Year and U.S. Amateur Champion in 1977.

Rye and fescue grasses join with fir, maple, oak, and ash trees to frame Witch Hollow's fairways, but the old-style beauty of the course never fully disguises her toughness. "Every hole has its own character," says Sorenstam. "It's beautiful scenery. . . . But most of all you have to hit the shots here. You have to work the ball off the tees, and you hit a lot of different shots. I think it's a great golf course. It's very fair, but also very tough," she adds. "This is one of the toughest U.S. Opens I've ever been to."

The toughest hole was the 394-yard 14th, which is a par five for normal play but can be turned into a par four for championships. For the men, it plays 470 from the back and with its water-guarded green it is either a very reachable par five or a very difficult par four. The USGA elected to use the ladies' tees for the Women's Open and reduce par to four.

The tee shot, played up to a crest, is quite inviting. There's a large bunker left and a couple of trees. If you should happen to really catch the tee shot, you have a huge advantage in that you'll carry the crest and get one or two clubs' worth of roll.

The green is the primary attribute of the hole (only 33.3 percent of the Women's Open field hit this green in regulation). Water guards the entire left side, and the back left extends out into the hazard, a part of the green where the flag is located only when the hole is played as a par five. To the right, where the pin is placed for par four play, there is a small bounce-in area, but it's not easy to find with a long second shot. Considering that the 14th averaged .538 strokes above par for the tournament, Stanford's chip-in birdie from the back fringe to briefly pull even with Lunke in the 2003 playoff was among the gutsiest shots of the year.

"When she made that chip," says Lunke, "I thought maybe it's her day, maybe this is the way it's supposed to be." It wasn't, of course, but as far as Cupp is concerned, the hole did its job.

"That's how tough, functional golf holes should work," he says.

Hilary Lunke made a name for herself in the hard-fought 2003 U.S. Women's Open at Pumpkin Ridge.

To anyone who has ever limped off the 18th green humiliated by Quail Hollow, it will come as no surprise that the course was originally designed by a Marine.

After graduating in 1937 from the University of Georgia with a degree in landscape architecture, George W. Cobb spent several years as a landscape architect for the National Park Service. In 1941, he joined the Marines as an engineering officer. His first course design project: overseeing Fred Findlay's design for the golf course at Camp LeJeune. Five years later Cobb completed his first solo design, also a military course, at Cherry Point (N.C.) Marine Corps Air Station. Cobb went on to become one of the southeast's better known course architects. Close to Bobby Jones, the Savannah native not only served as an architectural consultant to Augusta National, but in 1960 he co-designed the famed club's par-three course with his legendary friend.

Cobb's Quail Hollow design played host to 11 Kemper Opens on the regular Tour and seven Paine Webber Invitationals on the Senior Tour between 1969 and 1988. The course began hosting PGA Tour events again in 2003 when the Wachovia Championship debuted, six years after a crowd-pleasing Tom Fazio redesign. Quickly the course has earned a reputation for difficulty. The last three holes present what may be the most punishing triumvirate on the PGA Tour.

"I really can't think of tougher finishing holes on Tour than 16, 17, and 18 on this golf course," says Arron Oberholser, who finished second behind Joey Sindelar at the 2004 Wachovia. "You can't really throw TPC (Sawgrass) in there because you have a reachable par five in No. 16. I would be surprised if you could find three finishing holes tougher than these three."

Upon playing in the inaugural Wachovia in 2003, Charles Howell III was similarly impressed with the challenge he'd faced. "You could have a U.S. Open here tomorrow," said Howell. "It's definitely the toughest PGA Tour golf course I've played outside of a major."

Testing as Nos. 16 and 17 are, they cannot match the 478-yard 18th for sheer muscle. Fazio took a hole that was fairly benign before the re-design and turned it into a hole that keeps players on edge until the last putt falls. He did so by lengthening it and moving the fairway and green to bring a creek into play.

On the downhill tee shot, the player is faced with a large bunker on the right and a creek that runs malevolently up the entire length of the narrow fairway on the left. The second shot is uphill all the way and forces similar decisions: The right side of the green is well bunkered. The left is guarded, again, by the creek.

Off the tee, says Nick Price, "you've got a bunker which is just the perfect distance off the tee... Anything left on either the tee ball or the approach is dead. In fact, if you hit it left it's a double-bogey." The reward for a heroically accurate tee shot is a discomfiting uphill approach: 200 yards or more to the green is not uncommon. "It's one of those holes," adds Price, "that if you play it at even par for the whole week, you'll feel like you played it at two-under because it's more like a par four-and-three-eighths. If you're not on your game, you can make a big number there."

David Toms did exactly that in the 2004 Wachovia. After dominating the field for 71 holes, Toms came to the 72nd tee with a six-shot lead. Then he hit the wall. "I wasn't nervous," said Toms. "I'm sitting there with a six-shot lead and felt like I got past 17 without a disaster, the tournament was mine."

Toms, who had driven well on the hole all week, tried to give this one a little something extra—famous last words. "My game plan was to make a birdie and finish off in style," said the 2002 PGA champion. He ended up beyond the gallery to the right.

He pitched his second through the fairway and into the hazard on the other side. He played his third from the hazard, advancing it down the fairway. After landing his sand-wedge fourth on the green, a rattled Toms four-putted from about 50 feet for a quadruple-bogey eight and a mere two-shot victory.

Toms reviewed a memorable week capped off by his struggle with the home hole. "I went from being in total control and picking my targets and knowing what I was trying to do," said Toms, "to all of a sudden being totally different."

No. 18 can have that effect.

Opposite: David Toms managed to win the 2003 Wachovia Championship despite his eight on the demanding home hole. This sand wedge was his fourth shot.

Quaker Ridge *Golf Club, Scarsdale, New York* ~ *6th hole*

Depending on one's point of view (or handicap), the New York metropolitan area is either blessed or burdened with some of the toughest golf courses in the world. A trip to the south and west from the city brings Baltusrol and Pine Valley into view. Head east to Long Island and you'll find puzzlers such as Deepdale, Shinnecock Hills, and National Golf Links of America. To the northeast, I-95 is as tough on golfers as it is on motorists. In Mamaroneck you'll find the flagship of New York golf in Winged Foot, and even tranquil Fairfield County in Connecticut weighs in with the fierce Stanwich Club. But for decades one of the most challenging courses in an area rife with difficulty has been camouflaged among these better-known giants. Hidden in the leafy shadows of Scarsdale is A. W. Tillinghast's 1926 gem, Quaker Ridge.

Located virtually across the street from Winged Foot, and sitting in the giant shadow cast by its famous neighbor, Quaker Ridge is easily overlooked. But the course, built on a site with a storied past as both a Quaker meeting place and an American outpost during the Revolutionary War, is quietly counted by cognoscenti as among the toughest in the game. During the 1974 U.S. Open, Jack Nicklaus was asked if that year's host course, Winged Foot (West) was the best golf course in the world. His response: "It may be, but let me tell you, you have quite a golf course down the street."

American history became golf history in 1914 when the Metropolitan Golf Links purchased land in the area and leased it to the Quaker Ridge Field and Country Club. The next year John Duncan Dunn, Scottish-born son of Tom Dunn (the most prolific course designer of the late 1800s), was hired to lay out a short-lived golf course. When the club encountered financial problems less than a year later, a handful of members bought the land, created Quaker Ridge Golf Club, and hired Tillinghast, who presented the club with a brand new golf course by building 11 brand new holes and thoroughly revising another seven.

Tillinghast was fond of saying that "a round of golf should permit 18 inspirations." No record of how many agitations he liked to see, but judging by his work in Westchester County alone, it's plenty. Quaker Ridge is extremely punishing off the tee, even more so than its better-known neighbor. The fairways are hard and they feature unthinkable grades. An abundance of out of bounds and trees can rattle even the coolest player. Rees Jones, who prepped the course for the 1997 Walker Cup, the highest profile event ever staged at the club, says it's one of the most demanding driving golf courses in the world.

The brutal 443-yard sixth hole is typical of Quaker Ridge. It encompasses the sloped fairways, the narrow efficient landing area, and the overall rockiness of the site. The fairway slopes with determination from right to left. The landing area is very

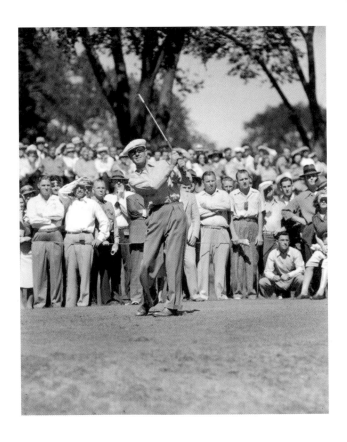

146

narrow. The player tends to favor the left side but, like the Walker Cuppers who struggled with No. 6 in 1997, you can also get blocked out by the trees there.

"I think that's what was happening to them in the Walker Cup," says Jones. "And on top of that, the green is not that large and the bunkers around it are quite deep."

Quaker is best known among area amateurs for hosting the Hochster Memorial, one of the Metropolitan Golf Association's most sought-after amateur titles. Initiated in 1934, the invitational 36-hole medal play championship is limited to 60 players. Even with fields that have included such august names as Dick Siderowf, Jess Sweetser, Willie Turnesa, and George Zahringer III, par has rarely been threatened.

Quaker Ridge has hosted three Met Amateurs and two Met Opens. The 1936 Met Open was particularly historic in that the field included Tommy Armour, Johnny Farrell, Paul Runyan,

and Gene Sarazen. But the title was stolen by a little-known Texan who made the event his first significant competitive title: Byron Nelson.

Tough as the course is, it's unlikely that Quaker Ridge will ever host a PGA Championship or a U.S. Open. While the Walker Cup (won handily by a U.S. team familiar with the course) and Met area championships have proven the course's mettle, Quaker Ridge lacks the one essential required by all major championships: It doesn't have a practice area. That deficit and the fact that when the club finally did host the Walker Cup, it was overshadowed within a few weeks by Winged Foot's PGA Championship, assure continued quiet pride for Quaker Ridge.

Opposite: The 1936 Met Open at challenging Quaker Ridge was won by a fresh-faced 24-year-old Texan named Byron Nelson.

In the chronology of a profession that includes such boldface names as Pete Dye, Tom Fazio, The Joneses, C. B. Macdonald, Alister MacKenzie, Old Tom Morris, Jack Nicklaus, Seth Raynor, Allan Robertson, Donald Ross, and A. W. Tillinghast, George C. Thomas is but a blip. He designed only 18 golf courses in his career and several of those no longer exist. Yet some students of golf-course design argue that had Thomas been more prolific, he might be remembered today as the greatest designer ever.

In 1920, Thomas (he liked to be addressed as Captain) took his sizeable inheritance and moved his family from Philadelphia to Beverly Hills to more closely pursue his true vocation—botany. Once in California, Captain Thomas joined Los Angeles Country Club and was asked to lend his horticultural expertise to a redesign of the club's existing course as well as the creation of a new 18. The new 18, known today as North Course, is among the best in the state.

In 1922, local powerbrokers Frank Garbutt and William May Garland were heading an effort to build a golf course for the Los Angeles Athletic Club. They asked Thomas for his opinion of the proposed setting. He felt that the property could not produce a championship golf course, but one "good enough" for the LAAC. Garbutt and Garland swallowed their pride and offered Captain Thomas the job. He accepted the assignment on two conditions: first, that Billy Bell supervise the construction, and second, that the project be given unlimited resources. Nearly $250,000 and 15 routing plans later, LAAC, which would soon be renamed Riviera Country Club, had its "good enough" golf course.

Thomas died in 1932, but Riviera has become part of American golf mythology. In addition to hosting 43 Los Angeles Opens (now known as the Nissan Open), Riviera has hosted the 1948 U.S Open, the 1998 U.S. Senior Open, and two PGA Championships (1983 and 1995).

While its role as a playground of Hollywood royalty earned the course early notoriety, it was Ben Hogan's performances at Riviera that assured the club a place in golf history. He won the L.A. Open in 1942, 1947, and 1948. Hogan also won the first of his four U.S. Open titles at Riviera in 1948. Then, in 1950, only 11 months after nearly losing the use of his legs in a head-on collision with a Greyhound bus, Hogan lost the L.A. Open to Sam Snead in a playoff in his first tournament back. A handful of golf courses have since called themselves Hogan's Alley over the years (Carnoustie and Colonial among them), but Riviera may have the most sentimental claim to the title.

In his book *Golf Architecture in America,* Thomas wrote extensively about course difficulty and almost always in favor of it. No hole at Riviera better represents Thomas's philosophy than the relatively unknown second. It's the toughest scoring hole in the Nissan virtually every year. A 463-yard par four, it plays back opposite the par-five first hole, uphill and into the wind. From the tee, a row of trees to the left guards the practice range. The landing area is full of precisely the little rolls and uneven lies that Thomas describes in his book. Thus, the second shot is the real key to the hole's difficulty. Even though Tour players are hitting five-, six-, and seven-irons into the green, it's a slightly uphill approach to a narrow well-guarded target. On the right is the hill to the clubhouse covered in the course's trademark Kikuyu grass. To the left, three large bunkers stand sentinel. The green is difficult to putt because a large ridge separates it from front to back.

Todd Yoshitake is the head professional at Riviera. He says much of the hole's difficulty arises from its location, i.e., the contrast between the scenic ease of the first hole—teeing off with the wind at your back to a 75-foot drop-off—and the sudden uphill reality of the 2nd. "The course really starts on No. 2," Yoshitake says.

Although No. 2 comes early in the round, Doyle Corbett played himself out of a tournament there. It happened in 1998, at the U.S. Senior Open. In the second round, the head professional at Sun Valley Golf Club cut his three-iron approach into the severe Kikuyu-covered slope to the right of the green. It would have been a lost ball, replayed from the fairway, had it not been for a marshal who must have thought he was being helpful when he pointed out the barely visible ball to Corbett. Ten shots later Corbett holed out for a 12.

Opposite, bottom: Ben Hogan's name was inexorably tied with Riviera after his valiant comeback appearance in 1950. Sam Snead turned back the sentimental favorite in a playoff.

Considered by astute observers to be the best golf course in England, Royal Birkdale was a late addition to the British Open rota. Although the course dates to 1889, it was not until a 1932 makeover by architects Fred Hawtree and J.H. Taylor that the course was considered Open-worthy. The new and improved Birkdale was quickly scheduled to host the 1940 Open Championship, but World War II intervened and Birkdale's debut was delayed until 1954.

Those lost years have more than been made up for. Over the second half of the 20th century, Birkdale's distinctive, nautical looking clubhouse has played host to eight Opens. The list of winners is dominated by great names: Johnny Miller, Arnold Palmer, Peter Thomson (twice), Lee Trevino, and Tom Watson, to name a few.

As a measure of the esteem in which Birkdale is now held, the Royal and Ancient Golf Club of St. Andrews chose the club to host the 100th Open in 1971. After a heroic display of putting, Trevino emerged victorious and completed an amazing run during which he also won the U.S. and Canadian Opens.

Five years later, Birkdale was the scene of Seve Ballesteros's coming-out fiesta. At what would ultimately become Johnny Miller's Open, the 19-year-old Ballesteros stunned the golfing world by leading the field at the halfway mark and again after 54 holes. Waywardness eventually proved the undoing of the mercurial Spaniard. The fairways at dune-covered Birkdale are notoriously unforgiving, surrounded as they are by a cruel mixture of long rough, blackberry, scrub grass, and yellow primrose.

In championship play, the toughest hole at Birkdale is the sixth, a 480-yard, uphill par four (it normally plays as a par five). In the 1991 Open, it extracted an average of 4.59 strokes, although Ian Baker-Finch birdied it in the final round on his way to a five-under 29 on the front nine and a winning 66.

While the dunes at Birkdale frame most of the holes, the sixth is an exception in that a ridge runs across the fairway in the landing area of the drive. That cuts down the roll of the tee shot and makes the hole play even longer than its considerable yardage. The dune also serves to make the second shot a blind one unless the drive is long and down the left side of the fairway. Of course, as difficulty would have it, the approach to the green is not as open from the left. Completing the challenge of the drive is a bunker that cuts into the right side of the fairway, from which there's simply no way to reach the green in regulation.

Imagine, then, how the sixth played in the third round of the 1998 Open when it was played in a howling crosswind. Many players had to use a driver for their second shot; that is if they were lucky enough to find the fairway off the tee. Not a single birdie was recorded that day, but there was one very noteworthy bogey—one that ultimately enabled Mark O'Meara to claim the championship. O'Meara was one of the players who went at the green with a driver for his approach, but he pushed it badly into some deep undergrowth. It seemed unlikely the ball would be found, and after about three minutes, O'Meara began to walk back down the fairway to play another ball under a stroke-and-distance penalty.

Before he played another stroke, the ball was found and picked up by a spectator. A confusing situation ensued; a debate over whether the five-minute allotment for finding a ball also applied to identifying the ball. Eventually O'Meara was allowed to take a drop at the spot where the ball had been found. Twice the dropped ball rolled closer to the hole, and ultimately he was allowed to place it. O'Meara knocked his third onto the edge of the green and made a bogey where a few minutes before it appeared he would make a triple bogey or worse. On a hole like the sixth at Birkdale, bogey is sometimes cause for celebration.

Mark O'Meara's magical 1998 season peaked at Birkdale, where he claimed his second major championship. The key to his victory may have been a third-round bogey at the stout sixth hole.

Not until the 1970s did the world wake up to the delights of Royal Dornoch. While not quite cut off from civilization, this remote section of north Scotland requires both determination and patience of its visitors, though new bridges and recently improved roads have made the trip somewhat easier than it used to be. The chances of a British Open being played in such a remote location are, well, remote. But the improvements in infrastructure have meant that both the British and Scottish Amateur championships made multiple visits to Dornoch in the latter years of the 20th century and into the new millennium. Even the rock star Madonna found the place, if only to get married there (as did former European Ryder Cup skipper Sam Torrance some time before).

The village of Dornoch holds an importance in the world of golf far beyond its almost peerless links. For it was in Dornoch that Donald Ross was born. The influence of this golf course on the young Ross, who would become one of the game's most prolific and admired designers, is clear after only the briefest look. Almost every green at Dornoch is raised above the level of the fairway. Almost every less-than-perfect shot is shrugged off either left or right, short or long, asking endlessly difficult and teasing questions of almost every approach shot. And it is just that same theory that Ross applied to what many see as his best course, Pinehurst No. 2 in North Carolina.

Nowhere is Ross's theory more apparent than on what many believe is Dornoch's toughest hole. "Foxy," a 445-yard par four, is well named for its ability to fool even the best players—and it has no need of a bunker to do so. On this hole, sand is notable only for its absence.

On the tee, it is difficult to know where to hit. Three mounds dominate the horizon on the left side. To the right, beyond a very narrow strip of fairway, are more mounds that stretch all the way up the right side.

The ideal shot is to the left, past the mounds, but that requires both accuracy and power to spare. A drive to the right leaves a harder line to the raised green. Left at least affords the chance to run an approach up the steep bank at the front of the green, a bank that doubles in height on the right side.

And what a green! A plateau, it sits atop a promontory that is broad enough on the right side, but narrows gradually to the left, where it is also extremely shallow. For many unwitting golfers, the result of that shallowness is a chip back from over the green.

A tough hole. A great hole. And one where Donald Ross learned his lessons well.

Opposite, bottom: Royal Dornoch's elevated greens had a lifelong influence on the golf course design portfolio of native son Donald Ross.

The Open Championship is, for good reason, closely associated with the great courses of Scotland. The claret jug conjures images of Scottish links, firth-born gales, and gorse far more readily than it does an English setting. But despite the fact that the Royal and Ancient prefers to leave the word "British" off the title, the Open is still very much a British affair. Since 1969, it has been played in England 15 times, with six of them at the course known colloquially as Lytham.

The course was designed in 1897 by George Lowe, Jr., who like many from Carnoustie, Scotland, left the region as a young man and took golf with him. Soon after landing a job as a green-keeper at St. Annes, Lowe was hired by the club to design a course at a new location. Several designers have made revisions, including Tom Simpson, Herbert Fowler, and the renowned duo of Colt and Alison.

At 6,905 yards Lytham may be shortish for a modern major championship, but that lack of length is more than made up for by insidious subtleties. Driving the ball accurately is critical here. In some cases, the emphasis on driving accuracy is even more pronounced as the hazards on many holes lie close to the optimal line. Like many courses throughout the U.K., the narrow greens run precipitously off at the sides, in many cases feeding even well-struck balls into greenside bunkers.

Royal Lytham has several very tough par fours on the back nine, with the 467-yard 17th earning the nod as the toughest. A dogleg right-to-left, a drive down the left towards the bunkers shortens the hole, but leaves a blind shot to a green that is guarded by two bunkers that cannot be seen from the fairway. A drive down the right will leave a long approach. The chain of bunkers that runs up the entire left side of the hole, many of them of the deep, walled variety, is more than enough distraction. To the right is what one author described as "real wilderness." Aside from steady nerves, the only element helping the intrepid par-seeker is the prevailing wind.

The 17th hole robbed Jack Nicklaus of the British Open in 1963 when, certain that a 4-4 finish would seal the title, Nicklaus played a two-iron through the green and into heavy rough beyond. Three shots later, he carded a bogey five. To this day, Nicklaus insists that the 1963 Open was his most regrettable loss. Seve Ballesteros won two Opens at Lytham with superb scrambling, but otherwise the list of winners at Lytham reads like a Who's Who, not of length, but of accuracy: Dave Thomas in 1958, Bob Charles in 1963, and Gary Player, who in 1974 wisely opted for a one-iron on most of Lytham's driving holes to beat Peter Oosterhuis by four shots. Player survived an adventure at the 17th in the final round, where, leading by six strokes, his ball was nearly lost in deep rough to the left of the green until it was found just before the end of the five-minute limit by his caddie, Rabbit Dyer.

The most acclaimed triumph over the 17th at Lytham was undoubtedly that of Bobby Jones in 1926, who came to the hole tied with Al Watrous. Jones, in search of his first British Open title, pulled his tee ball into what was then a sandy wasteland, but is now a chain of bunkers. Watrous, after driving in the fairway, hit the green with his approach, leaving Jones to face a bunker shot of some 170 yards (the hole was shorter in those days) over fairway bunkers, rough, and greenside bunkers. The claret jug rested in the balance. Jones wrote of his mindset as he stood over the shot: "An eighth of an inch too deep and...the shot expires right in front of your eyes. And if your blade is a thought too high...I will dismiss this harrowing reflection." His mashie-iron shot came to rest on the green, well inside Watrous's ball. Watrous was so undone by Jones's heroics that he three-putted the hole and went on to lose by two strokes. Today, the club Jones used for that shot is on display in the Lytham clubhouse and a plaque alongside the left-hand bunkers commemorates the moment.

Opposite, bottom: Gary Player nearly lost a ball on the 17th hole during the 1974 British Open at Lytham, but one hole later he was congratulated on a four-stroke victory by Peter Oosterhuis.

When Royal Melbourne was preparing to build a new course in 1926, the club decided it wanted to hire the best golf architect in the world. After consulting with the Royal and Ancient Golf Club of Scotland, club officials determined that Alister MacKenzie was their man.

MacKenzie's best work, such as Augusta National and Cypress Point, was still ahead of him, but the R&A's recommendation was more than sound. In fact, the Composite Course at Royal Melbourne that MacKenzie helped to create is ranked, along with the aforementioned two courses, among the top eight in the world by *Golf Magazine.*

Although MacKenzie spent only nine weeks in Australia, his influence was felt greatly in that country. In addition to designing Royal Melbourne, he found time to plot a layout for New South Wales in Sydney and to advise on some 20 courses in the Melbourne, Sidney, and Brisbane areas. Even now, nearly 80 years later, many credit MacKenzie's visit with the popularity of the sport throughout Australasia.

MacKenzie the visionary needed someone to carry out his plans once he left the country, and for that he selected Alex Russell, a former Australian Open champion. Russell had gotten a head start at Royal Melbourne, since the club assigned him the task of laying the groundwork for the new course even before it hired MacKenzie. Russell would go on to design a number of courses, including the East Course at Royal Melbourne, a second 18 that followed shortly after the completion of MacKenzie's West Course in 1931.

With its scrubby elegance and awesome difficulty, Royal Melbourne holds a unique place in the hearts of Australians. Local golf course designer Michael Clayton has been quoted as saying that along with the Sydney Opera House the golf course is "one of only two man-made things in Australia of world-wide significance."

The West course's wide fairways and oversized greens are deceiving (remember, MacKenzie was a noted camouflage artist). In fact, it's not unusual for a visitor to hit most of the fairways and still play bogey golf. That's because the true challenge of Melbourne lies in those oversized greens. Because the greens are so large, they are relatively easy to hit. But being on one of Mackenzie's greens is one thing, successfully navigating it is another. With the firmness, speed, and movement of these renowned surfaces, Melbourne, which has hosted 16 Australian Opens, can lay claim to being the four-putt capital of the world. Putting here is a constant struggle.

Nowhere is that more true than the sixth hole of the West Course. This hole, incidentally, also plays as the sixth hole on what is referred to as the Composite Course, which was first devised for the 1959 World Cup and has since been used in Australian Opens. This course incorporates 12 holes of the West Course and six of the East Course, and is considered better for spectators because it includes no road crossings. Confusing matters, however, the 18 holes of the Composite Course were played in a different order at the 1998 Presidents Cup, and recently the annual Heineken Classic has followed that order. In that configuration, this plays as the fourth hole.

The West sixth is a classic dogleg right of 450 yards that starts with an elevated tee. Its typically large fairway is guarded on the right first by scrub and then by large, deep bunkers. The ideal shot carries the trouble on the right but comes to rest in the right side of the fairway. The farther left the tee shot runs, the more it brings into play the deep bunker guarding the left side of the green. Assuming a 270-yard drive, the approach will leave 180 uphill yards to an amphitheatre green that is heavily bunkered and frighteningly contoured.

Even among Melbourne's famously dynamic greens, this one is lethal. In the 2004 Heineken Classic, Ernie Els took advantage of benign conditions to shoot an extraordinary 60 in the first round and took an eight-stroke lead after 54 holes, but Royal Melbourne bit back in the final round, especially on this hole. Els's second shot flew into a back bunker, from where he painfully learned just how tough this green site can be. Facing an awkward lie, he had to play sideways to a spot behind the green. He tried to play a delicate chip to a green sloping away from him, but hit it so softly that it failed to carry the slope right in front of him and the ball rolled back to his feet. His next attempt went 20 feet past and two putts later he had a triple bogey.

The triple sent Els reeling to a 42 on the front nine, which cost him his entire eight-stroke advantage over Adam Scott. Showing remarkable resilience, Els rallied with a 32 on the back nine to claim the title.

In the 1959 World Cup, Canada's Al Balding played his approach to the back of this green and promptly four-putted. Putts from the side are no bargain either: Local knowledge has these putts breaking one foot for every foot in length, meaning even a two-foot putt will break two feet.

Opposite, bottom: Australia's Royal Melbourne is one of the supreme tests in the game. Ernie Els found that out the hard way during the 2004 Heineken Classic, though he emerged with a victory.

One of the quaint aspects of golf the world over is that so many holes have fitting nicknames. Nowhere is that more true than at Royal Portrush in Northern Ireland, specifically at the brutally difficult 215-yard 14th hole known as "Calamity".

And indeed, calamity is exactly the fate of any golfer stricken with a propensity for what is euphemistically called a fade, more properly a slice. While the left side of Portrush's most famous hole is no bargain—thick rough amid some hillocks awaits the player who favors the port side—anything right is, in golfing parlance, gone.

In this case, that's a long way gone, down a gaping 75-foot-deep chasm that has destroyed many a promising scorecard. Only the most precise of tee shots is capable of finding the distant green, a feat made even more difficult by the ever-present and varying winds of the Irish Sea. Then there is the magnificent scenery, capable of distracting even the most hard-hearted soul. It is difficult to know where to look. Or where not to. The hills of Inishowen rise in the west. To the east are the White Rocks, limestone cliffs beyond which lies the old Dunluce castle and the majesty of the Giant's Causeway. Further afield, the dim outline of Scotland's southern Hebrides can be discerned on a clear day, as can the Donegal hills. The 14th hole at Royal Portrush presents one of the greatest 360-degree panoramic vistas in all golf.

Originally designed by Old Tom Morris and opened in 1888, Royal Portrush was remodeled by Harry Colt in 1933. At the time, Bernard Darwin, the doyen of British golf writers, was moved to write that Colt had created "a monument more enduring than brass." Clearly, the men at the Royal & Ancient Golf Club of St. Andrews agreed: A mere eighteen years later, Portrush hosted the only Open Championship that has so far been played outside Great Britain.

The winner that year was Englishman Max Faulkner, a cocky soul who before the final round was signing autographs proclaiming himself, "Open Champion 1951."

Such audacity is needed on Calamity's exposed tee. That and a sound technique, one able to rise above the mind games created by the likelihood of disaster down below. The canny or less ambitious player aims short and left to leave a relatively straightforward pitch to the flattish green, thereby eliminating the possibility of a very big number. The bold go for the putting surface in one. Make it and a satisfying three beckons. Miss and, well, some tired souls are down there still.

One last thing: At Portrush there is no let up. After Calamity comes No. 15, known as Purgatory.

Opposite: Northern Ireland's Royal Portrush is the only course outside of Scotland and England to host the British Open. That 1951 championship was won by England's Max Faulkner.

If the experts are to be believed, golf is as much mental as it is physical. And nowhere is that maxim demonstrated so graphically as on the 550-yard 14th hole at Royal St. George's. "The Suez Canal"—the hole is named for the ditch that runs across the fairway at around 330 yards—is one of golf's big bullies, a hole that relies on visual intimidation.

That mental torture is evident right from the start. When you stand on the tee, the refuge provided by the fairway is narrow indeed. On the left there is thick rough. All the way up the right is out of bounds, and beyond that lies the neighboring Princes course (where Gene Sarazen won the Open in 1932). In the 1985 Open, American Peter Jacobsen first lost his drive in the rough on the left, then over-corrected with his second ball and went out of bounds right. "I never thought I'd be hitting my third shot on this tee until Saturday," he quipped.

Eight years later, Bernhard Langer and Greg Norman arrived on that same tee vying for the Open title. Having birdied the previous hole, the German had the honor. Not that it did him any good. Langer's drive sailed out of bounds on the right side.

Having observed his companion, Norman stepped up and smashed a terrific tee shot miles down the middle. Five holes later, he was Open Champion for the second time.

Back in 1985 again, Sandy Lyle made the unlikeliest of birdies at the 14th in the final round. A pulled tee shot left him with nothing more than a pitch back into play, short of the Suez Canal. Into the wind, the Scot then struck a mighty two-iron to 35 feet and holed for his four.

"It didn't dawn on me until then that I had a chance to win," said Lyle after his one-stroke victory.

Since those momentous happenings, the 14th has become even tougher. It's been lengthened by 43 yards by moving the putting surface back and slightly to the right, even nearer to the out of bounds. The green, previously flat, is now heavily contoured, to the point where, in some conditions, it is possible to land on the surface and still bounce out of bounds, which makes going for the green in two a risky business. If all of that isn't enough, the prevailing wind is into the player and slightly from the left.

This is one intimidating hole.

Sandy Lyle's unlikely birdie in the 1985 British Open would be even less likely today as the 14th hole at Royal St. George's has been significantly toughened.

Even non-golfers have heard of the Postage Stamp, the satanic little 123-yard par three that is probably, yard for yard, the most difficult hole in all golf.

It is also, for good measure, the shortest hole on the British Open rota, falling ironically only two holes from what was for a long time the longest Open hole, Royal Troon's 601-yard sixth hole.

Much has happened in this outwardly unobtrusive corner of Ayrshire, a mere few miles from Prestwick, where the Open began back in 1860. In 1950, the German Herman Tissies took 15 shots to hole out on the Postage Stamp. Then, in contrast, in 1973, the 71-year-old Gene Sarazen, making a sentimental return to the championship he had won at Princes in 1932 and 50 years on from missing the cut in his only previous visit to Troon, aced the hole in his first round. One day later, he returned, hit his tee shot into the cavernous right-hand bunker—and holed out for a deuce. The old 1-2, without ever touching the green.

And what a green! Nestled between a high mound on the left, complete with three more bunkers (installed before Troon's first Open in 1923 to keep players from using the mound to bounce onto the green) and the deep depression from which Sarazen emerged, the putting surface is reasonably long but frighteningly narrow (25 feet) and, it must be said, somewhat flat. It is getting there that's difficult. Depending on wind conditions, finding the putting surface in less than two shots can take anything from the merest flick with a wedge to a full-blooded punch with a long iron. Doubling the difficulty, the

dune to the left of the green has the effect of shielding the putting surface from the elements. Many is the man who has leaned into a strong breeze on the tee and looked up to see the flag hanging limp. The result is rarely pretty for one so confused. The very shortness of the hole is a strength: In a strong wind one of golf's toughest tasks is the low shot with a lofted club.

On Royal Troon's eighth, normally brave men and women have, on occasion, been known to play short of the green, where there are no bunkers, for fear of reaching double figures. Perhaps that's what former Curtis Cup golfer Maureen Madill should have done while playing in the Helen Holm Trophy (the Scottish Ladies Stroke Play Championship). The Irishwoman hopelessly plugged her tee shot in the back right bunker, and with her mother caddieing and standing above as she hacked away, Madill kept going until she reached the green—in 16 shots. With each unavailing swing, her mother solemnly counted out the number of the shot.

Even the game's top players have trouble with the Postage Stamp. In 1989, Greg Norman opened the final round of the British Open at Troon with an incredible run of six straight birdies. But he bogeyed the eighth, hitting a nine-iron into a bunker. It was the only bogey in a round of 64; he would lose to Mark Calcavecchia in a playoff.

The Postage Stamp has never thought much of reputations. When Tiger Woods arrived at Royal Troon for the 1997 Open, he did so as holder of the Masters title. In the fourth round, he took six at the shortest par three he will ever play in an Open. Even the man who may turn out to be the greatest golfer of all time couldn't lick the Stamp.

Septuagenarian Gene Sarazen's sentimental return to Troon in 1973 became a sweet one when he aced the Postage Stamp hole.

The back nine at Royal Troon might be the hardest nine holes in golf. Thanks to the course's mostly out-and-back design, eight holes on the back play directly into the prevailing wind. These are hefty holes that make for a stern test even in rarely seen calm conditions. The back nine measures an intimidating 3,713 yards from the championship tees; compare that to the 3,462 yards on the usually downwind front nine. At Troon, a player needs to go on the offensive early; birdies can be had over the first six holes, but starting at the turn, the name of the game is defense.

The hardest hole on this hardest nine is undoubtedly the 11th. When the wind howled in the players' faces in the first round of the British Open in 1997, the back-nine scoring average rose to 40.16 and the average on No. 11 was a nightmarish 4.92. That's an average worthy of a par five, which, ironically, is what the hole had previously played.

The Railway Hole, as it is known because of its close proximity to a busy railway line on the right side, has undergone a couple of transformations. It was a short par four until the green was moved 160 yards prior to the 1962 Open Championship, making it a 485-yard par five. While it was still a potential birdie hole, the relocation of the green had put the putting surface within yards of the railroad tracks, a menacing out-of-bounds danger for those who tried to reach it in two.

In 1962, Arnold Palmer played No. 11 in four-under en route to his second consecutive Open Championship win. That same year, however, Jack Nicklaus found out how much trouble the Railway Hole can cause. Fresh from beating Palmer in a playoff at the U.S. Open, the 22-year old Tour rookie hit two shots onto the railway and carded a 10. Tom Watson eagled the 11th in the final round on the way to a one-stroke victory in 1982, but Mark Calcavecchia barely survived it when he captured the Open title seven years later. His drive finished in deep rough on the right, his second, too low, caught a hump and ended up under a thorn tree. After getting punctured by the tree while taking his stance, Calcavecchia hacked out into the fairway, hit the green with an eight-iron, and made a 40-footer for a par that helped him to secure a playoff against Wayne Grady and Greg Norman.

Disasters and near-disasters notwithstanding, the 11th was the easiest hole relative to par in 1989, a fact that didn't sit well with the folks at Troon. So, eight years later, the hole was shortened to 463 yards and played as a par four (unlike other cases of converted holes in championships, the regular tees at No. 11 have also been moved up so that it plays as a par four for everyone). The option of playing safe on the second shot had been eliminated. Now everyone would have to go for the green in two.

No. 11 didn't treat first-year professional Tiger Woods any better than it had treated Nicklaus in his rookie season. In the first round, Woods drove into the gorse on the right, advanced his second only 50 yards, and ended up making a triple bogey.

The 11th has only one bunker, a small gathering pit at the left front of the green. But the tee shot still induces fear. Gorse bushes and thick rough on both sides make it impossible to reach the distant green in regulation if a drive strays more than a few yards from the fairway. Trains whistling by on the right are not only a distraction, but an out-of-bounds threat as well.

The gorse on the right seems to have a magnetic influence on tee shots. In 2004, Ernie Els was battling for the lead down the stretch when his drive landed in a gorse bush in the same area that had once bedeviled Woods and Calcavecchia. In fact, his ball really was *in* the gorse bush, lodged in some branches well above the ground. "I don't think I've ever seen that happen," said Els. It left him with a risky baseball swing, but he managed a memorable par.

Earlier in the week, Els had made an ace on Troon's Postage Stamp eighth hole. Surely, such heroics on two horribly difficult holes would propel Els to victory. Not quite. He ended up in a playoff, where he suffered a disappointing loss to upstart Todd Hamilton.

Opposite, bottom: Ernie Els found his hopes for a second claret jug temporarily suspended by a bush on the 11th hole in the final round. He recovered for an out-of-the-ordinary par, but it didn't lead to a title.

Toward the end of the 20th century, it looked as though major championship golf had pretty much written off the Pacific Northwest. After all, no major had been played in the region since the 1946 PGA Championship. Despite the fact that that last championship, contested at Portland Golf Club, produced a more-than-worthy champion in Ben Hogan, major championship golf has long favored venues such as, say, Tulsa in August, over a return to the cool, shady Northwest.

That changed in 1998 when the PGA Championship came to Sahalee Country Club, located in the suburb of Sammamish northeast of Seattle. The club, with 27 holes originally designed in 1969 by Ted Robinson, had long desired to host a major. In 1992, it undertook a serious top-dressing program that not only brought a drastic improvement to turf conditions, but reaffirmed the club's commitment to championship golf. Four years later, Rees Jones was hired to update Robinson's bunkering and prepare a long-term plan for the tree-lined course.

Come the 1998 PGA, the club's work was done and the players' work was just beginning. For starters, the golf course was unfamiliar to virtually the entire field. Secondly, Sahalee is situated on 320 acres of forest. Towering cedars and ages-old firs harangued the field like something out of the *Wizard of Oz*. Even after Rees Jones removed a few hundred trees, the course remained a narrow tunnel of cedar, fir, and hemlock.

"If your driver is off just a little bit, you're going to struggle," said Retief Goosen, who missed the cut. "A couple of times I hit it in the middle of the fairway and still had to hit a fade on my second shot."

No hole played tougher in the 1998 PGA Championship than the 18th. As a 475-yard par four, it averaged 4.49 strokes per player.

"It was a brute," says Jones.

The tee shot is one of the more delicate on the course. While Jones did remove many trees, he simultaneously narrowed Sahalee's fairways by growing and extending the ryegrass rough. As a result, the 18th played, like so many of Sahalee's holes, even narrower than it looks.

"It's a very tight shot off the tee," says Jones. "Plus, it's a long hole so the guys are reluctant to throttle back. If they do go with a shorter club, it just leaves them that much longer a shot into the green."

The hole normally plays as a par five of 530 yards. The problem for the PGA Championship field was that with the tee moved up 65 yards, the landing area for the tee shot was an awkward one, just where the fairway turns to the left (though the hole's lone fairway bunker was taken out of play because the pros were easily able to fly it). If a player hit a driver and did not hit a draw, he was liable to run through the fairway. A miss on either side of the fairway brought Sahalee's ever-present trees into play.

"It was a par five anyway," says Robert Allenby. "It felt like a par five."

For the player who found the fairway, the approach shot was long, but fairly straightaway. A trademark bunker placed about 100 yards in front of the green featured (what else?) a protruding tree, but the hazard and the arboreal pest were removed in 2002 for seeming too penal. A new bunker now stands about thirty yards left/front of the green and another threesome of bunkers guards the putting surface itself. Unlike most of Sahalee's greens, this one has very little contour, other than a significant slope in the back. However, it can be hard to read.

Sahalee also hosted the 2002 WGC-NEC Invitational, for which the 18th was defanged. To the relief of the players, it was played as a par five.

Vijay Singh's first major came amid the looming trees and narrow fairways of Sahalee.

St. Nom-la-Breteche *Golf Club, Paris, France ~18th hole*

For more than three decades since its inception in 1970, the Trophée Lancome has been a perennial presence on the Paris social calendar. No one really does a sporting event like the French. Chic is the word that comes to mind, as expensively clad spectators stroll the elegant fairways of the St. Nom-la-Breteche Golf Club, some 15 miles west of the French capital near the Palace of Versailles.

Over the years, many of golf's greats have visited St. Nom. And more than a few have won there. The likes of Seve Ballesteros, Billy Casper, Sergio Garcia, Sandy Lyle, Johnny Miller, Colin Montgomerie, Jose Maria Olazabal, Mark O'Meara, Arnold Palmer, Gary Player, Nick Price, Vijay Singh, and Ian Woosnam all have lifted the distinctively sculpted Lancome trophy aloft.

All have had to deal with the 18th hole at St. Nom in order to do so. Unusually, it's a closing par three. Playing to 195 yards from a tee high atop the hillside to a green set in front of the beautiful clubhouse, the 18th is a hole that makes things happen.

In 1998, David Duval came to the tee one shot ahead of both Mark O'Meara and Miguel Angel Jimenez of Spain. That advantage, however, did not last. A slightly pushed tee shot by Duval finished in the pond to the right of the green and led eventually to a double bogey.

Next up were O'Meara and Jimenez. Perhaps in response to Duval's watery failure, both hit their tee shots well left of the putting surface. The American, who earlier that same year had won both the Masters and the British Open, could do no better than a bogey to tie his compatriot Duval.

Last to play was Jimenez. Showing a flair previously unseen in any of his play, the stoic from Malaga chipped in for the unlikeliest of birdies and a two-shot victory. The footprints from his dance of joy across the putting surface can surely be seen yet.

It is no surprise that the last hole at St. Nom is so often decisive. This is a hole with the power to intimidate and enhance even the smallest inkling of doubt in the back of the mind.

"A combination of things makes this such a difficult hole," says European Tour professional Raymond Russell, a regular competitor at the Lancome. "There is the water on the right side, of course. And a bunker over there, too. The bunker actually comes into play even more when they stick the pin back right on Sunday. The green slopes that way from front left to back right and narrows more to the rear.

"Adding to the intimidation factor is the fact that this is the final hole and also that the tee is so elevated. You can see all the trouble from up there and it is hard to gauge the distance correctly. You see a lot of shots finishing well short there, especially if it is windy.

"Left is no bargain either. Or long. The sensible play is a shot to the front edge of the green, where you can take your chances. But this is a hole where three is always a good score."

But five is not. Just ask David Duval.

Opposite, bottom: Miguel Angel Jimenez's unlikely chip-in birdie on the 18th at St. Nom-la-Breteche turned back two of the world's leading players at the 1998 Trophée Lancome.

Ben Hogan once said of Seminole Golf Club that "if you can play well there, you can play well anywhere." Of course, those words were spoken at a time when terms such as "coefficient of restitution" and "variable face thickness" had yet to enter the game's lexicon.

At the time it opened in 1929, Seminole—the first great golf course in rapidly developing Florida—was regarded as long. But even as technology has caught up with Seminole's sea-level length (the highest point on the seaside course is only 65 feet above sea level), the ever-present wind and the precision of Donald Ross's enduring design make it one of the most confounding and exhilarating golf courses in the world. Unlike some 1920s courses that have been obsoleted by modern equipment, Seminole can always rely on grueling winds and a strategically demanding layout.

Assisted by T. Claiborn Watson, Ross did some of his best and most original work at Seminole. Most noticeable is his bunker design. Replete with flashing and raised lips, it is unlike any other work in Ross's portfolio. But what keeps Seminole in the vanguard of the game's toughest venues is the seamless combination of wind and exacting design.

Hogan flatly called the sixth hole "the best par four in the world." But that was in the persimmon era when the world's best players were hitting driver and then four- or five-iron into the green. Back then, managing the angle into the green here required deft skill and planning. Today No. 6 has been largely tamed. It's not unusual to see players reach the green in regulation with an iron off the tee and a nine-iron approach.

But Seminole still has its moments. The long par-three eighth is a tester. The ingenious one-two punch of the 17th and 18th holes represents one of the most memorable finishes in the game. The enduring test of Seminole, combining wind, length (thanks to a new back tee), accuracy, and a devilish putting surface, is the fourth hole.

Most of the play at Seminole takes place between December and April. During that time the prevailing wind is out of the north. The fourth hole, a 465-yard par four from the new tee, plays directly into that wind. That makes this straightaway hole a bear. Even a muscled drive of 270 yards will leave an approach of some 195 yards into the wind. While the fairway provides ample room for short drivers, it narrows after the 280-yard mark. But it is the approach into the green, whether played with a three-wood or a three-iron, that commands respect. Even in the rare instance of playing a middle or short iron here, hitting the green is no bargain.

The fourth is one of the more heavily bunkered holes on a heavily bunkered golf course. A series of shortfall bunkers guards the left center of the fairway and leads to a squarish green that slopes aggressively from right to left and front to back. The green is masked by a classic Ross false front. A miss to the right leaves an awkward downhill chip: Read no chance. As a result many players miss the green to the left and face the decision of a bump, chip, putt, or flop shot into a legendarily firm and fast surface.

Regardless of their score on No. 4, wind-whipped players have long found comfort in Seminole's locker room, the finest in the game. With post-round refreshments readily available, this throwback to the rustic elegance that was Florida in the 1920s is an escape in itself. Adorned with plaques bearing virtually every household name in golf, politics, and Hollywood, there is no more evocative setting in which to lick one's wounds.

Opposite, bottom: Ben Hogan believed that the sixth at Seminole was the best par four in the world. Were he alive today, he might concede that the fourth is now tougher.

There are older golf courses in the United States. There are tougher layouts. Plenty of clubs have hosted more major championships. There are truer links courses, even on Long Island. But when it comes to the trifecta of historical significance, architectural genius, and difficulty, there may be no better golf course in America than Shinnecock Hills.

In 1894, Shinnecock Hills was one of the five founding clubs of the USGA and two years later the second U.S. Open ever played was contested at Shinnecock. That was on the long disappeared original links, which underwent several revisions. One was by Charles Blair Macdonald, the leading golf course architect in the early days of American golf, a Shinnecock Hills member, and the designer of National Golf Links next door.

But in 1927 it was discovered that the Sunrise Highway would be extended and barrel through part of the course, forcing the club to go back to the drawing board. Twelve new holes would be built on newly acquired property and, of the other six, only the third and seventh remained intact from Macdonald's course. The assignment fell to the partnership of William Flynn, who handled the creative end, and Howard Toomey, who handled execution and finance. Day-to-day oversight of construction was handled by a young up-and-comer named Dick Wilson.

The new course, which opened in 1931, has enjoyed inclusion on virtually every course ranking ever published and is widely recognized as the finest of many fine Flynn-Toomey designs. Their use of the prevailing wind is ingenious, helping on the longer holes and hurting on the short; the links-like bounce-in areas in front of many greens offer relief to the shorter hitter who may struggle to reach the correct landing area on this rolling topography (does Corey Pavin ring a bell?). The greens are among the firmest in the game, the rough and bunkers unyielding, yet under most conditions (the final round of the 2004 U.S. Open excepted) Shinnecock is not overly penal and retains a strong strategic element.

"It just doesn't get any better," wrote Johnny Miller in *Golf World* in 1995. "Shot for shot, based on shot values for testing skills, Shinnecock is America's best." The current course at Shinnecock has crowned three U.S. Open champions. None was happier than Raymond Floyd who prevailed in one of the most weather-addled, tightly contested Opens in recent memory. By 1986 Floyd, then 43, had earned a place among the best in the game, but he had never won a USGA title.

He fought through severe weather early in the week and a leaderboard logjam late in the week (at one point Sunday afternoon there were nine players tied for the lead) to prevail over a gaggle of contenders that included Greg Norman, Chip Beck, Lanny Wadkins, Lee Trevino, Ben Crenshaw, Hal Sutton, and Payne Stewart. Of the difficult conditions in a frigid, rainy, windy first round, Jim Murray, the late great columnist for the *Los Angeles Times* wrote: "This was like climbing Everest after a lifetime of taking elevators."

Things were even tougher in the final round of the 2004 Open, when the USGA let the greens get away from them and become impossibly firm. In those circumstances, it was almost impossible for players to hold the seventh and 10th greens, making them play as the hardest holes of the week. The Redan-style par-three seventh became a monument to USGA misanthropy, and attracted the same type of fans who go to NASCAR races hoping to see a crash. In normal conditions, though, the seventh is no monster (it ranked ninth in difficulty in 1995).

Year-in, year-out, No. 6 is the toughest test for both the average player and the Tour pro. In 1995, it ranked first in difficulty, playing to an average of .41 strokes over par. In 2004, it played to .39 over and ranked behind only the aforementioned seventh and 10th.

At 474 yards, the split-fairway par-four sixth is nicknamed "The Pond" for good reason: The water hazard that sits about 65 yards short of the green is the only one on the golf course. The water is actually the least of a player's worries. With the prevailing wind blowing in the face, the first decision for the club player is the line of the tee shot. The left-hand fairway is within easy reach, but opt for it and you'll likely be playing for par at best, furthermore you'll bring the water in to play. Longer hitters will opt for the right side, meaning they'll have to carry the ball well over 200 yards into the wind and over bunkers, mounding, and nasty rough to an unseen landing area. A ball landing in the rough will probably have to be chipped out. A good drive will leave a long to middle iron into a small green that slopes from back to front and from left to right. Balls hit to the front right side of the green often end up in the rough.

The sixth hole's legacy of toughness was secured when it not only ended Tiger Woods's chances of winning the 1995 Open as an amateur, but it actually forced him out of the tournament. After playing out of some deep rough on the third hole Woods "tweaked" his left wrist. He kept playing until the sixth, where he hit a drive and called it quits because he was having trouble holding onto the club.

Opposite, bottom: After fighting horrid weather and a mind-bending golf course, 43-year-old Raymond Floyd finally had his day in the sun at Shinnecock Hills in the 1986 U.S.Open.

The effect of the wind at Shinnecock Hills can be judged by how the 18th hole played in the 1995 U.S. Open compared with the 2004 U.S. Open. In 1995, winner Corey Pavin needed a four-wood to get home. Nine years later, the players in the final round were using nine-irons and wedges.

The genius of Shinnecock is that no matter what direction the wind blows, it's always a challenge—and very seldom is there no wind at all. While in 1995, No. 18 played to an average of 4.39, ranking second on the course in difficulty, it still played to 4.31 even with the shorter approach shots of 2004 and ranked sixth.

The 450-yard par four is a dogleg to the left. Strategically placed bunkers guard the left side of the fairway, bringing bogey or worse to mind. The fairway simultaneously snakes, undulates, and climbs as it makes its way uphill to a green that is tucked to the left and heavily bunkered. In fact, the leftward curl of the last 100 yards or so of the hole is almost a dogleg unto itself.

The wind on "Home" as the hole is known, is generally crossing or in the face, as it was in 1995. A crosswind makes it especially hard to hit the fairway, and with treacherous Open rough, that means a struggle to make par. Players who hit the fairway under those prevailing wind conditions will have a long-to mid-iron approach, and seldom will they be blessed with a level lie. Proper club selection is vital because the green here defines severe. The slope runs from right to left and back to front. A putt from above the hole can easily wind up off the green.

While tough holes are often defined by catastrophes they've incited, the 18th will always be remembered for the way it was tamed. Pavin is among the very shortest hitters on the PGA Tour. In 1995, he came to the 18th tee with a one-shot lead over Greg Norman and the dubious title of "Best Player Never To Have Won a Major" hanging over his head. Pavin safely bunted a driver to the right side of the fairway. He had 228 yards uphill to the green.

"My main concern was just getting it on the green somewhere," said Pavin. "I thought about a two-iron and didn't think I could hit a two-iron far enough to get there." Pavin turned to his caddie, Eric Schwarz, who had similar doubts about the two. Schwarz said, "No, I definitely think it's a four-wood."

Pavin, who had missed the cut in six of his 11 previous Opens, aimed at the right edge of the green "put it back in my stance and just took it inside and hit it. When I saw it come off the clubface I knew it was a good shot."

Low and drawing toward the pin, the shot was nearly perfect. Pavin eagerly sprinted up the hill to see it land. "I couldn't resist," he said, "I had to run up the hill to watch it." The ball bounded about 10 yards short of the green and rolled up to settle about five feet from the pin. "It was the best shot I have hit under pressure," said Pavin. "It was the best rush I ever felt."

Although Pavin, who putted superbly all week, missed the birdie, his par was good enough to stave off Norman, who finished two shots back and racked up his seventh career runner-up finish in a major.

Shinnecock gives, but only sparingly.

Opposite, bottom: Though he missed the birdie putt, Corey Pavin's four-wood to the 18th at Shinnecock Hills in 1995 proved that accuracy could still trump power in a U.S. Open.

Shoal Creek *Golf Club, Birmingham, Alabama* ~*12th hole*

In 1997, four-time U.S. Open champion Jack Nicklaus was asked which of his 200 or so golf course designs could best host a U.S. Open. After a considerable silence, Nicklaus responded, "Shoal Creek."

The Alabama club is best known for the racial stigma that attached to it at the 1990 PGA Championship, when founder Hall Thompson said in a newspaper interview that the club would not admit blacks. The resulting furor led to dropped television sponsorship, protest threats, and a change in policy by the PGA of America, USGA, and PGA Tour that they would no longer hold events on courses that did not have black members.

It's uncertain whether any more majors will be played at Shoal Creek. But overlooked in the racial imbroglio is that the 1977 design is a landmark in Nicklaus's architectural career. In fact, between hosting the 1984 and 1990 PGA Championships, Shoal Creek hosted the U.S. Amateur in 1986. When one studies the list of clubs that have hosted both the PGA and the U.S. Amateur—a list that includes Aronimink, Canterbury, Oak Hill, Oakland Hills, Oakmont, Pebble Beach, and Southern Hills—Shoal Creek's place as more than a sociopolitical touchstone, but as a championship test becomes clear.

The beginnings of the course were inauspicious. Thompson made a cold call to Nicklaus, asking that the Golden Bear come visit his wooded property. Nicklaus was initially unconvinced that the property could sustain a golf course, but relented after studying topographical maps and laying out trial routings with his then lieutenants, Bob Cupp and Jay Morrish. As the course began to take shape, Nicklaus made a site visit he'll never forget.

"I walked the center lines of the front nine, tee-to-green, and started scratching my head," he writes in *Nicklaus By Design*. "I didn't really like some of the things I saw so I turned around and said I'm going to start walking this way for a while. I started walking the other way—green to tee. It just started feeling better to me. After a few minutes I said 'Guys, we're going to take this nine the other way.'" Like that, the front nine was reversed.

The toughest hole on the course is No. 12. A 470-yard par four, it's a relatively straight driving hole. At the turn of a gentle dogleg right, a turn marked by bunkers, the hole heads uphill to a long narrow green that features a big slope on the right and a gaping, deep bunker on the left. For the PGA Championships and U.S. Amateur, deep rough turned a difficult hole into an extraordinarily difficult one.

Buddy Alexander won the 1986 U.S. Amateur at Shoal Creek and recalls No. 12 as the hardest hole. "The irony of it is that I played that hole extremely well during the course of the week," says Alexander, now the head golf coach at the University of Florida.

In the tension of the 36-hole final match, the 12th was halved both times around, in vastly different ways. Both Alexander and Chris Kite made bogeys in the morning. "I had about a two- or three-footer to win the hole and I didn't make it," recalls Alexander. The afternoon round was the same outcome, only more exciting, as both made birdies. "I holed it from the bunker, and Kite had about a 15-footer and he poured it right in on top," says Alexander.

As a test of golf, Shoal Creek distinguished itself in that amateur and in the PGAs won by Lee Trevino (1984) and Wayne Grady (1990).

"I'm not sure anything will ever be played there again," says Alexander, "and it's kind of a shame because it's a wonderful place."

Opposite, bottom: Wayne Grady overcame a difficult golf course to win a PGA Championship at Shoal Creek that was overshadowed by a racial firestorm.

Buffeted by the ceaseless winds of the central plains, Southern Hills is one of the most demanding tests in American golf. It has seduced, created, and devoured legends with God-like insouciance. Like the region that shaped its character, Southern Hills is hard country.

The lure of course difficulty has brought more than a dozen significant championships through the doors of this pink stucco clubhouse. In addition to three U.S. Opens (1958, 1977, 2001), Perry Maxwell-designed Southern Hills has hosted three PGA Championships (1970, 1982, 1994), two Tour Championships (1995, 1996) and an assortment of national amateur championships, including the 1965 U.S. Amateur.

The course has forged a reputation for excellent par fours. The 456-yard 12th hole is a landmark, regarded by both Ben Hogan and Arnold Palmer as one of the best in the game. Great as No. 12 is, and it is the *best* hole on the golf course, there is no doubt that the toughest hole at Southern Hills is the 466-yard 18th. The ideal landing area for the drive—and even the longest players use driver on this dogleg right—is a small plateau on the left side of the fairway. Otherwise, the player will be facing a long-iron shot from a downhill lie to very elevated green—a tough shot to pull off, even from the fairway. From the rough, forget it.

As if that's not enough, No. 18 is easily the most severely canted green on the golf course, sloping from back to front. Under major championship conditions it can be virtually impossible. During the 2001 Open, the hole averaged 4.442 shots for the week and drew the ire of the world's best players.

"All I can say," said Tiger Woods, whose streak of four straight major championship wins came to an end in Tulsa, "is that if you hit a good solid shot in the middle of the green, there is a chance of that ball rolling 40 yards off the green. That's a pretty harsh penalty for a good solid shot."

Asked for his impression of No. 18, Sergio Garcia said, "It's too difficult, too impossible. I don't know how to describe it."

Even the USGA agreed. Fred Ridley, chairman of the 2003 Championship committee, said "Certainly, No. 18 is probably the most difficult finishing hole ever in a U.S. Open Championship."

In fact, during the practice rounds, the USGA realized that the green was too fast for its severe slope and ordered it to be cut slightly higher. That made it a different speed from the rest of the greens, but alleviated the problem of approach shots backing up and rolling off the front of the green.

Difficulty in an Open and complaints about it are nothing new. In fact, the 18th at Southern Hills has been humiliating the best players in the world all its life. Consider this grisly fact: Of the six major championship winners crowned at Southern Hills—Tommy Bolt, Dave Stockton, Hubert Green, Raymond Floyd, Nick Price, and Retief Goosen—only Bolt parred the 18th hole in the final round. The other five carded bogeys and still won.

Goosen's 72nd-hole bogey was part of a collective nine-putt spasm that stunned the golf world and only reinforced 18's reputation as a man-eater. First Mark Brooks three-putted to finish at four-under. Next came Stewart Cink, who three-putted from 15 feet, ultimately causing him to miss a playoff. Finally Goosen simply had to two-putt from 12 feet for the win. He ran his first putt two feet past the hole and missed the comebacker. The mood at the 18th was Van de Velde all over again, with a little Hindenburg thrown in.

Goosen would recover completely. He one-putted eight of the first ten holes in the Monday playoff and went on to beat Brooks by two shots over 18 holes. To no one's surprise, Goosen bogeyed 18.

Opposite: On the final hole of regulation at the 2001 U.S. Open, Retief Goosen added his name to a distinguished list of players who have struggled on the 18th hole at Southern Hills.

Robert Trent Jones is the father of modern golf-course design. He is not only among the most prolific architects ever (roughly 500 original designs to his credit), and among the most honored, but he had a way of embracing the past while envisioning the future. Perhaps that is why Jones, who died in 2000, was called on to redesign, restore, or prepare so many legendary layouts—among them Augusta National, Baltusrol, Oakland Hills, and Winged Foot—for modern major championships.

Jones was interested in challenging the better player (a sentiment that won him few fans among PGA Tour players). His philosophy that "every hole should be a hard par and an easy bogey" is reflected in nearly every course he touched.

Among his most difficult layouts is Spyglass Hill in Pebble Beach, California. Named for the craggy lookout in Robert Louis Stevenson's *Treasure Island,* the golf course sits majestically above the Pacific coast, weaving between the water's edge and fairy-tale forestation. A public facility that opened in 1966, Spyglass is a relatively modern golf course but its ascent to the top drawer of PGA Tour layouts was quick. One year after the course opened, it replaced august Monterey Peninsula Country Club in the Bing Crosby National Pro-Am. Not only did Spyglass hold its own alongside Pebble Beach and Cypress Point (Cypress would be replaced by Poppy Hills in 1991), but it earned a reputation among tour players as the most difficult of the three courses and among the toughest courses in all of northern California. Jack Nicklaus once remarked that while Pebble Beach and Cypress Point inspired him to play golf, Spyglass inspired him to go fishing.

"The whole course, I think, is by far the hardest course of the three," says Pat Perez, who in 2002 finished second in what is now known as the AT&T Pebble Beach National Pro-Am. Jim Murray, the late Pulitzer Prize-winning columnist for the *Los Angeles Times,* once offered a more colorful opinion. "If it were human," wrote Murray, "Spyglass would have a knife in its teeth, a patch on its eye, a ring in its ear, tobacco in its beard, and a blunderbuss in its hand."

The 16th hole epitomizes Jones's philosophy and Spyglass's difficulty. A 468-yard par four downhill sharp dogleg right, it first poses a demanding left-to-right tee shot. Anything but a long powerful fade will leave plenty of dogleg to contend with on your next shot. Assuming you've safely navigated the dogleg, the 16th requires one of the most feared shots in the game: a long approach off a downhill lie to a well-protected green. Even Tour pros might need a longish iron to reach a back hole location. It's not unusual for those who do attack a rear pin to end up over the green, where a veritable jungle of rough combines with a sloping green to make the comeback chip virtually impossible.

"Spyglass is a pretty good representation of dad's thinking and it's one of his tougher golf courses," says Rees Jones, the second of two sons who followed their father into the business. "He built those greens much like the Dunes or Peachtree: They're elevated greens and long holes, so you have to hit the target. Because they're elevated greens, the bunkers are deep, and they're hard to recover from whether you're in one or around one. I used to play that course in the AT&T. I remember 16 as one of the holes I could never even reach in regulation."

Matt Gogel shot an 81 at Spyglass in the 2001 AT&T Pebble Beach National Pro-Am. "There is more variety on that course than any of the three we play," says Gogel. "With some of the ocean holes, then some of the holes that are reminiscent of Augusta, and then some of the holes that are just brutes, I mean you really have to play well."

In 2002, Gogel won the tournament, with a 67 in his round at Spyglass.

Opposite, bottom: Matt Gogel has seen both the beauty and the beast at Spyglass Hill during the AT&T Pebble Beach National Pro-Am.

William F. Gordon is among the most underrated of golf-course architects. "I don't know if Gordon is *the* all-time most underrated," says Ron Whitten, architecture editor for *Golf Digest*, "but he's probably in the top ten."

Gordon's work is best known in Pennsylvania. Of his 63 original golf-course designs, 45 of them were in his home state. In 1953, Gordon teamed up with his son David. Ten years later they created Stanwich, the third of their three courses in the state of Connecticut. It would be among the toughest of all their designs. After visiting the Stanwich site, Gordon laid out a menu of possibilities: "An adequate but not outstanding" course for about $300,000; an "interesting and challenging" course for $375,000; a "superb and aesthetic" course for up to $485,000. Founding member Jim Linen's response: "Let's see how the $485,000 version would look."

Little known outside the northeast, Greenwich's Stanwich Club has long been regarded as the hardest golf course in the Nutmeg State, a reputation backed up by a course rating of 76.4 and a slope of 146 from the back tees. The triple-witching difficulty of Stanwich—length, tightness, and extremely slick greens—has been obvious to New York metropolitan-area golfers for decades. But the course was finally introduced to a global audience in September 2002, when the club hosted the U.S. Mid-Amateur Championship, its first-ever USGA championship. The reviews were chilling. British Mid-Amateur champion John Kemp said: "These greens are absolutely the most difficult I have ever seen." In the quarterfinals, it took six tries for defending champion Tim Jackson to successfully mark his ball on one green. With no blade of grass tall enough to support it, Jackson's ball kept rolling away.

For club players, the 13th hole at Stanwich is, like any hole on the golf course, tough. But at 165 yards (which it measured during the stroke play rounds of the Mid-Am), it is at least parable. For the match-play part of the competition the tee box was moved back, leaving the hole to play anywhere from 199 to 215

yards. For Mid-Am caliber players, the water never really comes into play on the 13th, but with the severity of Stanwich's greens, the gaping bunkers on either side of the backward-L-shaped putting surface certainly do. The speed of Stanwich's greens is one thing, but combined with their diminutive size, sloping contours, and shoulders that encourage balls to trickle off the surface, they were criminal for the Mid-Am field.

"Those greens weren't built in an era when the Stimpmeter was running at 13-plus," says Brian Silva, who familiarized himself with the course during some remodeling work in 1985. "Those contours—at the speed they're played—make the greens very demanding, to say the least."

The 13th green slopes heavily from back to front, regularly rejecting even well-struck balls and sending them rolling off the green into a fairway chipping area. A tee ball sent over the green is almost a certain bogey. Any ball above the hole on the green promises an extremely challenging two-putt. For the Mid-Am finals the USGA tucked the pin in the remote back left tongue of the green, a move that brought all the risk factors in the green complex into play. That left three basic options on the tee shot:

~ Fire it over the left-hand bunker and hope you hold the back of the green;
~ Start at the middle of the green and draw the ball toward the pin;
~ Play to the middle of the green and risk rolling off, facing a difficult putt, or possibly even leaving yourself with a chip from the putting surface over some fringe.

From 200-plus yards that's a tall order. The 13th was such a mindbender, even for skilled, experienced competitors like finalists George Zahringer III and Jerry Courville (between them they hold 13 Metropolitan [N.Y.] Golf Association Player of the Year titles), that strategy dominated the duo's table talk during the lunch break that preceded the final 18 holes.

"At lunch we talked about how to play the 13th hole," says Zahringer. "I mean it's virtually impossible, unless you make a 10- or 12-foot second putt, to make par. So we talked about maybe playing a more aggressive shot, but you sit back there on that back tee, and it's 205 yards or something to the pin, and you say, 'Oh, my God, why would I aim at that?'"

Opposite, bottom: The 13th hole at Stanwich had local legend George Zahringer III scratching his head during the final match of the 2002 U.S. Mid-Amateur Championship.

Torrey Pines *(South Course), La Jolla, California ~* 4*th hole*

When the legendary George C. Thomas stopped designing courses in 1927, his assistant Billy Bell was free to pursue his own projects. Bell, a visionary in his own right, quickly became the most prolific and one of the most acclaimed designers in the West. Bell's son, Billy Jr., trained under his father, and when the senior Bell died in 1953, Billy Jr. took over the business. Between his solo designs and those on which he and his father collaborated, young Bell worked on some 200 golf courses, mostly in California and Arizona.

The most acclaimed of those courses is clearly the South Course at Torrey Pines (the Bells also designed the North Course). Nestled between a ridge overlooking the Pacific Ocean and a craggy hillside, Torrey South offers all that's beautiful and challenging about California golf: ocean views, wind, fog, rain, trees, and diverse topography. No surprise that the PGA Tour has played here every year since 1968.

There were a couple of moderate redesigns in 1977 and 1988, but the most recent and most meaningful remodeling was undertaken in 2001 by Rees Jones. It not only brought the course's difficulty in line with its beauty, it vaulted Torrey South into the big leagues: In 2008, the course will host its first U.S. Open. That event means three things: Long, Rough, and Fast.

The fourth hole is already there. Jones completely redesigned it, adding length, shifting the fairway closer to the canyon on the left, and then sliding the green toward the canyon. "Basically, if you go over, you go in the canyon," says Jones.

There's a very difficult hole location on the left side where a bunker guards the green. Jones invokes the wisdom of 1982 U.S. Open champion Tom Watson, who once said of Winged Foot: "There's just places where you can't miss these greens." Sometimes, says Jones, "you just have to decide not to go for the pin at Torrey Pines, you don't want to short-side it."

The easier play is coming up the right side. The green is aggressively contoured with a major transition from the deep portion on the right down to the little tongue on the left behind the bunker. Jones's advice: "Two-putt and get out of town."

At 483 yards from the tips, No. 4 is plenty long (the Tour sets it up at 471 for the Buick Invitational). To add that touch of USGA agony, it not only plays uphill, but it generally plays into the wind. Open contestants, Tour players, and everyday amateurs, all will need a long, steady tee ball if they hope to have a reasonable second shot at the green. There are two reachable fairway bunkers on the right, and while there is rough and forest on the left, *far* left is only an option for rock-climbers and scuba divers. The drop-off to the ocean looms so large that some players actually play to the extreme right, playing the fifth fairway all the way up to the green.

Although it has a narrow neck at the front, the green slopes from back to front and toward the ocean. It's guarded by two greenside bunkers on the front left and enough ice plant to send a chill through Tiger Woods. Woods, who grew up in nearby Cypress, California, and has played the course countless times, says, "On No. 4, when there is a front left pin, if you go right at it and you pull it about six feet, you're in an ice plant."

"It's pretty tough," says Jones. "You can't go long, you can't go left, you can't go short, and the green contour makes you hit the right section of the green."

Come 2008, even a 483-yard par four will probably not intimidate the world's best players by sheer length, so Jones, who is nearly obsessive about green contour, has embedded the hole's true difficulty in the putting surface. "Like the contours at Congressional or Spyglass, you're just not home when you think you're home."

Jones's new-look South has been favorably if cautiously received by Tour players.

"I don't think there's any question it can handle the U.S. Open," says Phil Mickelson. "I think it's exactly what the USGA has historically liked in the past, a golf course that's very long, tight, demanding on drives, greens that are very difficult with undulations and contours, deep bunkers. It's a very difficult golf course."

Opposite, bottom: Tiger Woods captured two of the first four Buick Invitationals after a Rees Jones redesign at Torrey Pines South.

TPC at Avenel, Potomac, Maryland ~ 12th hole

In its various incarnations, the land on which TPC at Avenel now stands has been a working gold mine, a horse farm, and an investment property. In 1986, under the supervision of then PGA Tour commissioner Deane Beman, it was converted into one of an expanding network of Tournament Players Clubs.

Because it operates as a private club, open only to members and their guests, Avenel is not as celebrated as, say, the TPC at Sawgrass, the flagship of the TPC courses, or Pete Dye's TPC Stadium Course at PGA West. But since 1987 it has more than held its own as a PGA Tour venue.

A few years earlier, the nearby Congressional Country Club (it's virtually across the street), longtime host of the Tour's Kemper Open, informed the Tour that since the club was going to be focusing on securing a U.S. Open bid (Congressional had not hosted the Open since 1964 and would secure its second in 1997), it would no longer be hosting the Kemper.

From the beginning, course architects Ed Ault, his son Brian, and Tom Clark envisioned a fan-friendly and user-friendly golf course. While this description may be applicable to the course as a hole, it's certainly not descriptive of the treacherous 12th hole.

At 472 yards the dogleg left 12th is long, but length is the least of this hole's defenses. Rock Run Creek ambles throughout the golf course, but nowhere does it come more directly into play, either physically or psychologically, than it does on the 12th.

The creek runs down the left side of the fairway, then crosses in front of the green and turns to guard the right side of the putting surface. The tee shot is guarded by trees to the right as well as water left. The green features a spine running right down the middle (the brainchild of Ed Sneed, Avenel's PGA Tour player consultant), parallel to the creek. So, if the hole is on the right side of the green and you bail out to the left of the green to avoid the water, you'll be lucky to two-putt.

"The idea behind Avenel was to design some holes for birdies and others for bogeys," says Clark. "We find that a lot players bogey the 12th. They find the water with their first or second shot or they struggle with the green. There's something about a stream that runs the length of a hole. You can run water across a hole or put it to the side and people just fly it like it was nothing, but let it run the length of a hole and it becomes a real mental hazard."

During the 2003 Kemper, the field averaged 4.38 on the 12th, including 127 bogeys, 28 double-bogeys, and five scores of triple bogey or worse. In 1999, the hole proved decisive for Rich Beem, who broke through at Avenel for his first PGA Tour win (three years later he would become an "overnight success" with his win in the PGA Championship). On Saturday, he found the creek on his approach to the 12th.

In Sunday's final round, Beem at first thought he would play left, "but I just—there were a couple of nice fishes floating around the water, I guess," said Beem, who favored the riskier right side in all four rounds. "When I hit it, I knew it was going to be long enough to stay up. I just wasn't too sure after it hit the green; fortunately it stayed up. It wasn't up by more than a couple of inches, but it was up just enough to hang up there and give me a nice opportunity."

His final-round par proved vital in his eventual one-shot victory.

Rich Beem took the bold route on the 12th hole and captured his first title in the 1999 Kemper Open at the TPC at Avenel.

TPC at Sawgrass *(Stadium Course), Ponte Vedra Beach, Florida ~17th hole*

Given the exalted status of the TPC at Sawgrass Stadium Course, it's hard to believe that as recently as 26 years ago that land was a forlorn swamp. It's a credit to Deane Beman's vision and Pete Dye's fortitude that the course was ever built in the first place. In a piece for *Golf Digest* about the course, the late Peter Dobereiner wrote:

> Deane Beman sent for Pete Dye and said: "Behold this tract of jungle swamp. Pray turn it into the world's first golf stadium!" Dye glanced over the uncompromising acres of marsh and impenetrable scrub.
>
> "Certainly," Dye said. "Bring me a bulldozer and two quarts of Mountain Lion's Sweat."

What Dye wrought from the mucky canvas is one of the most widely enjoyed golf courses and most avidly followed individual holes in the history of the game. For many fans who gather around the 17th tee box, sunbathe along the shores of Lake Beman, or gaze in wonderment from the sofa at home, the 17th has largely surpassed the tournament itself in importance. It brought a dash of Evel Knievel to a genteel sport: No one ever tuned in to watch him land safely. Tales of greatness and failure at 17 are told every year during the Players Championship. What's more, since the Stadium Course is open to the public, thousands of average golfers have been able to compare their performance on 17 to that of the game's icons. Afterward, players of all levels either love the hole or hate it.

"I think it's great," says Sergio Garcia. "Any golf hole where you get to the tee and you think, 'Just hit it on the green' has to be good. It makes you think a lot."

"It's just a great hole," says Ernie Els, "And where it's situated [in the round], 17th hole, that's just perfect. You know that the hole is out there. All day, it's there."

And it's there largely by happenstance. Dye, who worked in close consultation with his wife, Alice, and Deane Beman on the design, had originally envisioned a small lake adjacent to, but not surrounding, the green. As fate would have it, the dirt around the site turned out to be perfectly suited for filling holes, leveling fairways, or building mounds on other parts of the golf course. Dye used the earth liberally, dispatching it to all corners of the golf course. Before long, all the soil surrounding the 17th green had been removed and the green stood above a dirt basin. It was then that the Dyes recalled an island green on the Ocean Course at nearby Ponte Vedra Club (also the 17th hole, coincidentally) and promptly built their own version.

When Greg Norman won the Players Championship in 1994, he scorched the Stadium Course, shooting 24-under par for four rounds. During his final round, it seemed as though the course had more to fear than he did. Still, like an approaching dentist appointment, the 17th loomed in his mind. "I have to admit," says Norman, "that the 17th flashed in my mind at the 15th hole. I knew it would be the shot of the tournament, but I immediately blocked it out of my mind." He later described the 17th as "under pressure, the hardest 137-yard par-3 in the world."

Strangely enough, no leader has ever blown his advantage by hitting it into the water on the 17th in the final round. More than a few contenders have drowned their final chances there, though, none more painfully than Len Mattiace in 1998. Trailing by one, Mattiace hit his tee shot into the water and, after a penalty, his third shot into the tiny bunker in front of the green. From there, he blasted into the water and ended up with an eight.

Opposite, bottom: Greg Norman admitted that even as he was devouring the TPC at Sawgrass in 1994, the daunting 17th hole loomed in his mind.

Perhaps no individual hole in golf has gained as much attention in recent years as the par-three 17th at the TPC at Sawgrass. It has clearly earned a reputation as one of the most intimidating holes in the game. But while the fans may take a breather when Tour players leave the island 17th green intact, the players know their work isn't done. Statistically speaking, the 18th hole plays even harder for the PGA Tour than the 17th (.31 strokes over par for the 18th and .11 strokes over par for the 17th from 2002 through 2004).

Stretching 447 yards from the tournament tees with a slight dogleg left, the home hole is an object lesson in visual intimidation. To the left is a daunting lake that runs the entire length of the hole. In fact, there is far more water on the 18th hole than there is fairway. With a mix of towering trees, gnarly rough, dirt, and pine straw, the right side offers little relief.

The tournament tee is set slightly to the left, exaggerating the effect of the dogleg, highlighting the water, and practically forcing the player to move the ball right to left. Only the wind can make this hole harder. "If the wind is coming off the water, boy, that's a hard hole," explains Chris DiMarco. "If the wind is coming down the right, it's not *as* difficult, and obviously if it's into the wind at all, it's a really hard hole."

The designer, however, insists that the difficulty is more mental than physical. "It happens that the first-place check is for $1 million or so," says Dye. "It's a difficult hole, but that first prize has a lot to do with how much pressure the players feel there. Even back when Jerry Pate won he hit driver and five-iron, so the stress is mental; it doesn't come from the physical difficulty of the hole. Think about the fairway, it's a lot wider than the

fairways we see in major championship golf. Look at the British Open fairways we saw at Royal St. George's. The 18th fairway here is twice as wide as they were."

The difficulty isn't so much the width as the turn to the left. A long hitter will go through the fairway unless he works the ball right-to-left off the tee or hits less than a driver. Lay back, though, and it makes for a more difficult second shot.

The green and pin are extremely well defended. To the left, again, is the omnipresent water hazard urging the player to favor the right side. So, naturally, that's where Dye installed a smattering of grass bunkers sprouting four- to five-inch Bermuda grass rough, and a sand bunker. Another lone bunker sits at the rear left of the green. More a safety net for pulled approaches than a hazard, this bunker reveals Dye's softer side.

The 18th is so tough that for two recent Players Championship winners a two-stroke lead going to the final hole almost wasn't enough. In 2002, Craig Perks inexplicably hit a driver off the tee, finishing in the right rough, blocked by trees. He had to chip out, then went over the green with a seven-iron. He finished in spectacular fashion, however, chipping in for a par.

Two years later, Adam Scott, also with a two-stroke lead, appeared home free when he found the fairway with his tee shot. Then he came over the top of a six-iron and hit it in the water, forcing him to get up and down for the victory. He chipped it to 10 feet and made the pressure putt.

Opposite, bottom: A two-stroke lead coming into the TPC at Sawgrass's intimidating final hole proved barely enough for unheralded Craig Perks at the 2002 Players.

The Legends of Golf was played here for only two years (1995 and 1996). PGA West is also the former home of the Skins Game (1986 through 1991). The Bob Hope Chrysler Classic was played here once, in 1987, never to return. Why? You might as well ask why a lot of recruits drop out of the Marine Corps.

While Pete Dye's work at PGA West is undoubtedly the product of its time, it may be the definitive masterpiece of bravado design. While some courses of the "my-track-is-tougher-than-your-track" era now seem as fashionable as plaid polyester slacks, Dye's course survives, and in fact thrives, as a monument to 1980s confrontational design. No, the tour pros aren't exactly lining up for tee times, but PGA West remains a destination, a proving ground for all levels of amateur players.

Picking a tough hole at this landmark is like picking a good Frank Sinatra tune. Where do you start? A glance at the hole nicknames alone makes it clear that the entire maze was designed with all the warmth of Caligula. Monikers such as Black Hole, Eternity, Moat, Second Thoughts, Alacatraz, and Coliseum get the point across quite nicely.

There are plenty of choices, but any list of tough holes has to include the sixth, known simply as "Amen." A par three, the sixth measures a healthy 255 yards over water. There is not a

bunker in sight, just water, water everywhere. Dye is infamous for his island green at the 17th at the TPC at Sawgrass, but at nearly 100 yards longer, this one is even more diabolical.

Brian Silva, named *Golf World's* golf-course architect of the year in 1999, is a student of Dye's design work. Speaking of the sixth at PGA West, Silva says, "That's one of the hardest par threes I've ever seen, much less played. I just get defeated when I stand on the tee."

Like just about any Dye tester, there is a bailout. On the sixth at PGA West it's off to the left. But this particular bailout is tougher than most: There is water to carry, just not as much of it.

The green is huge and relatively flat, offering some un-Dye like assistance to those who might be uncomfortable hitting an all-out driver over what looks like the Pacific Ocean from the tee box. Of course, this green isn't going to be the scene of many short birdie putts.

PGA West, which boasts five courses (by Jack Nicklaus, Arnold Palmer, Greg Norman, Tom Weiskopf, and Dye) has been a fairly regular stop on the PGA Tour since the property opened in 1986. But of the 15 times that the Bob Hope Chrysler Classic has been to the property, it's only played the Dye course once, the rest have been on the Palmer Course. During that week in 1987 at the Stadium Course the players sounded more like witch hunters than professional golfers. Reigning U.S. Open champion Raymond Floyd called the design "spiteful" and "hateful." Tom Watson said it was "awful and artificial." Bernhard Langer said it was "silly," and he finished *second!* The players actually drafted a petition and sent it to then PGA Tour Commissioner Deane Beman insisting that the course never host another Tour event.

Dye defends the design. "The professionals forget that the whole idea of a Pete Dye golf course is to require good players to hit a wide variety of shots," he writes in his autobiography. "Touring professionals have a much better overall game than they think they do, and I know they can handle this challenge."

Chi Chi Rodriguez had it right when he told the *Los Angeles Times,* "Most of the courses today, the guys [on Tour] shoot 20-under par and think they've accomplished something. They can't do it at PGA West because you can't hit it crooked and score. Golf was meant to be a game of skill, not just strength. To get around here, you have to have the skills."

Corey Pavin won the 1987 Bob Hope Chrysler Classic in its only visit to the TPC Stadium Course at PGA West.

Golf history is virtually synonymous with Scotland. Tales of the game's early days drip with mentions of royal bans and Scottish clans. The great courses of Scotland—the Old Course, Muirfield, Royal Dornoch, Carnoustie—are timelessly embedded in both the social fabric and sporting history of the country.

Upstart Turnberry, however, has quickly earned a place alongside the auld grey icons of the game. While its current course is not much over 50 years old—a relative greenhorn—Turnberry stands among the great tests of the game. In this case, youth has not been wasted on the young. Though wet behind the ears, Turnberry has paid its dues. Twice—during both World Wars—the courses of Turnberry were requisitioned for use as training grounds and hospitals. By the late 1940s, the early design work of architects such as Willie Fernie and Cecil Hutchison had been replaced by acres and acres of tarmac, airplane hangars, and cement.

In 1949, the deliciously named Mackenzie Ross (no relation to either legendary designer) was hired to bring golf back to Turnberry. Ross was assisted by James Alexander, an executive with then resort owner British Transport Hotels. Two years later, the Ailsa course opened to raves. In a region where the sport had been played for centuries, newcomer Turnberry was soon hosting the game's elite fields: the 1963 Walker Cup and the luminous 1977 British Open. Memories of 1977's "Duel in the Sun" between Jack Nicklaus and Tom Watson are firmly etched alongside the oldest and most cherished moments in the game. The visual cues of Turnberry—the Firth of Clyde, The Irish Sea, the lighthouse and noble Ailsa Craig, lend the place iconic stature. But as golf historian James W. Finegan wrote in his *Blasted Heath and Blessed Greens: A Golfer's Pilgrimage to the Courses of Scotland,* lore is "distinctly tertiary" here. Turnberry is all about the golf course.

The challenge of Turnberry is exemplified by the 454-yard ninth hole. Named Bruce's Castle for the nearby remains of a 14th-century Robert the Bruce fortress, the ninth combines awesome beauty with visual intimidation to create one of the most difficult and thrilling holes in the world; the only hole on the British Open rota in which the sea comes directly into play. The tee, an exaggerated version of that on the 18th hole at Pebble Beach, is set on a craggy seaside promontory, the last foot of arable earth this side of the island of Arran (Australian Jack Newton was nearly blown off the tee during the wind-riddled 1973 John Player Classic). Simply walking the narrow path from the eighth green to the ninth tee is enough to marvel at those who play from the championship tee.

Once safely aboard, the view is simultaneously inspiring and humbling. While the coastline—punctuated by Ailsa Craig and the world-famous lighthouse—captures the imagination, it's the tee shot that captures your attention: nearly 200 yards of carry over rock, sand, and roiling sea. If the tee shot itself is not exacting enough, there is the landing area. Even a perfectly struck shot is likely to roll off this infamous hog's-back fairway.

The second shot is a lengthy one, which when combined with sidehill lies, unpredictable winds, and a green so keenly canted that it repels even well-played balls, can bring the fairness of the hole—but not the difficulty—into question.

Victims of the ninth stand in good company. In the 1977 Open, two-time champion Lee Trevino fell out of contention when, in the third round, he played the eighth and ninth holes in a combined three-over par. In Michael Corcoran's book, *Duel in the Sun: Tom Watson and Jack Nicklaus in the Battle of Turnberry,* Ben Crenshaw confesses that it was the ninth hole that kept him from making a charge on that historic day. After eight holes, Crenshaw was within hailing distance, but Gentle Ben's hapless double bogey on No. 9 started a slide that left the championship to be fought out by Nicklaus and Watson. It also kicked off one of the more frustrating stretches of Crenshaw's career: From 1977 through 1981, Crenshaw would post British Open finishes of T5, T2, T2, 3, T8. He would never win the Open.

Opposite, bottom: Jack Nicklaus and eventual champion Tom Watson staged an epic battle for the British Open title at Turnberry in 1977

Valderrama *Golf Club, Sotogrande, Spain ~* 17*th hole*

When in 1984 tin magnate Jaime Ortiz-Patiño bought the 10-year-old Los Aves golf course, he renamed it Valderrama, billed it as "The Augusta National of Europe," and brought in original architect Robert Trent Jones for a redesign. Given the unlimited attention showered on the project (600 sprinklers for starters), Valderrama quickly gained acclaim as the best-conditioned course in Europe, affirming the Augusta comparison.

It became the site of the season-ending Volvo Masters on the European Tour and also has hosted the 1997 Ryder Cup and a couple of WGC-American Express Championships, and has been ranked by more than one publication as the best course on continental Europe. And, like Augusta National, its design has constantly been tweaked through the years.

For the most part, the results have been favorable. However, the redesign of the par-five 17th by Spain's own Seve Ballesteros in 1993 resulted in what may be the most disliked hole in international competitive golf.

The case has been made in this book that tough holes are not necessarily great holes. The 17th is a prime example. The hole is universally scorned. *The World of Professional Golf 2001* by the late Mark McCormack says, "To call the 17th hole at Valderrama goofy would be an insult to some goofy but charming holes... No, the 17th at Valderrama is simply bad."

"It's the worst hole we play all year," said Colin Montgomerie.

"Just a bad hole," added Stuart Appleby.

Lee Westwood succinctly describes the hole as "rubbish."

The plan for turning what was once a relatively dull 570-yard hole into an exciting, reachable par five by reducing the yardage and adding a pond in front was sketched out by Jones in 1988, but wasn't implemented then. But in this case the devil is in the details, and those were done by Ballesteros when the changes were finally made five years later.

While shortening the hole to 511, he installed a strip of rough across the fairway at the 290-yard mark to prevent long hitters from going at the green in two with a middle iron. As if that weren't gimmicky enough, he came back in 1995 and added seven large mounds to the landing area. Now players were not only assured a second shot of at least 220 yards, they often had to play it from a sidehill, downhill, or uphill lie.

If the mounds weren't enough to give them second thoughts about going for the green in two, the green complex certainly was. The putting surface slopes dramatically from back to front. For those who would consider taking an extra club on the second shot, Ballesteros assured that going long was not a safe play. There are two bunkers behind the green, and a shot from that area to a green sloping towards the water is a frightening one.

Not that laying up eliminates the fear factor. In 1995, Ballesteros, who would captain the winning European team at the 1997 Ryder Cup, ordered the grass in front of the green to be shaved so that approach shots that were too short would roll back into the pond. As a final touch, the fairway in the lay-up landing area was reduced by half.

One of the memorable images from the 1997 Ryder Cup is Tiger Woods putting into the water on 17. In fact, Woods's relationship with the hole is severely strained. In the 1999 WGC-American Express, he hit a low-spin nine-iron and still watched the ball back up off the green into the pond. His triple bogey cost him the lead, but he went on to win the playoff.

One year later, in the same event, Woods found the water twice in the first three rounds. Still, he trailed by only one shot as he came to the 71st. But Woods almost predictably found the water yet again. This time he made double bogey and finished fifth. It was the fourth time in five rounds that Woods had made a splash at the 17th. Woods was not alone. In the final round that year, the last four groups played the hole to an average of 6.25 strokes, unheard of for a par-five played by the best players in the world.

"Every ball I've hit in the water, though, has been good shots," says Woods. "It's just indicative of the hole. It's not a very well-designed hole…just walk along the bank, look how many balls are in the water."

Oddly enough, the WGC-American Express debacles came after the hole was redesigned yet again, by Roger Rulewich, and the green's slope reduced. "We did everything but tear the whole green apart," Rulewich said before the 1999 WGC event at Valderrama, and some would say he should have taken that

step. Defenders of the hole say that it is very playable when the green is maintained at member speeds and that, even under the faster conditions of a tournament, the field generally plays the hole under par. But when the green becomes especially crusty, it becomes clear that the putting surface is still too severely sloped, and there is a disturbing randomness as to whether an approach shot is destined to pull back into the water or not.

To Rulewich's credit, he did eliminate some of the hole's excesses. He took out the strip of rough across the fairway while lengthening the hole to 540 yards, and also got rid of the mounds in the fairway.

Still, the greenside debacles continue. In 2000, Mike Weir won the WGC-American Express despite a triple bogey in the second round, when he hit two balls in the water.

With the Volvo Masters returning to Valderrama in the last few years, Darren Clarke added his name to the list of victims in 2004. Leading the tournament in the second round and six-under for the day through 16 holes, the Irishman hit three balls into the water and made an 11.

Opposite: This third shot by Tiger Woods to the 17th hole at Valderrama finished in the water, leading to a triple bogey, but he still managed to win the 1999 WGC-American Express Championship. It's one of many struggles Woods has had with the infamous hole.

Every profession has its perks. Whether you're a lawyer who attends Bar Association conventions in Bermuda or a salesman who enjoys the annual meeting in Palm Springs, mixing work with pleasure is nothing new.

Same with the PGA Tour. What better place to stage a mid-January tour event than the Waialae Country Club, Hawaii's most elite private club situated between the majestic Koolau mountain range to the north and the Pacific Ocean on the south?

But images of laid-back professionals sipping cold drinks on the southeastern shore of Oahu are misleading. While the par-70, 7,060-yard Seth Raynor/Charles Banks-designed course is largely accommodating to the best players in the world, it can be extremely stingy in places. In fact, Waialae consistently places at least one hole in the PGA Tour's annual ranking of the top 50 most difficult holes.

The meat of the golf course is the opening six holes. (The nines are reversed for the Tour event and are described here in the order in which the Tour plays them.) "That's a tough stretch of holes," says Retief Goosen—and that was before he made a nine on the first hole in 2004. Chris DiMarco adds, "You just try to survive the front, get to the ninth, and make a charge."

Five of the opening six holes are long par fours. Average distance: 452 yards. The early "breather" hole is anything but: the 203-yard par-three fourth is tightly bunkered.

Any of the first six holes can play as the toughest, depending on the wind direction—and the wind usually does blow here. In recent years, the 488-yard par four first has been the hardest nut to crack. After ranking in the top 30 on Tour in difficulty for two straight years, the first stepped it up a notch in 2005. It will probably finish the year in the top 10 thanks to a scoring average of 4.457 as the pros combined for only 20 birdies all week against 162 bogeys.

Raynor and Banks designed several holes on each of their courses patterned after classic holes in Scotland. The first at Waialae is an homage to the Road Hole at St. Andrews—one of the toughest holes in the world. Like its inspiration, the first is a dogleg to the right with out of bounds to the right on the tee shot (Goosen hit two tee shots out of bounds on the way to his big number). There's no road next to the green, and no bunker as deep as the one to the left of the green on the Road Hole. But whereas the St. Andrews hole is open in front, the difficulty of the approach at Waialae comes from having to carry a large bunker guarding the front of the green.

The hole used to yield birdies and eagles as a par five, but in 1999 the tees were moved up slightly to play as a par four, just like the Road Hole. In fact, this version is 27 yards longer (it's still a par five for members). That was one of a number of changes that turned Waialae from a scoring paradise into a significant test.

Golf-course architects Raynor and Banks did most of their work along their native East Coast. Their collaborative and solo work—courses such as Yale and the Country Club of Fairfield in Connecticut, and Whippoorwill in New York—can still be enjoyed. Sadly, Waialae was Raynor's second-to-last design. After collaborating with Banks on Waialae and Mid-Pacific Country Club, also in Honolulu, Raynor returned to the United States and went directly to Palm Beach, Florida, for the grand opening of his new nine holes at the Everglades Club. He died shortly thereafter, and Banks died five years later.

Opposite, bottom: The PGA Tour's Hawaiian swing is not all luaus and grass skirts. Chris DiMarco says the first six holes at Waialae in the Sony Open in Hawaii are a matter of survival.

Wairakei Golf Course, in the center of New Zealand's North Island, lies at the heart of the country's geothermal region. In fact, the par-five 14th was nicknamed The Rogue after a geyser that, before the course was built, was located next to where the green currently sits. When the course was designed in the late 1960s by Commander John Harris, Peter Thomson, and Michael Wolveridge, the erupting geyser was covered, redirected, and replaced with a golf hole that taunts with subtlety and illusion.

PGA Tour professional Phil Tataurangi is a New Zealander and has a home near the course. He has played Wairakei innumerable times, and he has never come close to reaching the 14th green in two. His respect for the hole derives from the fact that it requires three good shots to have any chance at par.

"There are few par fives in the world where every shot is demanding," he says. "When you get to most par fives on the Tour, you're looking at going for the green in two or an easy lay-up and you're thinking birdie. With the 14th at Wairakei, you're happy to walk away with par."

From the tee, there are few clues of the difficulty that lies ahead. The setting for the 600-yard test is a wind-protected valley, and the hole bends to the right in the distance. The tee shot is toward a mountainside of pine trees, and a decent drive can put you in or near some shallow bunkers that sit at the dogleg. What you can't see from the tee, however, is that the fairway narrows to just 16 yards between those bunkers—the first evidence of this hole's subtle dangers.

As you approach the corner, the magnitude of the difficulty becomes more apparent. The 300-yard outlook to the green is stunning, and there's the highly unusual sight of a 100-foot pine tree sitting in the middle-right of the fairway. It's not a wide or sprawling tree, but it's more than enough to limit your options. A perfect drive allows you to play to the left of the tree—and the ideal play is a shotmaker's delight: a mid-iron fade around the tree, which will leave you short of another fairway bunker in the distance, as well as put you in the middle of the fairway for your third.

"You can play to the right of the tree," says Tataurangi, "but it's generally a much harder shot to execute. The biggest snare on this hole is trying to hit your second too far. Another option is to hit a low shot under the tree's branches and put it just beyond the tree. I try to leave myself a three-quarter mid-iron shot into the hole."

If you end up in a position to approach the C-shaped and two-level green with your third, you'll realize that it's often difficult to keep the ball on the green, and even tougher to stop it below the hole. The entire green is elevated by about 30 feet, sloped from back to front, and it's only 15 yards deep in some areas. Many players have watched their shots pitch safely on the green, only to see them trickle back into either of the two bunkers in front of the green. "Because the green is elevated," says Tataurangi, "you can't see all of the green and it's difficult to judge the distance. When you ultimately do find yourself on the green, every putt breaks outside the hole, so you don't want to leave yourself a par putt of more than a few feet."

The hole is relentlessly demanding. The length is not daunting to a strong player, and its perils are obvious in retrospect, but the hole is always capable of reminding you who's in charge.

Left: Native New Zealander Phil Tataurangi has never reached the green in two on the 14th hole at Wairakei, where he says par is a very good score.
Opposite: A tree in the middle of the fairway complicates things on the 14th hole (left). Small but deep bunkers, like the ones on the 15th (bottom right) are part of Wairakei's challenge.

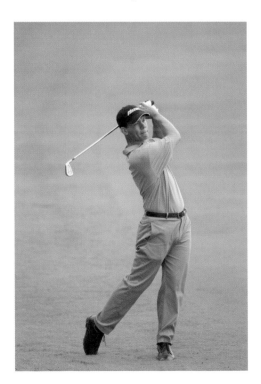

The PGA Tour only started coming to Westchester Country Club's West Course in 1967, but it has never left, so this Walter Travis design is one of only a handful of golf courses to have hosted a PGA Tour event for each of the last 37 years.

The list of titleholders at Westchester—Ernie Els, Raymond Floyd, Hale Irwin, Jack Nicklaus, and Arnold Palmer among them—reads like a Who's Who of U.S. Open Champions. There's a reason for that. Westchester's traditional design mirrors that of the classic U.S. Open venues. Furthermore, for many of its years on Tour, Westchester's West Course has been played just prior to the U.S. Open. Its small undulating greens, its insistence on accuracy, and its thick rough have made it an ideal warm-up for the national championship.

The Open is typically about length, rough, accuracy, and speed of greens, but ultimately it's about survival. The same can be said for the 12th hole at Westchester. Of all the holes played every year on the PGA Tour since 1989, this 473-yard par four (a par five for members) has played the toughest.

The genius behind the 12th (it's actually the third hole for member play; the West Course nines are reversed for the Buick Classic) is Walter Travis. A native Australian who moved to the United States at age 23, Travis was one of the most acclaimed players of his era. After taking up golf at 35, he virtually domi-

nated the American amateur scene, winning the U.S. Amateur three times in a four-year span (1900, 1901, 1903). In 1904, he won the British Amateur and in 1902 was runner-up to Laurie Auchterlonie in the U.S. Open at Garden City Golf Club, where Travis was a member (he would later do redesign work there).

In the three Buick Classics beginning in 2000, the field played the 12th hole in .35 over par. Over that same period they played the 11th in .31 over par, giving the course a fearsome 1-2 punch. No. 12 begins with a narrow plateau fairway that features newly restored bunkers to the left and right. At about 250 yards out, the fairway crests and runs down into a valley that eventually climbs up to a green that sits well above the level of the original fairway. The club of choice off the tee varies by player; a driver leaves a shorter second shot but a two-iron leaves a level lie. The green is protected by bunkers left/front and a small bunker to the right. Designed to accept short-iron approach shots as a par five, it is a difficult target for Tour players, who are playing a mid- to long-iron approach that is hard to stop on the elevated green.

A bad miss to the right of the green is jail: During member play the ball will roll all the way down the side slope and into the trees at the base of the hill. For the Tour event, the grass on the hillside is grown to rough length. The longer grass may stop the ball, but it also leaves a troublesome pitch back up to the putting surface. In 2003, Joey Sindelar was just off the 12th green in two. "I could not hit the ball on the green from six steps off. It was a double. You have to be patient through that stuff and expect that everybody is going to get one or two of those."

In June of 2000, after carding a first-round 67 in which his only blemish was a bogey at No. 12, John Maginnes offered this rationalization: "On that hole, par is really about four-and-three-quarters; so to make a five there, you're not really losing a whole lot to the field."

Ernie Els is one of a list of U.S. Open champions who've also won at Westchester Country Club, where small greens and thick rough make for an excellent pre-Open test.

Given the venues it has been selecting and the dramatic finishes it has been eliciting in recent years, the PGA Championship, once seen as the least of the four majors, is now among the shinier jewels in the grand-slam crown. Consider the 2004 edition contested at Whistling Straits.

Pete Dye's homage to the linksland origins of golf, Whistling Straits is part of a golf nirvana built along two windswept miles of Lake Michigan by bathroom-fixture magnate Herbert Kohler. Many developers and designers have attempted to emulate the natural splendor of ancient links golf courses. Most have failed. And while no one can out-design Mother Nature, Dye's work here thoroughly captures the random, lunar quality and windblown exhilaration of Scottish or Irish golf.

This accomplishment is all the more remarkable when you consider that this 560-acre parcel pocked with mounds and hillocks and 50-foot elevations was originally flat. "Not pretty flat," says Dye. "It was flat, period. Pool-table flat." Briefly used by the U.S. Army as an antiaircraft training facility, it nearly became a power plant until Kohler acquired the property and Dye got his hands on it.

At that time, the bluff dropped about 80 feet straight down to Lake Michigan. Since the bluff had been sloughing off into the lake, the Army Corps of Engineers allowed Dye to cut it down by 60 feet. That left Dye with a lot of sand and dirt, 800,000 cubic yards of which he used to create the spectacular yet natural-looking mounds and elevations he envisioned. While he was at it, Dye sprinkled bunkers everywhere he looked. No precise count has been made, but there are well over a thousand of them.

The layout makes the most of the waterfront. Eight holes play directly on the water, and the views of Lake Michigan—available from all 18 holes—make a convincing case that you're actually on the other side of the Atlantic.

Opened in 1998, Whistling Straits was awarded the 2004 PGA Championship only two years later. Dye's creation is so visually intimidating that even the pros feared that the course was too tough for them. More than one predicted that an over-par score would win. Dye, always happy to get inside players' heads, demurred, and predicted a winning score of eight- to ten-under.

Dye was right—the magic number for reaching the playoff was eight-under 280. This was due in part to the PGA of America's easing off on the set-up by moving some tees up in the early rounds and in part to the fact that the wind didn't blow hard until Sunday, when the course finally showed its teeth.

Whistling Straits boasts a variety of holes, including a few that can be considered birdie holes. On the other hand, the hard holes at Whistling Straits are *really* hard. Three of the course's par fours measure at least 500 yards from the championship tees, the first three par fours to break that barrier in a major championship. The toughest holes come down the stretch, the 518-yard par-four 15th, which during the final round had even big hitters straining to reach the green, and the 500-yard par-four 18th, which goes by the nickname "Dyeabolical."

Many visitors to Whistling Straits come away pronouncing it a great golf course except for the last hole. With a forced carry over Seven Mile Creek and adjacent wetlands on the approach shot, and a hard-to-find lay-up area, it may be too much for the average golfer, but the PGA Championship demonstrated that it's a great stage for final-hole drama in a major. The championship tee is set well below the highest point of the fairway, leaving a drive that travels first uphill and then downhill. The tee shot requires some choices—play safely to the right and leave a longer second shot or go down the left side, which requires a carry of some 270 yards over sand and rough but leaves a shorter approach. The fairway ends abruptly at the foot of the downslope, so depending on the wind and how long a player hits the ball, driver might be too much club.

The green is shaped like a three-leaf clover in back, with a long stem forming the front. When the flag is on the left or right "leaves," it's a long carry over sand (and water on the left) to attack the pin.

In 2004's final round, Justin Leonard, playing in the final pairing, came to this hole with a one-stroke lead in regulation. He hit what he thought was a perfect five-iron right at the flag, but it came up just short and landed in the bunker. His bogey dropped him into a playoff. Earlier, Chris DiMarco hit a six-iron to 15 feet, but he couldn't sink the birdie putt that, it turned out, would have won the championship for him outright. Ernie Els, another early finisher, played his second to the "safe" middle of the green, then three-putted for a bogey that ultimately left him one behind.

Clinging to a one-stroke lead when they reached 18 in the three-hole playoff, Singh was conservative with a three-wood tee shot. That left him with a nine-wood to the center of the green and two putts for the victory. It wrapped up the biggest title in a nine-victory season for Singh and a smashing debut for Whistling Straits.

Opposite, top: The ninth (foreground) and 18th holes.
Opposite, bottom: The pinnacle of Vijay Singh's remarkable 2004 season was his win in the PGA Championship, helped by his controlled mastery of the 18th hole at Whistling Straits.

Winged Foot is an embarrassment of riches. It's been blessed with colorful characters such as longtime head professional Claude Harmon and protégés such as Jackie Burke and Dave Marr. Its proximity to New York City gives the club a vibrancy that makes so many other "great" American clubs pall in comparison. Then, of course, there are the two Tillinghast courses nestled up next to each other like two necklaces in a jewel box. How spoiled is Winged Foot? During the 1929 U.S. Open, in which Bobby Jones turned back Al Espinosa in the playoff, many of Winged Foot's members took a pass on following the greatest player in the game around their West Course. Instead, while Jones and Espinosa chased history on the West, the Winged Foot members slummed it—they played the East Course.

Lots of golf clubs have two or more 18-hole courses. Few have two Tillinghasts and even fewer have two Tillinghast gems. And while the West Course with its nearly unrivaled collection of stout par threes and par fours has soaked up the spotlight and taken its rightful place alongside the great courses in the world, the East Course has stood modestly in the shadows. The West—a slightly tougher course (75.2 course rating and 141 slope from the back tees vs. 73.8 and 141 for the East)—has hosted just about every possible significant championship in the game: four U.S. Opens (it will host its fifth in 2006), a PGA Championship, two U.S. Amateurs, and a Walker Cup. The East has had a glimmer of the spotlight, hosting two U.S. Women's Opens and a U.S. Senior Open, but it is still waiting for an invitation to the big dance. If the West, which is perennially ranked in the top 10 courses in the United States, is the belle of the ball, than the East, recently ranked as high as 39th in the nation, is more like the girl next door—in pearls.

The East might not have the championship pedigree that the West enjoys. But knowledgeable members and longtime local competitors will tell you that while the West is longer and richer in history, the East actually requires greater diversity in shotmaking. Yes, Nos. 1, 10, and 18 on the West have certainly earned their stripes, but the hardest hole of the 36 holes on this tree-lined campus may well be No. 17 East.

"I've played a lot of par threes all over the place and it's about the hardest one I know of," says Winged Foot's longtime head professional and former Tour pro, Tom Nieporte. Although the hole features neither water nor bunkers, Nieporte likens it to the famed 16th at Cypress Point. "You miss the green and you're pretty much finished." And it's even tougher now that a new back tee was installed before the 2004 U.S. Amateur (qualifying rounds were played at both courses), lengthening the hole from 210 to 232 yards.

For a major championship venue, Winged Foot's overall terrain is surprisingly flat. Very few holes feature a dramatic change in elevation. The plainness of the landscape simply underscores Tillinghast's genius. The 17th hole on the East, however, is a precipitously downhill par three, with the drastic downhill slope making the proper yardage difficult to gauge. Adding to the calculus is the fact that nearly the entire front third of Tillinghast's green is actually a false front that repels even well-struck balls.

From the tee it appears as though a draw might be the play, but too much of a draw will land you in a greenside swale, and par is pretty much out of the question. "If you hit a push, it's even worse," says Nieporte. "And if you short-side yourself on either side, you're just not going to make par unless you can hole a 40-foot putt." Even if you miss the green left and the pin is back right, Nieporte says, "a good player has a one in ten chance at par."

The green itself, raised dramatically, is among the most difficult of all 36 at Winged Foot. That's saying a lot when you consider that for decades critics have considered 10 West to be among the most befuddling greens in major championship golf.

Nieporte says of Tillinghast's design: "They must have taken a bulldozer and piled up all the earth in the area to make that green. It's got to be 25 feet high." Furthermore, it's difficult to hold and even harder to read. It's half House of Horrors, half Mona Lisa. Says one member: "The green feels as though it slopes away from you no matter where you're standing."

"Everybody struggles with it," says Nieporte, who adds that there's no shame in avoiding the green complex altogether on the tee shot by laying up short, which affords the least severe pitch shot. A lay-up, a chip, and a putt or two may be the answer.

Opposite, bottom: Ryan Moore was the medalist at the 2004 U.S. Amateur on Winged Foot's East and West Courses before winning the title on the West in match play.

By 1900, the New York Athletic Club (NYAC) had become the world's preeminent amateur sports enclave. Its members were (and still are) distinguishing themselves in the Olympics and other world-class competitions. By 1920, the club's symbol, the winged foot of Mercury, had become a globally recognized symbol of athletic excellence. In 1921, a group of members proposed that the club build a golf course, but the measure was rejected. Undeterred, the maverick group created a club of its own, appropriating the NYAC's winged-foot logo and setting out to build a golf club worthy of the Athletic Club's tradition.

A. W. Tillinghast received succinct direction: "Give us a man-sized course."

Man-sized they wanted—Big and Tall Shop they got. Tillinghast removed some 7,200 tons of rock (most of which went into the construction of the clubhouse) and 7,800 trees. His thinking on subduing the unfriendly terrain is classic: "Often it is necessary to get from one section to another over ground which is not suited to easy construction, but that troublesome hole must stand right up with the others. If it has not got anything about it that makes it respectable, it has got to have quality knocked into it until it can hold its head up in polite society."

A long golf course (today it measures 7,226 yards from the tips; par 70), Winged Foot has always felt even longer because the routing is forged through corridors of trees and into small greens. The design is purely strategic in that nearly every challenge is visible from the tee. The small greens slope drastically, and they're not only hard to read, but they run dangerously fast. Finally, the bunkering is pure Tillinghast. The fairway bunkers suggest the shot (draw, fade, etc.) while the gaping greenside bunkers place the ultimate stress on the approach. Winged Foot embodies Tillinghast's belief that "a controlled shot to a closely guarded green is the surest test of a man's golf."

The 1929 U.S. Open not only confirmed the course's place on the national stage, but it solidified the reputation of the 18th hole as one of the game's great tests. A par-four dogleg left measuring 452 yards (in Bobby Jones's day it played 419), 18 West has played a decisive role not only in Winged Foot's history, but in golf lore. In the final round of the 1929 Open, Bobby Jones stood on the 18th tee needing a par to tie Al Espinosa. Jones drove the ball solidly but pulled his approach. After barely clearing the front-left bunker, Jones's ball came to rest in the deep greenside rough. Standing with his feet well above the ball, Jones played a niblick to about twelve feet. He had to one-putt in order to force a 36-hole playoff. His 12-footer was largely downhill and broke severely from left to right. Consistent with Jones's putting philosophy of "reaching the hole with a dying ball," the ball died on the lip, teetered, and fell in for a 79. In the next day's playoff Jones eviscerated his opponent, beating him 72-69—141 to 84-80—164.

Fifty-five years later, Greg Norman holed an even longer par putt to reach a playoff. After his second shot veered sharply right into the grandstand, Norman took a drop and pitched 40 feet past the hole, then stunned the crowd by sinking it. Unlike Jones, he didn't win the playoff, falling flat against Fuzzy Zoeller, 67–75.

On a given Saturday in spring, Winged Foot is an ego-shrinking test. Under U.S. Open conditions, it can be nearly impossible. The 1974 Open raised the bar for difficulty in the national championship. In the first round, not a single player broke par. Sandy Tatum, who was then head of the USGA championship committee, was asked if the USGA was trying to embarrass the best players in the world. "No," he said. "We're trying to identify them."

Opposite, bottom: Losing by eight strokes to Fuzzy Zoeller at the end of an 18-hole playoff at the 1984 U.S. Open, Greg Norman pulled out a white towel.

Yale University was founded in 1701, but it took some 225 years for Yale to get serious about golf.

In 1926, two years after the school was given a gift of 700 acres of swamp and woodland, the university hired Charles Blair Macdonald and Seth Raynor to turn the sprawling acreage into a golf course. Macdonald, a Chicago-born stockbroker who picked up the game as a student in St. Andrews, Scotland, was one of the pioneer golf-course architects in the United States. His design of the original Chicago Golf Club (nine holes in 1892 and another nine in 1893) made it the first 18-hole course in the United States. Early in his life, golf-course design was Macdonald's passion. Even for designing landmark private courses such as Lido, Mid Ocean, National Golf Links, Piping Rock, and Sleepy Hollow, Macdonald never took a fee.

Raynor (an engineer by training) had been hired by Macdonald in 1908 to survey the site of National Golf Links of America. By 1915, they had become partners. Macdonald, who was 18 years Raynor's senior, eventually began to ease out of the business while Raynor went on to his own storied career.

The work of Macdonald and Raynor—both their collaborations and their solo work—represents one of the most respected golf-course design portfolios in the game. Of all the golf courses they created, none is tougher than Yale. And of all the holes at Yale, none is tougher than the 10th.

There are a lot of hard holes in this world. The 10th at Yale is not only hard, just getting to the tee is a trek. After getting beaten up by the downright medieval ninth hole, a long par three with a Biarritz design, an intimidating all-water carry, and a lobotomized green, players must trudge up (and I mean up) a worn dirt path, dodging rocks and tree roots, to the 10th tee.

Once on the tee you're greeted not by a cart girl, but by a climbing slab of parched grass crowned nearly 400 yards later by a mono-brow cross bunker and a thin glimpse of what *appears* to be putting surface. To a golfer huffing from the walk to the tee, the 10th hole looks much more suitable as a ski slope.

The 10th is a straightaway par four. At 396 yards from the back tees, this hole gives new meaning to the word uphill. Immediately off the tee, the fairway elevates to block out any sight of the landing area. A 240-yard drive will put you in the swale. Whereas you couldn't see the landing area from the tee, now you can't see the flag. The fairway is lined with dense forestation on both sides, and the green is 40 feet above the fairway. The common mistake here, urged on by gravity more than human error, is to be short. Macdonald and Raynor thought of that in advance: A deep trap extends across the front width of the green to catch short shots. The green itself is double tiered so that the rare approach shot that does find the green needs to be accurate.

In the 1970s and 1980s the Yale course fell into serious disrepair, but in recent seasons it's received the time and attention deserving of its landmark design, and the course is now ranked 69th in the U.S. by *Golf Magazine.* It has hosted a spate of prestigious championships, including two U.S. Junior Nationals, the 1991 NCAA Eastern Regional championships, the 1991 ECAC Men's Championship, and the 1992 ECAC Women's Championship. During the 1991 NCAA Eastern Regionals, 360 rounds were played by the best collegiate players in the East. Only 21 of those rounds were below par.

The 10th hole at Yale, designed by C.B. Macdonald (shown) and Seth Raynor, is virtually medieval in its toughness.

Acknowledgments

Publishing is a collaborative exercise. I would like to express my gratitude to the many people who helped out in the researching and editing of this book. This project simply could not have been completed without the help and insight of dozens of individuals. Chief among them is Margaret Kaplan, my friend and editor at Harry N. Abrams, Inc. Thank you for everything, Margaret. Golf course designer, Rees Jones, was not only an invaluable and generous source for my research, but he went above and beyond the call by graciously agreeing to write the Foreword for this book. I am grateful for his thoughtful cooperation.

Others who added immeasurably to this book include Jack Nicklaus, Tom Fazio, Pete Dye, Brian Silva, Bob Cupp, Bobby Weed, Tom Clark, Dean Knuth, Rod Milford, Todd Yoshitake, Jim Finegan, Brian Gerrard, Tom Nieporte, Bill Safrin, Craig Harmon, Paul Harney, Jack Druga, Bruce Patterson, Suzy Whaley, Buddy Alexander, The Golf Writers Association of America, Ron Whitten, Geoff Shackelford, Gary Van Sickle, Ed Sherman, Lorne Rubenstein, Jim Herre, Frank Jemsek, Carol McCue, Shelley Smith, Peter Morrice, Jimmy Roberts, John Huggan, Pete Wofford, Kevin Morris, Jeff Freeman, Mike Stoltz, Jon Crisler, Jim Farrell, Chuah Choo Chiang, Scott Tolley, Marilyn Keough, Diane Jackson, Cameron Reid, E. Clayton Gengras, Jr., John Zimmers, Charlie Millard, Hiro Watanabe, Petro van Bosch, Mike Cullity, Bob Denney of the PGA of America, Phil Stambaugh of the PGA TOUR, and Craig Smith, Beth Murrison, and Pete Kowalski of the USGA.

I would like to extend my deepest gratitude to David Barrett, who edited this book for Abrams. David is as golf-knowledgeable and dogged an editor as there is. Both the reader and the writer were fortunate to be in his capable hands. Finally, I would like to thank my wife, Eileen, and my family for their patience, interest, and support.

Photo Credits

Above: Bay Hill Club and Lodge,18th hole

Public Courses

OPEN TO THE PUBLIC

Ballybunion Golf Club, Ballybunion, Ireland
www.ballybuniongolfclub.ie
Bay Hill Club and Lodge, Orlando, Florida
www.bayhill.com
Bayonet Course, Seaside, California
www.bayonetblackhorse.com
Bethpage State Park, Farmingdale, New York
www.nysparks.state.ny.us/golf
Blackwolf Run (River Course), Kohler, Wisconsin
www.destinationkohler.com
Carnoustie Golf Club, Scotland
www.carnoustiegolflinks.co.uk
Casa de Campo (Teeth of the Dog), La Romana, Dominican
Republic
The Challenge at Manele, Lanai, Hawaii
www.manelebayhotel.com
Cog Hill Golf and Country Club (No. 4 Course), Lemont, Illinois
www.coghillgolf.com
Colbert Hills Golf Club, Manhattan, Kansas
www.colberthills.com
Concord Resort and Golf Club (Monster Course), Kiamesha
Lake, New York
www.concordresort.com
Doral Golf Resort and Spa (Blue Course), Miami, Florida
www.doralresort.com
Giant's Ridge (The Quarry), Biwabik, Minnesota
www.giantsridge.com
Glen Abbey Golf Club, Oakville, Ontario
www.glenabbey.com
Harbour Town Golf Links, Hilton Head Island, South Carolina
www.seapines.com
Karsten Creek Golf Course, Stillwater, Oklahoma
Kauri Cliffs Golf Course, New Zealand
www.kauricliffs.com
Koolau Golf Club, Oahu, Hawaii
www.koolaugolfclub.com
Ocean Course at Kiawah Island, South Carolina
www.kiawahresort.com
Old Course at St. Andrews, Scotland
www.standrews.org.uk
Pebble Beach Golf Links, Pebble Beach, California
www.pebblebeach.com
Pinehurst Resort and Country Club (No. 2 Course), Pinehurst,
North Carolina
www.pinehurst.com
Royal Dornoch Golf Club, Dornoch, Scotland
www.royaldornoch.com

Royal Portrush Golf Club, Portrush, N. Ireland
www.royalportrushgolfclub.com
St. Nom-la-Breteche Golf Club, St. Nom-la-Breteche, France
Spyglass Hill Golf Course, Pebble Beach, California
www.pebblebeach.com
Torrey Pines (South Course), La Jolla, California
www.torreypinesgolfcourse.com
TPC at Sawgrass (Stadium Course), Ponte Vedra Beach, Florida
www.tpc.com/daily/sawgrass
TPC Stadium Course at PGA West, La Quinta, California
www.pgawest.com
Turnberry (Ailsa Course), Ayrshire, Scotland
www.turnberry.co.uk
Wairakei Golf Course, Taupo, New Zealand
www.wairakeigolfcourse.com.nz
Whistling Straits (Straits Course), Kohler, Wisconsin
www.destinationkohler.com

LIMITED ACCESS
*The courses listed below are open to the public only during
certain days or hours and may include other requirements such as a
handicap card. Arrangements generally must be made in advance.
Play on these courses is sometimes included in the itinerary of tours
from golf-travel companies.*

Kingston Heath Golf Club, Melbourne, Australia
Muirfield, Gullane, Scotland
New South Wales Golf Club, Matraville, Australia
www.nswgolfclub.com.au
The Oxfordshire, Thame, England
www.theoxfordshiregolfclub.com
Paraparaumu Beach Golf Club, Paraparaumu Beach,
New Zealand
www.paraparaumubeachgolfclub.co.nz
Royal Birkdale Golf Club, Southport, England
www.royalbirkdale.com
Royal Lytham and St. Annes Golf Club, Lytham St. Annes,
England
www.royallytham.org
Royal Melbourne Golf Club (West Course), Black Rock, Australia
www.royalmelbourne.com.au
Royal St. George's Golf Club, Sandwich, England
www.royalstgeorges.com.
Royal Troon Golf Club, Troon, Scotland
www.royaltroon.co.uk
Valderrama Golf Club, San Roque, Spain
www.valderrama.com

MEDINAH (NO. 3 COURSE) 13TH HOLE

Editor: David Barrett
Designer: Robert McKee
Photo Research: Laurie Platt Winfrey, Cristian Pena, Carousel Research, Inc.
Production Manager: Stanley Redfern

Library of Congress Cataloging-in-Publication Data

Millard, Chris.
  Golf's 100 toughest holes / by Chris Millard ; foreword by Rees Jones.
    p. cm.
  Includes bibliographical references and index.
  ISBN 0–8109–5010–3 (hardcover : alk. paper) 1. Golf courses. I. Title: Golf's
one hundred toughest holes. II. Title.

  GV975.M48 2005
  796.352'06'8—dc22

                    2005012655

10 9 8 7 6 5 4 3 2 1

Harry N. Abrams, Inc.
100 Fifth Avenue
New York, N.Y. 10011
www.abramsbooks.com

Abrams is a subsidiary of